DREAMING SALLY

A TRUE STORY
OF FIRST LOVE,
SUDDEN DEATH
AND LONG SHADOWS

DREAMING SALLY

JAMES FITZGERALD

RANDOM HOUSE CANADA

PUBLISHED BY RANDOM HOUSE CANADA

www.penguinrandomhouse.ca

Random House Canada and colophon are registered trademarks.

Page 351 constitutes a continuation of the copyright page.

Library and Archives Canada Cataloguing in Publication

FitzGerald, James, 1950–, author
    Dreaming Sally : a true story of first love, sudden death and long shadows / James FitzGerald.

Includes bibliographical references and index.
Issued in print and electronic formats.
ISBN 978-0-345-81453-1
eBook ISBN 978-0-345-81455-5

    1. FitzGerald, James, 1950–. 2. FitzGerald, James, 1950– —
Childhood and youth. 3. Authors, Canadian (English)—Biography.
4. Coincidence. 5. Grief. I. Title.

PS8611.I888A34 2018   C818'.603   C2018-900733-8
                                                 C2018-900734-6

All interior photos are courtesy of the author.
Book design by Kelly Hill
Cover art: (photo) courtesy of Margaret Rayworth; (frame) © Dinga/Shutterstock.com
Interior art: © Dinga/ Shutterstock.com

Printed and bound in Canada

10 9 8 7 6 5 4 3 2 1

Penguin
Random House
RANDOM HOUSE CANADA

For Katy

CONTENTS

PART IV

PART V

PROLOGUE

No wonder I'm feeling anxious. Over four decades have passed since I saw George Orr, back in the sixties, back when we both loved an eighteen-year-old girl named Sally. Our adolescent triangle was undone by a catastrophe as sudden as it was uncanny, yet an unspoken bond has endured between us.

Unspoken till now.

It's an October Sunday in 2010 and on the five-hour flight from my home in Toronto to his in Vancouver, I mull over our recent exchange of emails. After years of hesitation, I have asked permission to capture the full story, our story, in a book. Or will George think of it as strictly his story? Only if he consents will I plunge in.

He loves and hates the idea of my writing about Sally and her impact on our lives. Yes, a book can heal, but a book can re-traumatize. After the summer of Sally, we both became journalists, lurking on the thresholds of power, sticklers for the facts, maybe even the truth. Yet George, a gifted professional communicator, has never been able to bring himself to record his version of events of August 1968.

In his late twenties, George quit Toronto to reinvent himself in British Columbia. Now in his sixties and twice divorced, George has at last found happiness with Anne, his third attempt at a life partner. His three children from his first two marriages know nothing of the turbulence of his youth, but he felt compelled to show my email about Sally to his twenty-six-year-old daughter, Lily, and her response was swift: "Dad, you're a journalist. You expect people to open up to you. What goes around, comes around."

And so George emailed back: "I respect my daughter's opinion. I'm in."

After checking into a North Vancouver bed and breakfast, I find my way to his address at the appointed hour of noon. As I descend a steep driveway leading to his split-level house, as I ring the doorbell, I remember our first—and only—meeting shortly after Sally's death. The image of George's bearded Byronesque face—brooding, forbidding, looking half mad—had been permanently branded on my memory. When the door swings open, the face appears, now clean-shaven and crowned with silver hair. His smile and handshake break the tension faster than I imagined.

When he introduces his partner, Anne, I'm struck by her physical similarity to Sally, especially the contours of her eyes and mouth. I blurt, "Thank you for tolerating my intrusion." She murmurs some reassuring words, but I can sense that she's uncomfortable with my mission. Why wouldn't she be, knowing the shadow that Sally has cast on her partner?

After lunch in a glassed atrium overlooking Burrard Inlet, George leads me down to a cluttered basement office.

I know my end of the story, but not his. And vice versa. When I pull out my digital recorder, he smiles wryly. He knows my reputation as a buster of secrets through my two published books: *Old Boys*, an oral history in which I invaded the privacy of three hundred graduates of Upper Canada College, the exclusive Toronto boys' private school to which we were both indentured at birth; and *What Disturbs Our Blood*, a dark family memoir in which the privacy I invaded my was own.

As we talk, the connections and similarities between us pile up like a bed of falling leaves; if we are not full-fledged doppelgängers, we are close enough. We both have younger brothers named Michael whom we initially treated cruelly, then reconciled with. We both love music passionately yet never picked up an instrument. Both of our paternal grandfathers served as majors in World War I. His grandfather founded an insurance company, which his father obediently took over; my grandfather founded a medical laboratory, and my father similarly followed suit. Both our fathers were "old boys" of Upper Canada College, both naval officers scarred by the horrors of the North Atlantic, each of their combat vessels sinking a single Nazi U-boat, both becoming functioning Irish-blooded addicts, radiating the charm of Irish-blooded addicts. Both our mothers went to the same private school, St. Clement's in Toronto, and both were bright, iron-willed, housebound "old girls," chronically resentful of the weaker sex known as husbands. Their charming husbands.

Each set of parents, Orr and FitzGerald, envied their children and the emerging personal freedoms of the sixties. The attitude they projected toward their children was implicit but all the more coercive for that: Reach for the sun—but never outshine us. George and I had evolved along parallel tracks into tellers of stories, iconoclasts and ironists of Irish-outsider temperament and inclination, uncomfortable with, even contemptuous of, our inherited class privilege; the best part of our privilege was the freedom to have our cake and spit it out.

One of my own preoccupations—the emotional vulnerabilities of men, especially "leaders," born or made—strikes close to George's heart. George reveals that he was a classmate of Michael Ignatieff, an Upper Canadian–White Russian aristocrat groomed for greatness. They both were precocious; high expectations dogged their paths: nothing short of the prime minister's office would do. For different reasons, that destiny remains unfulfilled.

Why does George's path seem so mysteriously intertwined with mine? Why, over the years, has something compelled us both to hoard transcripts, letters, photos, artifacts, mementos? Why do we collect evidence and stock our memory palaces to the point of overkill? Why do we love the same films, the same books, right down to the same bars of music, the same poetic and comical phrases?

Why were we crazy about the same girl?

"It feels like we're archetypal characters in an unfinished, unfinishable novel," I tell him. "Who were those guys all those years ago? What happened to them? Where did they go? Or not go?"

I hear footsteps on the basement stairs; it's Anne, coming down to check the spinning clothes dryer. Her eyes say it all: *Why is this stranger opening up old wounds?* But she's too late: we've already embarked on a mutually risk-fraught experiment in honesty.

Three hours have passed, or is it more like forty-two years? As I follow George to the door, we pass by a cardboard box stuffed with old letters.

George takes one off the top and thrusts it into my hand. "This is the last letter Sally wrote me from West Germany that summer. I never read it. Too painful. Take it with you."

For a moment, I feel as if the basement is flooding. Sally's favourite song was "The Letter" by the Box Tops. We danced to it all that summer. Instantly I am pulled back to that overcast Tuesday afternoon of August 13, 1968, a day when entire worlds died and others were born. The day Sally died.

PART I

We each experience the world as the inside of our mother's body.

—MELANIE KLEIN

ONE

James Loves Sally

From the back seat window of my mother's Nash Rambler, I counted the short white lines stitching the black asphalt, the monotonous zipper of Highway 11 lulling me into a low-grade trance. The fifty-mile trip due north of Toronto unfolded with the unbearable slowness only a child knows. To kill time, I played obsessive word and number games in my head—*I am ten years and eleven months old . . . Highway 11, take me to heaven*—interrupting myself only to ask in my still-unbroken voice: "Are we there yet?"

At last, the car swerved right onto Innisfil Line 3, and over the railway tracks we rumbled, mother, sister, brother and I, then past the Lefroy Harbour turnoff, through the remnants of old-growth forest, toward the familiar cluster of lakeside cottages. As my excitement mounted, I pictured the sandy bay beyond, in the lee of a windy tip of land that curved like a woman's hip under the August sun, holding in its shelter a clutch of splashing children I longed to join.

After helping unpack the car, I rushed to slip on my bathing suit, tying the frayed white cord at my belly button. I took a slim path that cut through soft, shin-high grass, skirted the cedar hedgerow, then skipped down a brief descent of rough-hewn planks to dig my toes into the communal sand of De Grassi Point, Lake Simcoe.

The city boy, starved of tenderness of touch or kindness of word, would soon be born, or reborn, on what everyone called "the baby beach." In the years ahead, I could and would revisit the place in my memory at will.

I first saw Sally in a makeshift Sunday school, held in the McMurrich cottage, where we droned in unison the Anglican hymn "All Things Bright and Beautiful." She was six and I was five, both skinny, long-legged offspring of doctors who were colleagues at the University of Toronto. The McMurriches were a first-generation De Grassi family, a species of rural aristocrat stretching back to the 1890s, and Sally was related by blood. She was already enrolled in the all-girls private school Branksome Hall, and from birth I had been programmed to follow my father Jack's path to the other side of the mirror, the equally exclusive all-boys private school, Upper Canada College.

Sally was now a slim-hipped, wisecracking, eleven-year-old tomboy with brown eyes and curly hair, a ready laugh and a distinctively raspy voice. She was known as "Juno" around the point because she tended to run her words together, like, "Juno if you trap fireflies in a bottle, they'll die?" Personality to burn.

Most nights after dinner, kids gravitated through the tall grass of the commons to her cottage on the north side of the point, where she waited for us. The weathered structure echoed Sally's last name, Wodehouse—pronounced "wood house"—suggesting equal parts vulnerability and stability. Her parents, George and Jane, seemed affable and outgoing, their overlapping laughter, lit by after-noon cocktails, sifting through the screens of the veranda. I already towered over Jane, nicknamed "Tiny" for her five-foot, one-inch stature, a wild contrast to her robust six-footer of a husband. Sally's sixteen-year-old sister, Diana—round-faced, quiet, serious—seemed to occupy another universe from us.

We kids loved playing Capture the Flag and our favourite, Kick the Can. I could never wait for my turn to be It. I tried to kick the can as far as I could, as everyone scattered to hide, often in the nearby grove of pine trees that cast a prickly carpet of needles and cones. A fast runner, I revelled in the darting and deking, the exhilarating tension between capture and liberation. Like extra-innings baseball, the game was theoretically endless and I yearned to keep playing in the dark.

When nightfall chased us inside, we'd play Hangman, or Rock, Paper, Scissors, or, if I felt brave, engage in a staring contest; we were not quite ready to play doctor. I loved aggressive card games like War and Pig but especially Cheat. A game of chance that rewarded badness was too good to be true, and I won, won, won, gleefully slapping the killer cards hard on the tabletop as we gulped down sweating glasses of Kool-Aid and licked clean our Cheezies-coated fingers. One time, as Sally shuffled the next hand, I was mesmerized by a moth banging crazily against the screen, longing to merge with the light bulb, creating a halo behind her tanned face.

During the day, we liked to visit Mr. Ed, the grey-haired local postman and handyman who stocked a small barn with massive chunks of ice insulated with sawdust. Ed waved us into the back of his pickup truck and we rumbled over the two miles of sun-dappled gravel into the village of Lefroy, where we split a five-cent banana Popsicle on the metal edge of the fire-engine-red mailbox. One day, John Rogers, dubbed "Roar" by his grandkids for his gruff voice, stopped our joyriding in the back of Ed's truck: "You kids might fall out and crack your heads." He was the Godfather of the North Point, and his word was law. A burly, leonine stockbroker with startling tufts of grey hair on his bronzed chest, Rogers had bankrolled the newly erected Upper Canada College clock tower, which loomed within eyeshot of my Toronto home. Every summer, Roar Rogers opened his long, white dock at the tip of the point, between the baby beach and the Over-Forty dock, as a communal gathering place. Sally and I now spent hours on a diving platform twenty yards out from the dock, anchored at the spot where the sandbar surrendered to unknown depths.

Afraid of the dark waters on the far side of the platform, I preferred to jump off the diving board feet first. At first, Sally and I graded each other's cannonballs from 1 to 10, but soon she surged ahead, executing graceful swan dives and jackknives while I hesitated. Pulling herself up the ladder, she flattened her unruly tangle of hair with her long fingers, then curled her thumbs under the elastic rims of her bum-clinging bathing suit, snapping it back in place. She shot me a look—scaredy-cat —and once more dived into the deep. Disgrace and desire forced me to follow suit, and for the first time ever I hit the water headfirst.

It was the afternoon of August 6, 1962, weeks short of my twelfth birthday. We had arrived at the point from the city only days earlier, and everyone was talking about the sudden death of Marilyn Monroe. I hadn't seen Sally for nearly a year, and I found her down on the dock on the tip of the point, wearing an unfamiliar tight, dark blue bathing suit. She was lying on a towel on her back, perfectly still, eyes shut against the flood of sunshine. My stick-thin tomboy friend had acquired a new, winter-grown body of bumps and curves. Enthralled, I turned a silent thought over and over: *So THIS is what everyone is talking about. . . .*

As I slipped past, I cast a fleeting shadow over her body, and her head jerked up. I unfurled my towel and stretched out on it, face down.

"Hi," I said.

"Hi."

Her unusual aloofness unsettled me. It seemed we were starting from scratch. My mother captured the scene with her box Kodak, my insanely long legs shooting across the dock at a right angle to Sally's feet, but the image failed to capture my inner tumult. It seemed only yesterday we were thrusting the heads of dandelions under each other's chin—if your skin shines yellow, it means you love butter. Less than a year ago, winning a laugh from Sally had been as good as a kiss. But now?

That August our circle expanded to include the fast crowd, led by a muscular, crewcut prep boy with the enviable name, Stephen Love. Despite the impact of the new Sally, I was also nursing a quiet crush on Marilyn Price, a pretty blond Branksome classmate of Sally's—a smart aleck who spat out "Get lost!" and "Drop dead!" when you said nothing in particular. But Marilyn was sweet on Steve, not me, and so we went round and round, clanging the sides of the invisible triangle, even as I struggled to remain loyal to Sally.

As if answering a prayer, Steve one afternoon proposed a game of Spin the Bottle. Marilyn was fated to take her life by her own hand, but in this patch of time, six eleven- and twelve-year-olds sat cross-legged and vibrating in a circle on a sun-swept veranda. But when the mouth of the twirling Orange Crush bottle stopped, pointing straight at my groin, I panicked and fled down to the dock, chased by the scalding laughter of sweet-scented girls. The lesson was as clear as it was cruel: in school, I regularly stood first in spelling and Steve Love last, but in real life the body ruled the mind.

At the annual regatta, I couldn't wait to show off my swimming prowess to the assembled throng, but most of all to Sally. I dived off the platform, landing with a chest-smashing splash, and began wind-milling my arms stroke for stroke with Brian Love, the brother of Steve, all eyes watching, all mouths shouting, our hands slapping the nylon cord at exactly the same moment, our mad sprint ending in a dead heat. But the organizers had made no allowance for ties, so Brian Love received the first-place medal, and John Stevens the second place. Someone thrust a flashlight in my hand as a consolation prize, but I was inconsolable in my bitterness. Did I not finish first?

Days later, Brian's mother pressed into my palm a disk she had bought and engraved herself. "I felt badly that you did not receive a medal, too," she said, smiling at me with the palpable warmth that seemed to emanate from all mothers but my own. In our family, "love" was a four-letter word.

One night, after dusk scattered our gang homeward in all directions, I hung back to stargaze with Sally, raising our fingers to trace the points of the Big Dipper. As if reading my hope, she invited me into her cottage to watch TV, a black-and-white job with rabbit ears that pulled in a fuzzy signal from the nearby town of Barrie. In the dim light, I held my prize flashlight under my chin, shooting spooky shafts of light into the shadowed sockets of my eyes, and moaned like a ghost. I still liked nothing better than making her laugh, especially when she bit her upper lip to stop from exposing her gums.

It was just the two of us, alone together, no parents, no sister, no other kids, no spinning bottles. The interior of her place was unusual, with a living room that was open to the rafters like a court-yard, the bedrooms tucked around the perimeter of the second floor as if they were gazing down on us. I spread out on the sofa and Sally slouched in the chair beside me, the two of us engrossed by a World War II drama.

But soon a familiar, insidious feeling of entrapment choked me; it was late August, and the buttery flow of summer was ebbing away. Then Sally announced that she was leaving for the city the next day so she could go on an outing with Marilyn, and I fell into a well of premature mourning. The endless summer was a liar.

When the day came to pack up our car and head south, I felt as if I was leaving the only truly good thing I had ever known; the only place where joy flowed, unadulterated; the only sliver of time and space where the chronic anxiety of the city gave way, fleetingly, to an animal state of self-forgetting.

Days earlier, wandering alone in the woods, attempting to fill the gap Sally had left, I had found a wriggling dark pink salamander. Scooping my prize into a glass Mason jar, I dropped in leaves of lettuce to sustain it, but the creature quickly died and then liquefied. I buried the jar like a coffin in the narrow laneway beside our cottage, placing a rock on top to mark the spot. I promised myself, the son and grandson of forensic-minded pathologists, that when I returned the next summer, I'd dig it up and find a skeleton, a memento mori perfect in its whiteness.

But later that fall, my parents announced that we were not renewing the cottage rental for the following summer of 1963. They gave no reason for their decision, which felt like a death without a funeral.

I passed the next three summers at an all-boys camp farther north, taking week-long canoe trips into the mosquito-infested bush with pimply classmates, fending off the occasional homosexual advance inside our leaky, fart-ridden pup tents. As part of earning my Bronze Medallion for life-saving skills, I was forced to perform mock mouth-to-mouth resuscitation on an uncooperative fourteen-year-old boy. My first kiss but not my last medal.

We never returned to De Grassi as a family. While I envied Sally's unbroken connection to the point, all those Mays to Octobers piled one atop another, I nearly forgot her.

TWO

The Importance of Being George

I f my childhood load was heavy, George Benjamin Orr was growing up similarly burdened. If he became a rebel, it was not without cause.

One day in 1960, he was invited to tea by Alan Stephen, whose genial manner and Oxbridge accent perfectly suited his position as headmaster of an exclusive all-boys prep school. "Orr, I've had my eye on the two boys in your class who could be prime minister one day. There's you and there's Michael Ignatieff," Stephen said.

Oh, God, George thought. *Now I'll have to do my homework.* He was twelve years old. It felt like a life sentence.

Regardless of his class standing, the shy boy had much to puzzle out, especially as he was recuperating from a large blow. At the start of Grade 5, his parents had pulled him out of Owen Boulevard Public School, where he'd known the same boys and girls forever, and enrolled him in Upper Canada College. When he passed under the stone archway of his "alma pater"—no girls allowed, no questions asked—he lost all connection with his peers, and himself. A random caning by a free-ranging blond psychopath was but one of countless "character-building" humiliations of the British colonial–style snob school that delivered a home truth: a single tear was blood to the sharks. When punched in the face in the mandatory boxing tournament for seven- to thirteen-year-olds, George thought his head had exploded, and he preferred to keep his head. He simply quit, stepping over the ropes and out of the ring. Thinking outside the box.

Although three previous generations of Orrs had proudly worn the blue-and-white old-boy tie and crested blazer, the family lived four miles to the north in the suburbs of York Mills. The homes of both sets of George's grandparents stood mere blocks apart, and the Christian name George had been passed down continuously on both sides of the family: six preceding Georges inhabited the dual streams of his bloodlines. Although no one said it aloud, he had someone big to live up to. Maybe several someones.

George was not fond of his paternal grandfather, a manipulative, alcoholic bully who was the co-founder of a successful insurance brokerage, Mulholland-Orr. While George's father, George Jr., insisted on the nickname "Mac," he could not resist being shunted down the tracks of the family business. If Mac had ever possessed the stamina to counter the inexorable will of his own father, his service in World War II had beaten it out of him. Even at twelve, George was at least dimly aware of the plight of his father and dreaded becoming the third-generation insurance man.

Just as I, in my own way, dreaded becoming a third-generation medical man, following the pattern of my father and my paternal grandfather.

In the summer of 1939, freshly graduated from UCC, Mac Orr had held the world by the tail. Handsome and athletic, gregarious and quick-witted, the six-foot teenager was a track star poised to glide into the winners' circle of Toronto high society. But the outbreak of World War II hijacked his future. Instead of running for Canada at the Olympics, Mac joined the Royal Canadian Navy at age seventeen. His class background ensured a commission, and by the time he was twenty he was a lieutenant on the HMCS *Calgary*, a 110-man Flower-class corvette that had been bulked up with depth-charge throwers and anti-aircraft guns in order to escort convoys of unarmed munitions vessels between Canada and England, fending off wolf packs of invisible Nazi U-boats. The corvette's living conditions were appalling, the pervasive stink of vomit speaking to the plight of beardless young men plucked from the prom and dropped into the maw of mass murder. Lieutenant Orr was trained to follow orders: During a battle, never risk more lives by slowing down to pick up survivors of sunken ships. Follow orders he would, but abandoning merchant sailors to perish in the flaming waves failed to square with a Christian conscience.

Together with two other warships, the corvette sank the Nazi submarine U-536 with depth charges off the Azores in 1942 and assisted in the D-Day landings in Normandy in 1944. At war's end, Mac, at twenty-three the youngest-ever commander of a Canadian corvette, pried off the vessel's two-foot-tall brass bell, mounted it on a wooden stand and lugged it home.

His teenage sweetheart, Dorothy Benjamin, a pretty, strong-willed, well-bred graduate of the girls' private school St. Clement's was there to meet him. To Dorothy, known as Do (pronounced Dough), Mac was a shining naval hero; somehow she managed to ignore the fact that three years of combat had arrested his growth.

Soon they were married; soon she was pregnant. All her life, Dorothy had been indulged by her beloved father, George Benjamin III, a successful businessman. But in the ninth month of her pregnancy, her father died of a heart attack in his sixties; twelve days later, her son George was born. Never speaking of the trauma of her own life—or the tripling of the name of George in father, husband and son—Dorothy soldiered on, giving birth to a second son they called Michael.

For six years, the family nestled under the umbrella of both sets of parents. Then, in 1953, Mac relocated his young family to a functional two-storey three-bedroom brick house he built on a dirt road in York Mills, overlooking open farmland. Their new home was miles below the gold standard of Rosedale and Forest Hill, a hard fact of no small importance to Dorothy, who in the face of other deficits in her life, had become a devout social climber.

By the end of her twenties, Dorothy found herself a rules-bound stay-at-home mother. She did not think to indulge her sons with hugs or stories or play but insisted they tightly grasp the social niceties. University-educated, more talented and intelligent than the average housewife, she reconciled herself to roles within charitable organizations like the Imperial Order Daughters of the Empire, still thriving in repressed, deferential Toronto.

As Dorothy plotted an upward trajectory, Mac drank. While veterans typically buried their scars in silence, Mac's Irish tongue was loosened by shots of Canadian Club rye. Year after year, his two growing boys were held captive by his vivid tales of horror and heroism on the deadly North Atlantic, streaked with guilt and sentimentality and white-hot bursts of profanity. What could they make of a father driving the hull of his corvette over the bodies of hapless sailors? A chain-smoker, Mac routinely flicked the butts of his Player's Navy Cut "Flat 50" cigarettes—standard issue for Canadian sailors—into the toilet bowl and, each morning, mustering a wordless response, young George targeted the floating tufts of tobacco with bursts of piss.

Dorothy gradually realized she had married the wrong man and the dream of her life would never happen. Driven by the intensity of the premature loss of her father and her disappointment in her husband, Dorothy began to reinvest her ambitions in her first-born son. Not that her mothering improved. George and Mike rarely saw their parents; after the ritual family watching of the six o'clock news, they left the boys alone and pursued a hectic social life. By then, George knew the playbook cold.

One day, George was furtively smoking cigarettes with his Grade 9 friend Patrick in the third-floor bedroom of Patrick's Glencairn Avenue home. Suddenly a bulky fourteen-year-old kid backed through the window off the eavestrough. For reasons he will never understand, George grabbed a pellet gun and shot the boy in the butt, and from such a random event a deep bond was born.

Stewart lived down the street at number 297 and fitfully attended Lawrence Park Collegiate. An indulged, fearless, chain-smoking, sex-obsessed, learning-disabled, rough-and-tumble public-school kid, Stewart was like a shot of penicillin to the prim private-school mould, a Huck Finn of Irish-Icelandic-Geordie blood, unafraid of his own id, bursting to strike out for the territories and surrender to all impulse.

Stewart and Patrick pulled George like a water skier in their wakes. They experienced him as quiet and private, slightly out of sync with reality, not sure he was really there, but a shared irreverence sealed the threesome's alliance. George was soon introduced to the art of boosting cigarettes, skin mags and random merchandise. They stole flags from libraries, made prank phone calls and whipped eggs at the door of a prominent violinist. For the sheer hell of it, they jumped fences at 3 a.m. and splashed in backyard pools, then cruised the nearby posh girls' school Havergal College, where teenage boarders flung open their windows and flashed their boobs.

George felt like he had made it to Grade 9 on charm; now he was just trying not to drown. Besides his delinquent forays with Stewart and Patrick, he channelled his aggression into contact sports and weekend rambles in the city's creek-fed ravines. Sharing a bedroom with his younger brother, George routinely bullied Mike until his sibling grew strong enough to hold his ground.

Girls remained alien life forms until a summer weekend in 1961 spent at Patrick's cottage in Shanty Bay on Lake Simcoe. George, Patrick and a guy named Doug Woods gravitated to a trio of girls, each equal parts bright, cute and mysterious.

That first summer, Alison Lay felt like another buddy. But the next summer, as the sextet meandered up a farm road in the warm dusk, past ruminating Holsteins, split-rail fences and shimmering piles of hay, just like that, Alison gently slipped her hand into his. As the kisses landed, he felt he had stepped on a downed wire. Summer jobs disrupted future contact between the two of them, but the enchantment of his first crush never died.

Only two summers later, a UCC classmate, Graham Woods, invited George to join him and another sixteen-year-old boy and his girlfriend on a ride up Highway 11 from Shanty Bay to Orillia. George wavered, then declined; within the hour, the three teenagers were crushed to death in a five-car pile-up. That same summer, another classmate, Eric Humphries, was killed by a bolt of lightning. No parent or teacher helped George cope with any of the deaths, and he experienced potent and lingering shame after he failed to attend the funerals.

He could routinely think of fifty things more interesting than school work and purposely streamed down from the bright kids' classes—2A1, 3A2, 4B1—retreating into a class by himself, fighting for a mind of his own. Over the dinner table, the headmaster's words survived as an oft-repeated family joke: "George Orr is one of the brightest but laziest students I've ever known." He felt for classmates such as Michael Ignatieff, the Boys Most Likely, the steady A-streamers, the straight-shooting, all-round, inside-the-circle Right Stuffers. They were willing participants in a powerful grooming process over which they had little or no control. In their hearts they wanted to do good and do well, but their personal authenticity was thrown under the school bus. They would never stop looking up to the teacher/father figures in anticipation of the coveted words "Good boy. Good job."

Bored to death by school but riveted by current events, George devoured the daily newspapers and CBC Radio. He began dreaming of entering journalism, a profession considered suspect by his parents; newsgathering ranked miles down the ladder from law, business and politics.

In November 1963, a bullet to the brain of an idealized Irish-American president turned everything upside down. TV news went live overnight, and so flowed the cacophony—the Bomb, the Beatles, *The Feminine Mystique*, Andy Warhol's soup cans, Ken Kesey's psychedelic bus, Martin Luther King Jr.'s dream, Malcolm X's nightmare, Freedom Summer, the Gulf of Tonkin, the Generation Gap, *The Medium Is the Message*, the Free Speech Movement. In 1964, the impassioned plea of the UC Berkeley student leader Mario Savio—"You've got to put your bodies upon the gears and upon the wheels . . . upon the levers, upon all the apparatus, and you've got to make it stop!"—pitched the first wild wave of baby boomers onto the beachhead of their parents' material dreams, the peace generation declaring war on the traumatized, alcoholic war generation longing for peace. The Boomers vs. the Bombed.

In this year of 1964, a swirling family drama caught George in its vortex. When Mac wanted to accept the offer of an executive position with a large American insurance firm, his controlling father branded him a traitor to the family. In a brazen act of emotional blackmail, the Orr patriarch threatened to walk out of his tony Alexandra Wood mansion and jump off the Bayview Bridge if Mac dared desert the family business. The ploy worked but forged an irreconcilable generational rift. At the height of the feud, Mac's invalid mother died; in a symbolic act of disavowal, Mac and his family were consigned by his father to the last row of the funeral chapel.

George now faced his own do-or-die moment. How does a sharp sixteen-year-old boy question power from within a power school? Leaders who mislead? Parents who blindly follow?

One evening at the dinner table, he rocked his captors with a pointed question: "Why do you keep wasting your money sending me to a school I hate?"

At the sound of the dropped cutlery, he launched a second depth charge: he wanted to pass up Grade 13 at UCC and enroll in journalism downtown at Ryerson Polytechnic—at the time not a university but a disreputable community college.

The parental phalanx returned fire: how dare our firstborn, our lawyer-businessman-politician-in-training, even contemplate breaking ranks? Of not taking one for the team, as we had? The words "disgrace" and "over our dead bodies" engulfed him, and the ultimatum was swift: "If you spurn UCC, you spurn the family. Move out."

So no journalism school but a small victory nonetheless: George was allowed to rejoin his beloved tribe of elementary school friends in Grade 13 at York Mills Collegiate. He moved his bedroom into the basement, where, immersed in a dreamy underworld of music and paperbacks, radio and TV shows, newspapers and magazines, he not only stripped off his despised blue tie but burned it. Under his graduating class photo, in the space for Intended Profession, he wrote, "Criminal lawyer." Let people guess whom he might prosecute first.

Crossing the threshold of a classroom half full of girls proved a welcome shock. Then came a second welcome shock: after he graduated, he spent July and August of 1965 travelling by bus through Western Europe with three dozen mostly private-school teens from across Canada. Run by Bernie Taylor, a Latin professor from the University of Toronto Schools, whose then all-male students were accepted according to ability rather than privilege, the European Odyssey was a North American knock-off of the eighteenth-century British Grand Tour; on that rite of passage young male aristocrats, graduates of Eton and Harrow, bought up crates of paintings and sculptures and spread their seed across the Continent before returning sated, and often syphilitic, to their inherited islands of privilege.

For George, Europe was not only where history was kept but also some notion of libertine sophistication. Yes, a guided tour was terminally bourgeois, but even in the slowly thawing Canada of 1965 the trip proved splendidly wild—fifteen boys, including a clique of UCCers, travelling in two Volkswagen vans along with twenty-five girls in a large bus, zooming from London to Paris to Vienna to Rome and through assorted country byways. It was sudden, exhilarating freedom, doing whatever you do when your parents aren't looking. George fell into the arms of Bacchus, but not Venus, though not for lack of trying.

Freshly turned eighteen, George wasn't intending to develop depth in any capacity, but Chartres Cathedral changed his life. Nick, the erudite twenty-one-year-old leader, knew the history of glass-making, stone masonry and flying buttresses cold. Different kinds of supporting arches? Built by hand? Original stained glass intact? Still standing eight hundred years later? George had died, gone to heaven and didn't want to leave.

That fall, he backed into the Glendon College campus of York University, opened four years earlier at Bayview and Lawrence Avenues, a short mile south of his basement catacomb. (His 63 per cent average had excluded him from the University of Toronto, his mother's alma mater, to her sorrow, not his.) He enrolled in psychology because it was the shortest line. Instead of gaining sublime insights into the human condition, he got lost in a Skinner box.

But his thwarted passion for journalism found a subversive outlet. He was hooked on a CBC Radio show hosted by Don Sims, a crusty newshound, broadcast live from midnight to 1 a.m. from the downtown Royal York Hotel where a roundtable of hard-drinking editors of the city dailies, the *Telegram*, the *Star* and the *Globe and Mail*, stuck analytical pins into the news of the day.

George routinely woke up at 11 p.m., quietly rolled his mother's box-like, two-tone blue 1963 Triumph Herald down the street and turned the ignition. Driving down Yonge Street, he felt as if he were headed for a rendezvous with a forbidden lover. At the hotel, he took a silent seat in a corner to listen to the old pros holding forth on the history of news, competitive journalism, context, accountability, speaking truth to power, comforting the afflicted, afflicting the comfortable. Asking questions. Difficult questions. He loved it.

When he got back home, he switched off the engine and coasted up the driveway. His head hit the pillow at 1:25, then the next morning it was up and off to behaviourist psychology class where, like the food pellets deployed in a maze of starving rats, all wellsprings of inspiration evaporated from the dream of his life.

THREE

Mother Moon

October 1962. Two months had passed since Sally Wodehouse had appeared to me like a revelation on the sunbathed dock of De Grassi Point. At twelve, I was a news junkie, spreading the evening paper on the living room carpet of our Toronto home, scanning the blurred reconnaissance photos of Soviet ships unloading nuclear warheads into the port of Havana. Impending doom, like sex, was testing my preadolescent comprehension. As I helped my mother stockpile cans of food, games of Monopoly and Clue and back issues of *Life* magazine in the damp, cramped freezer room under the basement stairs, I thought, *When I die, let it be sudden.*

Our fraught nuclear family was conducting its own protracted Cold War. In their youth, my parents had both yearned for the jazz bohemias of New York and Paris. Instead they got married and stayed put. A perfect recipe for domestic hell? Take two thwarted rebels, add a pinch of charm, wit and cynical glamour, project high expectations in opposite directions, toss into the rotating blades of the blender and repress. When my mother wanted a divorce, my father blocked her request in order to save face. I was the product of a born career woman without a career, oppressed by three needy kids, and a needy man-child who had never wanted kids.

From the moment of our births, it had been written that my brother and I would attend UCC. In my first year, I had thrived under my form master, Jack Schaffter, a former RAF pilot able to rip a phone book in half yet who responded tenderly to the acute sensitivities of an eight-year-old boy. "I am concerned," he wrote on my first report card, "about his extreme nervousness inside and outside the classroom." Only much later did I realize that this rarest of humans was the first and last person in my childhood who not only recognized my vulnerability but cared.

After Schaffter came a near-unbroken chain of brutes, bores and automatons, forcing me to build a fortress of mute endurance. One day after lunch in Grade 7, our bachelor master, an ex-Grenadier Guard, ordered six of us to appear at his boarding house apartment at day's end, where we would be caned for our "general attitude." The three-hour wait outside his bedroom door felt like sweating out a death sentence. I was called in first; bending over, I resolved not to give him the satisfaction of hearing me cry out, but the blows extracted the trickle of a tear. The next day, in the swimming pool where we were compelled to swim naked, the welts on my backside shone like a redeeming purple badge of courage. When news of the caning eventually reached my mother, she responded with a laugh.

I was learning my lessons well: Endure the ordeal. Turn the other cheek. We were future leaders, and leaders never complain.

This same fall of 1962, while I was still dreaming of my summer with Sally, our dog-faced science master crudely chalked the convoluted insides of male and female possums across the Grade 8 blackboard and formally introduced me to the clinical term "sexual intercourse."

First violence, now sex.

Never give a tongue-tied boy a *Roget's Thesaurus* for his twelfth birthday—he'd sooner play with words than girls. As Tony Hearn, another erotically starved British bachelor master, hammered home

grammar and punctuation, I was driven by fear and curiosity to memo-
rize long columns of vocabulary. One winter day, Hearn read aloud the
mythic story of the Spartan boy who hid a wolf cub under his cloak.
The cub gnawed at his viscera but the stoic boy dared not cry out lest
he betray his secret to the elders. When he fell over dead, intestines
spilling out, the Spartan nobility hailed the child as a paragon of
manly heroism. The story stuck in my mind, and guts.

. My father had written off his children, and I had written off my
father, obeying the invisible sign hanging from his forehead: Don't
give me any grief. In my drive to stay alive, I pinned my last best
hopes on my mother, mustering all the power of my despair to waken
her maternal instincts and soften her toughness. My mother never
indulged in daydreaming or naps and punished all who did; she was
more a human doing than a human being. If she caught me drifting
off, she intruded like a dream censor, rousing me from the forbidden
cave of my inner life.

In years to come, my mother would sporadically relate stories of
my early childhood with such cool matter-of-factness that I realized
she was immune to their very poignancy: that she was already overwhelmed by the demands of my toddler sister, so my birth triggered
a postpartum depression; that she surrendered me to an agency,
Mothercraft, for the first weeks of my life; that she could not breast-
feed; that I was a celiac baby, spitting up my food. I squirrelled away
her reportage to marinate in my memory palace, retroactive clues to
understanding her and thus myself.

An orphan in all but name, I was left to grapple alone with a per-
sistent buildup and backlog of unanswered questions. Why was the
parental bedroom door perpetually shut to me? If I cried, why did my
mother lock me in the nursery until I stopped, but even then did not
let me out? Why did night terrors routinely savage my sleep? Why did
I feel like a china plate on a wall? Why was my older sister, a frantic
bundle of perpetual protest, being drugged and strapped to the bed?

Why was my three-year-old brother running away from home? Did my experiences actually happen? Was I real?

When I was four or five, I dared to push open the bathroom door to find my mother soaking in the pink enamel tub, soap bubbles clinging to the black wall tiles. My eyes deflected from her pillowy breasts, landing inches westward on the circular smallpox-vaccination scar, no bigger than a nickel, indenting the filmy wetness of her tanned upper arm, alluring, sensational, out of reach. I beat a retreat to the hardwood floor of the nursery, where every day I had been drilled to obey the unspoken Royal Protocol: Never Touch the Queen.

It seemed I had but one strategy left: what if I planted myself on the living room floor a short distance from my mother's feet, my back turned to her? What if I sat perfectly still and undemanding, a toddler pretending to read an upside-down book, never speaking, never crying? What if I looked back over my shoulder, then tentatively wriggled backward inch by inch across the arctic tundra toward the fireplace of her body, as close as I dared? How could such perfect goodness fail to inspire a perfect love?

But she never reached down and pulled me up on her lap; never touched, kissed, cuddled or soothed me, never read me a bedtime story. I was compelled to withdraw into my imagination but never ceased attempting to engineer alternative routes up the cliff face that was my mother, negotiating endless hairpin turns, only to be cut off, each time, at the pass.

The TV camera of my head points to the Grade 1 classroom of Brown Public School. A withdrawn child, nudging on a state of autism, I strain to copy the six letters from the blackboard to form my first written word: m-o-t-h-e-r. The survival instinct is inventing solutions; maybe writing down words will compensate for my fear of speaking up. If the statue cannot love me with her body, I will spoon stories into her mouth, like alphabet soup, hoping she will give something back. If I master spelling and the tool of writing, if I entertain, if I amuse, if I enliven, something has to give.

My six-year-old hand drags a pencil over a page of foolscap, and out comes a tale of a boy starving for food and air, building a rocket to the moon, unaware there is even less food and air up there. Seemingly pleased, my mother, the moon, promises to keep the story and show it to me when I turn thirty, as if she alone controls the timetable of the one-way trip to Planet Janet, as if she alone knows she stands as my sole way out of the inner world into the outer. Perhaps, she hints, one day I will become a writer.

In Grade 9 math class, the ancient stone-faced master who caned my father a generation earlier routinely singled me out for humiliation. I didn't need to be clairvoyant to figure out that my father had been wildly and silently unhappy here. Why did he send us? Were we supposed to become replicas of him? I sank from the A to B stream.

Week after week, the math master told me to stand up and verbally work out a baffling equation; week after week, I burned in paralyzed silence; week after week, he stood and waited for the eternity of five minutes without offering a word of help. As the class sighed and squirmed, my tears dripped on the page so that I could no longer make out the equation. I felt like the ants I incinerated at recess with sun rays concentrated by my magnifying glass.

Mission accomplished: the waterworks ran dry, and I started giving as good as I got. I delighted in terrifying a phobic classmate with a rubber spider that raised panicked whimpers as he cowered on the grass. When I learned that the mother of a boy living across the street had died, I teased him viciously. Like Lawrence of Arabia, I was enjoying my own cruelty. I randomly tormented my younger brother, bruising his flesh with knuckle-driven "noogies" till the day he broke the spell with a slug to my face, and I desisted. Miming the protest movements of the times, he had taken to lying down, spread-eagled, in the middle of our street, stopping traffic, forcing a minimum ration of personal attention not to be found in our house or school. A gentle, undemanding character, Mike was the canary in the coal mine, and one day in a rare act of solidarity I joined him on the pavement.

My developing keenness for spies and double agents proved no accident, for one night over dinner our mother made a startling revelation. As twenty years had passed since the end of the war, she explained, her own contribution was now officially declassified. In the Rockefeller Center in Manhattan, she had worked in the British Passport Control Office, but the job was a cover; in fact, she was a "secret secretary" for Sir William Stephenson, the "Quiet Canadian" who ran the British MI5 spy network for Winston Churchill. Later, based in Guatemala City, she helped monitor suspected Nazi spies in Latin America. My daily strivings to decipher the enigma that was my mother assumed a whole new aspect.

In the summer of 1966, I found refuge from the city working on a raspberry farm near Port Hope, Ontario, that was owned by my uncle, David Ouchterlony, the organist of Timothy Eaton Memorial Church in Toronto. Like me, he was addicted to puns, so we had a field day. His wife, Kay, my mother's older sister, was everything Janet was not: warm, kind, simpatico. Hard physical work dispelled the trance of TV, radio and newspapers, and I thrived. In baking heat, I hauled irrigation pipes up and down hills and drove a tractor to collect the baskets of picked berries. Impersonating Huck Finn, I smoked a corncob pipe, assassinated groundhogs with a .22 rifle, counted passing boxcars and cooled off in the pond. For the first time since my summers with Sally, I lost track of time.

One humid August evening, I was invited on a double date. In the back seat of a '57 Chevy, my fifteen-year-old body was pressed up against the window by Linda, a girl who grew up on a neighbouring farm. Impressed with my pretentious vocabulary, she belted out the pop hit "James (Hold the Ladder Steady)" about a girl eagerly eloping, but I clung to the rung inside my chaste, airtight class bubble. Wasn't it written that I was supposed to marry Sally, or someone like her?

In the fall of 1966, entering Grade 12, I turned sixteen. My father's lifelong struggle to live up to the impossible standards of a distant, eminent father had collapsed into a nervous breakdown; he was drowning in his self-hate, but we all pretended everything was fine. The wolf-toothed pain now skewering my guts every day would not be diagnosed as Crohn's disease for another three years, but I knew that the consequences of asking for help were worse than the affliction.

I had recurring dreams of transferring to a hyper-idealized public high school where wholesome blue-eyed boys and girls in jeans and T-shirts played out the sunny enthusiasms of Mickey Rooney and Judy Garland Hollywood musicals. But when my sister left her private school for her final year at coed Oakwood Collegiate, she failed to integrate; I realized it was too late to change course and reverse the tide of our conditioning. To survive, some need to escape poverty, others to escape affluence, still others to escape both.

FOUR

George Loves Sally

I n the spring of 1966, George Orr, nearly nineteen, started a four-month stint working in a gold mine in the Northwest Territories after a lost first year at university. His father had procured him the job and a plane ticket to endless tundra, abysmal weather, tattooed roughnecks and mosquitos with the bite of vampire bats. A father's revenge. George learned much about life outside the box of upper-middle-class privilege. He worked as a carpenter's assistant at $75 a week, the first time he'd picked up a hammer or saw. The first thing he built was a coffin for a miner crushed in a cave-in.

In mid-August, he returned to Toronto, a muscular six-footer sporting a wispy black beard and a pocket full of cash. The first day back, he phoned Stewart, the childhood friend who'd introduced him to the elemental thrill of shoplifting cigarettes. Grown into a self-possessed, deep-voiced, broad-shouldered bear of a guy, Stewart had fallen three school years behind George owing to a reading disability. George's parents regarded him as a dangerous influence, but George loved him—the only guy he had ever known who had been true to himself from day one.

"I've met a girl named Gerrie," Stewart announced. "And she has a friend, Sally. Both are sixteen and going into Grade 12 at

Branksome Hall. How about a double date—one half of it blind?"

George's experience of private school girls had so far not been encouraging, but what harm could come of a single date?

On the sultry evening of Thursday, August 18, 1966, hours after the Beatles played a sold-out concert at Maple Leaf Gardens, Stewart wheeled his father's canary yellow Skylark into Chestnut Park Road, a Rosedale street studded with ten-foot-tall wrought-iron lamps and shaded by canopies of century-old elm and oak trees, a galaxy removed from the primal permafrost of the Far North. As George walked up to the front door of the genteel three-storey home and rang the bell, he was surprised by a queasy upsurge in the pit of his stomach.

There she stood, long and tall, like the song, oval-faced, her brown hair with its subtle tint of red curving to the shoulders. Sally Wodehouse was not smack-in-the-head gorgeous, but she radiated something exciting, something real, something *alive*.

At the Imperial Theatre on Yonge Street, a quartet of pink two-dollar bills produced tickets to *The Endless Summer*, a California surfer documentary. Afterwards, the foursome cruised back up to Fran's Restaurant on College Street, cramming into a leather booth for burgers and cherry Cokes. After four months with rank cigar-smoking miners, who attached the word "fuck" to each foul breath, George saw Sally as a delight—sweet, bright, witty, vivacious, fresh.

After steering the Skylark up Mount Pleasant Road, Stewart parked on a Rosedale side street and suggested the couples switch front and back seats. As George and Sally, the Two Virgins, chatted amiably up front, in the back Stewart and Gerrie thrashed like an octopus. From the radio blasted "Summer in the City," punctuated with the sounds of rattling jackhammers and Volkswagen horns, and the car literally rolled in sync with the rock. From the beginning, George and Sally shared something in common: *Don't look in the rearview mirror.* But somehow their conversation flowed freely across their three-year age gap.

The next day, George phoned Sally to ask her out, this time without Stewart and Gerrie. Once again braving the threshold of 30 Chestnut Park Road, he encountered the intimidating paternal figure of Dr. George Wodehouse, who led the young man to his lion's den at the back of the house. Pulling a fat cigar from his mouth, George the Elder fixed George the Younger square in the eye and, deadpan, intoned, "Before you two go out, I want you to know I'm head of the student medical health services at the University of Toronto. I'm responsible for thirty thousand students. I don't know if you've heard of the Coca-Cola douche, but it . . . does . . . not . . . work."

What George was thinking: *What the fuck?*

What George said: "I really like Sally, sir. But we're just good friends."

The second date dispelled the suspicion that their ease with each other was not an illusion: another movie, another dinner, another magic carpet ride of talk, talk, talk.

That fall George returned to York. After class he would borrow his mother's Triumph Herald and roll down Mount Pleasant Road to pick up Sally. Nestled in a thirteen-acre patch of Carolinian forest, the campus of Branksome Hall occupied the gilded Rosedale address of 10 Elm Avenue, its main building, Hollydene, a three-storey red-brick Victorian mansion with gables and chimneys and a porte cochère supported by four Doric columns. Accommodating six hundred students aged four to eighteen, Branksome Hall was one of the city's quartet of private, exclusive, Protestant, all-girl institutions, each accorded its own caricature, each holding a grain of truth: Bishop Strachan for snobs, Havergal for brains, Branksome

for egalitarians and St. Clement's (where George's mother went
to school), the poor cousin. Threading through knots of school-
girls in red blazers, green kilts, knee socks and black Oxfords,
George felt as if he was penetrating a forbidden enclave to retrieve
his Sally.

When Mrs. Wodehouse bought a blue Mustang with a white
canvas convertible top, Sally was transformed overnight into the
living song. On weekends, with George at the wheel, they would
"do the crawl" through Yorkville, the teeming enclave of two narrow, parallel one-way streets, a short five blocks south of Sally's
house, where young hippies were converging from all over Canada.

As they passed the dozens of coffee houses, clubs, art galleries
and head shops, George and Sally studied like curious anthropol-
ogists the barefoot, beaded and bearded, the body painted and
sandal shod, the panhandlers, potheads and pushers, the spaced-
out bikers and greasers and Jesus freaks, the jugglers and the
clowns, the rich-kid runaways expelled from houses and schools
not unlike their own. In the window of the Mynah Bird, a drop-
dead gorgeous go-go girl in leather boots and miniskirt gyrated
like an Eaton's department store mannequin jolted to life. The
acoustics of Joni Mitchell and Gordon Lightfoot radiated from the
doors of the Purple Onion, the Riverboat, the Penny Farthing; farther south, on Yonge Street, in bars such as the Colonial and Le
Coq d'Or, Robbie Robertson, Rompin' Ronnie Hawkins, David
Clayton-Thomas and John Kay, the future founder of Steppenwolf,
rocked out a tougher, bluesier, electrified rock 'n' roll. The bad
bohemian young were everywhere disturbing the sleep of the puri-
tanical old of Toronto the Good.

As reticent as he was ambitious, George had longed for somebody soft and sweet to pull him out of himself, and now the magical
Sally was obliging, listening closely as he released his true self into
the world; under her spell, a raconteur was being born. He was a

Canadian, he did exist and he actually felt articulate. It was all happening so fast, like some wildly exciting casino-run of dumb luck that he could scarcely believe, let alone control.

Mere months had passed since a bearded, slightly more worldly George Orr had drifted home from a rough-and-tumble summer job in a subarctic gold mine, delivered by a dream-like August evening to the drawbridge of a Rosedale castle, where he succumbed to the sly smile of a sixteen-year-old blind date. But even as he was captivated, as he grew almost reluctantly happy, he caught a whisper from the depths of his mind: *Be careful of what you wish for.*

From the start, George found the other members of the Wodehouse family a touch intimidating—George and Jane, intelligent, socially connected, opinionated, heavy drinkers and smokers, gladly unsuffering of fools, and the older sister, Diana, quietly envying the evolution of Sally into a social butterfly.

Even at nineteen, George was mature enough to empathize with the adults: Who is this young man our daughter keeps bringing home for dinner? How do we deal with him? Do we like him? Is he a keeper? Do we throw him back? If we throw him back, do we upset Sally and make it worse?

George soon learned that Sally's father had pulled scare tactics on every suitor of his teenage daughters and driven most away. As the Wodehouses realized that George was gaining traction, they began to include him in family birthdays, Easter, Thanksgiving and Christmas, the quartet-plus-one perching on stiff wooden chairs surrounding the hand-carved rosewood table positioned under the crystal chandelier. Having drilled her sons on the finer points of etiquette—work the silverware from the outside, don't spill, drool, or speak with your mouth full—Dorothy Orr had done her sterling best to raise a young gentlemen of manners, and he could pass muster.

Unlike George's father, a charming treader of water, George Wodehouse was a bold, balding, cigar-puffing figure who commanded a room with the overwhelming self-confidence common to many doctors. And he could hold his liquor: on weekends, the Wodehouses started drinking steadily at two but unflaggingly made dinner by six. George never saw Sally's parents drunk, an important lesson in image control.

A classic raconteur, the doctor told stories in ways the damaged Mac Orr could not match. In August 1944, near Caen in Normandy, he was commanding a casualty clearing station in an open battlefield. Under intense German fire, within the space of a hellish hour he tied tourniquets and bandaged thirty-five wounded young soldiers with arms or legs blown off, saving some lives, losing others. He was awarded the Military Cross.

After the war, Dr. Wodehouse got down to the business of doing good and doing well. When he met Jane Toller, the determined daughter of a privileged Maritimes family, he accepted that he occupied a slightly lower social station and let her drive him like a government mule; given his innate brains and ambition, his "marrying-up" worked as a comfortable contract of mutual gain.

In the Medical Arts Building at Bloor and St. George streets, he built up a private practice until 1950, the year of Sally's birth, when at thirty-four his career path curved dramatically upward. Appointed head of the University of Toronto's student health service, he occupied an office at 256 Huron Street, a Victorian house in the heart of the aptly named St. George Campus of the university, supervising a staff of doctors cross-appointed from city hospitals. Attached to Branksome Hall as the school physician, he performed the annual polio shots for anxious lines of kindergarten girls, promising a lollipop to those who succeeded in suppressing their tears.

He became a veteran observer of the gropings of countless hormonally crazed undergrad youth and their miserable outcomes from pregnancy to VD. A realist, Dr. Wodehouse co-authored a comprehensive paper on birth control, warning the reactionary, prudish, Victorian-minded administrators to avoid a head-on collision with the fast-advancing hordes of horny baby boomers. He believed that the University of Toronto still had time to forestall the worst-case scenarios erupting across American campuses—rashes of unwanted pregnancies, coat-hanger abortions, young women bleeding out, sometimes to death. Students wanted facts, not morals, but in a *Father Knows Best* world—and sometimes he actually did—as long as birth control remained illegal for the unmarried, the doctor-in-chief of the nation's largest institution of higher learning was bound to the letter of the law—even as an aspiring young pagan bearing his own Christian name was circling his own teenage daughter.

George felt as if he'd inherited a new set of parents more glamorous than his own. The Wodehouses occupied the top link of the food chain: house in Rosedale, cottage on Lake Simcoe, friends in high places, enjoying being on a first-name basis with Lester Pearson, the country's prime minister. George found Sally's confidence attractive because he didn't have any. Because she shunned nylons and lipstick, high heels and eyeshadow, beguilingly underplaying her own princess-ness, she rose even higher in George's estimations. A flat-footed, slightly androgynous tomboy who swore like a sailor, she wasn't dainty, and that's why she was fun—wedding natural charm to an emerging fearlessness.

She shared her mother's sharp tongue but nothing of the fastidious snobbery, the status-based airs and attitudes. Yet Jane had a hard time resisting George because he liked her, and she'd always wanted a son. Siphoning bottles of gin like the Queen Mother, she trolled for hints as to whether he had yet made love to her daughter, but she was too well brought up to raise the subject directly. Enticing as it all was, George remained unsure if he wanted to fly into the gilded cage of the Rosedale Chosen, where young lives were mapped out in advance of their living. He heard the violins, but he saw the strings attached.

The Orr and Wodehouse parents socialized on only two occasions: Jane, the social gatekeeper, maintained a genteel distance, anointing the Orrs "nice." Dorothy Orr approved of Sally but not only for her membership in the right club; in the bright light of the teenager she recognized her lost, unfettered self and looked forward to Sally's visits.

The deeper George ventured into Sally's lively social circle—much of it male—the faster her distressing popularity rose to meet him. Did she like someone better than him?

On the Victoria Day long weekend of May, 1967, days before Sally's seventeenth birthday, George first experienced the ritual spring opening of the cottage on De Grassi Point, the taking-down of the storms and the putting-up of the screens. Simultaneously, over four thousand hippies and their sightseeing admirers, inspired by San Francisco's Human Be-In of months earlier, flocked two blocks south from Yorkville Village to the lawns of Queen's Park to join the poet-singers Leonard Cohen and Buffy Sainte-Marie in the city's first mass Love-In. Arrest-and-freak-out-free, the event radiated a gentle calm of flute playing, dancing circles and flowers passed to passersby. The media were charmed.

Gradually Dr. Wodehouse was ceasing to perceive his daughter's boyfriend as an existential threat. Most weekends that summer, the two Georges drove up north together, with or without the females, chopping down trees or swimming on the sandbar. He could not pinpoint the day it happened, but young George came to believe Sally's father had resigned himself to him: she likes him, so I'll like

him. "Our house is your house" was the watchword, but the doctor
was equally clear on another score: no one sleeps with my daughter
under my watch.

That summer, Sally headed south to Cape Cod for a six-week stint
as an au pair, taking care of the unruly brat of a prominent family
neighbouring the fortified Hyannis Port compound of the Kennedy
clan. She wrote George letters complaining of the "madhouse" she
was enduring; since absence may make the heart grow fonder (or
colder), George drove down with Stewart for a week-long visit.
Returning through New York State, the young Canadians were
awestruck by the sight of open trucks crammed with thousands of
crewcut green-fatigued draftees streaming down the highway.

George acquired a new Honda 90, a meek excuse for a motorcycle that maxed out at 30 mph. Standing at the foot of his driveway
on Gordon Road, George let his buddy David ride around the block
helmetless. On his third circuit, a dog bolted into his path and David
slammed the brakes, hurtling over the handlebars, hitting the asphalt
on his forehead. To the horror of all, he convulsed on the road like a
fish out of water. Luckily, the accident happened in front of a doctor's
house; the doctor stuffed a breathing tube down the teenager's throat
and stayed with him until the ambulance delivered him to Sick Kids
Hospital. Emerging from unconsciousness several hours later, David
made out the faces of his parents and George and his parents. He
suffered only a concussion and some scrapes, and George's Honda
incurred nothing but a broken turn signal. But David's father couldn't
forgive George—and George didn't blame him.

That autumn George entered his third year of university and
Sally her final year of high school. In a friend's station wagon, they
drove Stewart up to Muskoka Lakes College for Grade 13, where he
was destined to be chosen head boy—then fired, rehired and refired

for his inevitable delinquencies, no small accomplishment. On the road north, Stewart indulged in a last thrash with Gerrie in the fold-down back of the car as Sally, clutching the dying vestiges of her prudery, interjected: "I know what you two are doing. Stop that!"

When distance broke Gerrie and Stewart up, George grappled with an irrational anxiety that he might also lose Sally. He had moved from Glendon College up to the main York campus at Jane and Steeles, a flat, bleak expanse of brutalist concrete and glass where students scuttled beaver-like through underground tunnels to evade the vicious winter winds. Then suddenly the light went on: George needed to focus on art history. In France, he had fallen in love with painting and architecture, then forgot he had.

As Canada's Centennial Year, 1967, drove to a close, George knew he was in deep with Sally. Which made him uneasy: *If your life seems too good to be true, it probably is.*

Sure enough, days later, Sally told him the bad news: her father wanted to send her on an Odyssey trip through Europe all of next summer.

To George, this could mean only one thing: she was leaving home. And she was never looking back.

FIVE

The Act You've Known for All These Years

During the Christmas holidays of 1967, my mother placed a green brochure in my hands. Under the carved face of a Roman sun god, I read a quotation from Lord Tennyson's poem "Ulysses":

> *I am part of all that I have met;*
> *Yet all experience is an arch wherethro'*
> *Gleams that untravell'd world, whose margin fades*
> *For ever and forever when I move.*

My maternal grandmother was shelling out US$1,375, roughly equal to a year's tuition at UCC, to send me on the two-month European Odyssey. Over July and August, twenty-six teenagers and two young leaders, mostly drawn from private schools from Halifax to Toronto to Vancouver, would tour Italy, France, Switzerland, Germany, Austria and England in four Volkswagen minibuses. I was puzzled that my grandmother, a prudish, pious, classically trained pianist who produced three offspring by having sex exactly three times, thought the trip was a good idea. Was the Odyssey an unspoken reward for surviving ten years at UCC?

I scanned two separate alphabetical lists of names, a pleasingly symmetrical thirteen boys and thirteen girls. Six of the boys were schoolmates whom I'd known forever, but as my eyes slid down the list of girls, I recognized no one until the last name leapt out at me: Wodehouse, Sally—Branksome Hall—30 Chestnut Park Road, Toronto 5, Walnut 4-4555. *The number I never called.* I was quietly thrilled that six years on, my playmate of the summer sandbar was magically re-entering my life. I remembered her, but had she remembered me?

But I had to survive till then. Every morning I felt like Gregor Samsa of Kafka's *Metamorphosis*, struggling to heave my giant cockroach thorax out of bed. I could not shake an unyielding inner pressure, as if I must immediately address the UN General Assembly without notes, singlehandedly solving world hunger, disguised as my own. Each morning in the Prayer Hall—where long hair currently posed the direst of threats to the manhood of Western civilization—I slouched in a hard wooden pew, a reluctant prefect taking roll call for bodies as absent as my own. I resented being forced to take maths, physics and chemistry, for which I had no aptitude or interest; in fact, I couldn't escape the feeling that I was the subject of some depersonalized, controlled, double-blind, longitudinal science experiment—a subject being turned into an object.

A disproportionate number of the school faculty were closeted homosexual men, adding a strange brew of homoeroticism and homophobia to the atmosphere we breathed. No one seemed to care when our algebra master, Walter Bailey, a tortured alcoholic of caustic tongue, spent an entire class reading aloud from a paperback of softcore homosexual pornography provocatively thrown on his desk by a student. A wretched teacher infected by a world-class cynicism, face flushed with a self-loathing that he dumped on us, he doubled as a wretched guidance counsellor. Weirdly, I felt empathy for him even as he felt none for us.

I stoically continued to ignore all signals from my body, including the intensifying bouts of cramping in my guts, the ceaseless cycles of constipation and diarrhea, symptoms of Crohn's, though I didn't know it then. I also tried to prevail over what turned out to be severe anemia. A strong swimmer, I had a few years earlier set a record in the backstroke and competed for the school's first swim team. When, because of leg-aching tiredness, I had to ask to be excused from the year-end meet at Hart House at the University of Toronto against the rival boys' private schools, the coach refused. In a suit of concrete, I finished dead last by a humiliating margin. I almost admired the dark simplicity of the centuries-old Master Plan: sink or swim in the social Darwinian piranha tank, and if you sink, you won't be missed.

On the night of Saturday, May 11, 1968, I was hanging out with Mike, a neighbourhood friend. We had formed the habit of watching old movies together, turning down the sound and ventriloquizing our own ad-libbed dialogue. Mike also possessed a bizarre facility for reading the scrolling names of movie credits backwards at lightning speed, a source of convulsive hilarity, especially when stoned; Ringo Starr will forever remain Ognir Rrats. The violence flowing from the nightly newscasts, meanwhile, kept us wondering: Why were masses of Sorbonne students throwing up barricades on the Left Bank of the Seine, hurling Molotov cocktails at security police?

A year older than me, Mike was home from his first year at the University of Western Ontario. He had hated every fucking second of it and had resolved to drop out and hitchhike to Kathmandu and beyond. I had just received early acceptance at Queen's University, unwittingly trading one austere Protestant enclave for another.

Until recently, Mike had lived half a block down Dunvegan Road at number 45. His mother, Millie, was one of those warm, sweet-smiling, sandwich-making wives who humanized the neighbourhood, gamely propping up their war-traumatized husbands; with her I basked in a kindness unknown at home or school. Her husband had recently sold their three-storey mansion to a nouveau riche hipster-architect who, on this very evening of May 11, was bent on razing the place in a wild "Destructorama" party, then erecting a red-brick townhouse in its place. When Mike decided to crash the bash, I was in.

We found the house jammed with over two hundred architects, artists and engineers clad in bell-bottoms, Nehru jackets and hard hats. Wielding sledgehammers and pick axes, the Beautiful People were doing their less-than-beautiful thing, ripping out the radiators, light fixtures and bathtubs as a live band rocked out "Light My Fire" and a hovering film crew shot the mayhem.

In the smoky din we threaded through the glut of bodies, brushing past a stoned dolt with a toilet seat hung round his neck. Up the staircase, I followed Mike through the rooms of his childhood, and as we passed the splintered Ping-Pong table, the screens ripped from the sun porch, the piles of shattered lathe and plaster scattered under the black holes punched in the wall, I watched his face redden. Turning into his parents' bedroom, we encountered a miniskirted goddess, wobbling in her intoxication, struggling to lift a sledgehammer. Snatching the tool, Mike started in on a wall. As a ring of guests recoiled from the intensity of Mike's psychodrama, the host appeared and demanded that we leave. Mike said, "What if it was my father who sold you the fucking place?" But to the new owner, the obvious anguish of the teenager cut no ice, and we were escorted to the street.

Only one teacher, who ran a redemptive Grade 13 English class, cared enough to let me explore who I was. Jay MacDonald was a trained actor who had studied under Vladimir Nabokov at Cornell University. A suspected homosexual, he was blessedly free of the *Lord of the Flies* perversity that infused the institution. Countercultural shrapnel was shredding the classical canon, and I was picking up the scattered pieces like a magpie, stuffing shreds of human compassion and conscience into the rows of glass jars arrayed inside me. I identified with the low raised up, from Jane Eyre, the plain, orphaned governess, to Pip, leaving flowers on his mother's grave, worshipping the beautiful yet coldly rejecting Estella who provoked his tortured vow, "I'll never cry for you again."

One day in class, MacDonald observed how many of the plots of the books we were studying were driven by multiple coincidences and the unseen hand of fate. When he remarked that such seeming contrivances in fact reflected archetypal truth, I was not buying in. Abandoned as an infant, Oedipus Rex not only unwittingly killed his father at a three-way crossroad but turned around and unwittingly married his mother? I mean, pull the other one.

On my own time, I had recently devoured *The Catcher in the Rye*. Holden Caulfield was a lanky, six-foot-three, seventeen-year-old, dyspeptic preppie, fending off phonies and a nervous breakdown, and so, astonishingly, was I. For our end-of-year assignment, MacDonald invited the class to pen a parody of any of the books we had studied over the year. I couldn't believe my ears—I was being granted permission to speak with my true voice. The sentences poured onto the page, and within an hour I had spoofed the plot of *Jane Eyre* in the sulky, injustice-collecting, teenage tones of Holden Caulfield.

At the start of our next class, MacDonald announced that during the last five minutes of the lesson he would present "a new interpretation of *Jane Eyre*." I thought, *That'll be interesting*, not dreaming he'd read out my paper. Which he did.

"Well, if you really want to know about it," went the opening sentence, "my crummy life started out pretty depressing, being an orphan and all."

As MacDonald reduced the class of twenty-five to hysterics, the nail-biting introvert with churning bowels sat at the back of the class, beside himself, his cover blown. My parody ended: "All I can say is that I'm goddamn glad that nothing too way out or too coincidental has happened in my life so far, because I want to sell a lot of copies of this book I'm going to write, and I don't think too many people go in for the long, unbelievable stuff every guy and his brother are writing these days."

As the laughter subsided, MacDonald asked the class, "Now, who do you suppose wrote this piece?"

No clue.

"It was Mr. FitzGerald."

Twenty-five heads swivelled as one, fixing me with an incredulous stare. *Him?* The hunched-over nonentity, the mute beanpole who disappeared years ago? Such intense scrutiny would normally deliver a splash of psychic napalm, but instead I felt like a swallow released from a dark, empty place.

Still, there was a catch: in the sanctum of my inner world I found *Jane Eyre* a poignant, tender love story, but I was conditioned to mock the very stuff that moved me: the sublime sufferings of Jane trapped in the frigid orphanage, her telepathic response to the voice of the blinded Rochester calling from across the heath. Being clever was safer than being real.

On June 6, I came downstairs for breakfast to find the headlines blazing another political horror: Robert Kennedy had been gunned down in Los Angeles only weeks after the killing of Martin Luther King Jr. At the table, I struggled to hold back my tears, puzzled by the power of my feelings. In the five years since his brother's murder, Robert Kennedy's character seemed to have deepened in a crucible of introspection and pain. Witnessing the hopeless poverty of the black ghettos and migrant workers, the privileged liberal was radically transformed by moral passion and genuinely championed the underclass. If anyone would have led us out of the wilderness, it was RFK, a rare figure in the pages of history. The potential you loved in others was ultimately your own.

As we watched the televised images of the funeral train bearing the flag-draped coffin from New York to Washington, massive, solemn crowds lining the tracks, I was stirred by an eerie sensation: I felt as if I was connecting with something unspeakable that might have happened in my own Irish family, backwards down the tracks, back to early childhood, back to before my birth. Thoughts that do often lie too deep for tears.

My father was now a broken man who saw his life as fraudulent, a wrong turn, all past fixing, the public shell of his Forest Hill utopia masking a particular private hell, his only escape route the quiet plotting of his own murder. It was no accident that with such a role model, I might wonder about his own father, my grandfather, a forgotten medical hero whose name was never mentioned in our house.

At the same time, rumours of the sexual predation of UCC students by masters whispered down the corridors of our daily lives as open secrets; in flashing, uncanny moments, I dared to suspect that the unlit underground of family and school were fused within a single circuit, haunted by monsters in disguise.

Within the slow-motion implosion of my own nuclear family, I was buffeted by a maelstrom of contradictory messages. Should I carry the torch? Or torch the carriers? Still, I was absorbing a vital lesson at home and at school: violence inflicted on children in the name of love was a Big Lie.

Many of my peers were set to seal their fates, either dutifully moving on to manage the inherited family wealth or splitting the scene for good. I was muddling around somewhere in the middle. I was disinclined to sleepwalk into the old boys' network, the whole point of my education; I preferred not to rule the unruly world but to hang backstage and watch.

Stripping off my blazer and blue tie for the last time, I retreated to the coach house for a private celebration. I dropped the holy disk on the turntable, the needle in the groove and twisted the knob to full blast. Uplifted by the power trio of Eric, Jack and Ginger, I merged with the blistering congress of guitar, bass and drums, and for a moment I found hard proof of the existence of God.

On Saturday, June 15, I boarded the Queen Street streetcar bound for 1 Fallingbrook Road, the home of Professor Bernie Taylor. Perched on the windy Scarborough Bluffs overlooking the white-capped blue of Lake Ontario, the three-storey wood-frame house was ringed by shade trees and a white picket fence. As Bernie, a strapping, grey-haired man in his mid-fifties, greeted me at the door, my stomach tingled at the prospect of meeting my summer companions.

Gathering in the sunroom, the boys gravitated to one side, the girls to the other. The opposite sex. Catching Sally's eye, I felt blood rush to my cheeks. *Play it cool, man.*

"Haven't I seen you somewhere before?" I tried.

I recognized her answering smile across the gap of the years. The twelve-year-old was now eighteen, but I was relieved that she had not shed her quirks: the slightly raspy voice, the lowering eyelids and upturned upper lip, the long fingers casually hooking strands of reddish-brown hair around her ears, the expressions shifting from goofy to foxy, from plain to striking and back again, her body a touch ungainly, a touch graceful. An actual, familiar girl, one who knew me, and liked me, lost and now found. Love at second sight.

When Bernie touted the trip as "an experience you will remember for a lifetime," sniggers ensued—we weren't swallowing the propaganda. A savvy marketer who for the past twenty years had sold his trips in the living rooms of the well-to-do, Bernie recruited his leaders from the country's top private schools, cherry-picking the best and brightest—not necessarily the richest—head boys, head girls, team captains and promoted their star power to attract other students. A veteran of five Odysseys, Nick was Bernie's twenty-four-year-old protege and heir apparent, and as he stepped forward to speak, I liked him instantly: blond, blue-eyed, self-confident, quick-witted, charismatic.

We were asked to stand up, one by one, and say something about ourselves. When my turn came, I stammered something inane, my affectation of rock star coolness mocked by my turtleneck, cardigan and horn-rimmed glasses. But if I couldn't find the right words, it did not seem to matter. In my seventeen years, I had known the wondrous and the terrible, and their distressing proximity, but on that radiant June afternoon I had reason to hope my chronic worries were history. If I must obey a higher authority, let it be the Law of Attraction, and let it be Sally.

SIX

"I'm Never Going to See You Again"

When Sally told George she was going to Europe, he did not take it lying down. Terrified that the eight-week trip would give her endless opportunities to stray, he convinced himself that some private school snake-in-the-grass would triumph where he had failed on his own Odyssey in 1965. Full of passion, George swore up and down that he'd sooner rot in hell than let Sally cross the road without him.

She had come to know him as quiet and lovable, and seeing him act so possessively shocked her. "Guess what? I *am* going. What are you going to do about it?"

The more George protested, the more she resisted. If he was playing Othello, inflamed by the green-eyed monster, she was not about to channel Desdemona and expire under the smothering pillow.

Then it got worse. Dr. Wodehouse insisted that his daughter was not only destined for a nursing career but that she should train at the Royal Victoria Hospital in Montreal. George interpreted this latest paternal edict, on top of the trip, as part of a conspiracy to distance his daughter from her overanxious suitor.

Feeling as if it was a full-time job managing the two Georges in her life, Sally huddled with Gerrie to forge her own plan. First, she persuaded her best friend to come with her on the Odyssey. Then they both applied to nursing school at the University of Toronto for the fall of '68 and agreed that, one day, they would stand as each other's bridesmaid. When she returned home, Sally assured her boyfriend, she would be right where he wanted her.

On Christmas Night 1967, George was as usual invited to the Wodehouse family dinner. But as he scanned Sally's family members taking their set places at the polished rosewood dining room table, he felt his distance from their circle and the class codes conducted with such symphonic seamlessness by Dr. and Mrs. W. Here was the gilded box that to his eyes increasingly resembled a coffin; here was the rarefied heaven-on-earth his mother so unambiguously wanted for him. But did Sally want it too? As George sipped the cold vichyssoise from the monogrammed sterling silver spoon, he wondered how long before he would need the same spoon to tunnel out of prison. The question gnawed: *do I belong here?*

Past midnight, George and Sally ascended the staircase and lingered in each other's arms on the threshold of the second-floor guest bedroom. After Sally broke off their kiss, he watched her slip away into the darkness to her bedroom on the floor above.

In the dawn light of Boxing Day, he was jolted awake by a dream of primal intensity. As the phantasm of faces and voices melted away, he was left with a single thought drumming his head: *Sally will die in Europe this summer.*

Over breakfast, he could not help telling Sally the dream. As he watched her face fall, he knew he should back off but instead found himself begging her to drop out of the Odyssey. She was bewildered, then creeped out, then irritated. For weeks he had been badgering her to not to go, and now he was pulling this stunt?

Undeterred, George told the dream to his parents, Sally's parents, his friends, to anyone who would listen: "Sally will die in Europe this summer." Almost to a person, the response came back: "Get over it. She loves you. The dream is just a dream." The sole exception was his neighbour Graham Gillman. Destined to divert from a promising corporate path into a Buddhist monastery in Sri Lanka, Graham was the only one in George's world who actually knew how to listen. All the same, George could not shake a deepening sense of isolation.

Through the winter of 1967–68 and into the spring, George and Sally squabbled over petty things—which movie to see, which restaurant to choose, which route to take home. Soon they were making excuses not to see each other every day, since the less they saw of each other the less they made scenes. They loved each other, but their mutual irritation forced them apart until their attraction pulled them back together. The dream, the talking about it, the not talking about it, the dressing-downs and the making-ups, the lust, the mistrust, all mirrored the larger riotous, crazy, unravelling world. Soon only one thing united them: losing their virginity.

But where could they find the space and time? The third floor of Sally's house? George's basement? Her mother's Mustang? His mother's Triumph? Four no's spawned a single yes: one Saturday afternoon, feeling half his age of twenty, George booked a room in the King Edward, the venerable downtown hotel where the Beatles had slept. While Sally waited upstairs, George survived the worst fifteen minutes of his life summoning the nerve to buy condoms in the lobby drugstore.

But even their new physical closeness failed to relieve the dread simmering in George's chest as the date of Sally's summer Odyssey edged closer.

———

On the afternoon of Tuesday, June 11, George joined family and friends to watch the seventy-one graduates of the Branksome Hall class of 1968 gather in front of the Metropolitan United Church at Queen and Church Streets in downtown Toronto. Tradition called for all grads to wear a dress of pure white—nothing sleeveless, strapless or touched with colour—but the girls fashioned a creative mix of semi-dodgy designs: long-sleeved, short-sleeved, some high-necked and virginal, others daring a flash of cleavage.

A kilted highlander in full-dress regalia led the line of girls through the arched doors of the church and down the centre aisle to the front pews, his elbow squeezing from his bagpipe a primitive droning and chanting sound originally designed to spur Celtic warriors into the madness of battle but which, on this tranquil day, released nothing but an air of dignified poignancy. The principal handed out the diplomas in alphabetical order, Sally Lyn Wodehouse the last in line.

Piped out of the church, the grads returned to the school where they picked up bouquets of roses sent by family and boyfriends, then gathered behind the boarding quarters of Sherborne House to pose for the official black-and-white class photograph. For the final act, all were piped, two by two, through the gates of the Junior School, back to their beginnings, past the old Deacon House, while along the path, family and friends clapped and snapped photos as traffic hummed through the wooded ravine of Rosedale Valley Road. On the back lawn of Jarvis House, a three-storey Victorian, all gravitated to the shade of the maple tree planted in 1867, the birth year of Canada. Murmuring mothers in stylish hats spooned dishes of ice cream shaped like strawberries while cherubic kindergarten kids skipped across the grass, their kilts fastened with tartan suspenders.

Around the fringes of what was clearly a family affair, boyfriends such as George hovered self-consciously, disguised in jackets and ties, like untrained foxes circling the henhouse. George found himself dreaming of some kind of rescue mission, but he was still unsure whether it was Sally or himself most in need. A dreary clerical summer job confined to his father's insurance office had already induced a near-chronic lethargy. For her part, Sally exulted in the freedom promised by the soft June breeze. She was now done with the tight schedule of the swimming, badminton and basketball teams, all that jolly-hockey-sticks crap, the demerit points issued for drooping bloomers, the age-old "You can't be too rich, thin, smart and athletic" pecking orders.

On the red cover of the yearbook, under the school crest, the school motto was printed in silver block letters: "Keep Well the Road." Sally's friend Gerrie made the first real detour when she dropped out of the Odyssey only days short of their departure; for her, it was just a school extension course. She'd sooner hitchhike and backpack on her own. George was thrilled: maybe Sally would follow suit, and if she did, his terrible dream of her death could not possibly come true. But Sally did not quit the trip. Still, if George had chanced to read the lines inscribed under Sally's graduation photo, he might have felt his jealousy ease:

NICKNAME: *Just Plain George*
AMBITION: *To get married*
FAVOURITE SONG: *See You in September*

In the six months since George's ominous dream, he had failed to divert the inevitable. On the morning of Tuesday, July 2, 1968, together with Mrs. Wodehouse, he drove Sally in the Mustang convertible to the airport. In his head, he had shot and cut their parting scene from a thousand different angles, but when the inescapable moment came, if he felt anything at all, it was numb.

Stone-still, George watched Sally ascend the terminal escalator. With a final wave of her hand she swung right, dissolving like a cloud of vapour. A feeling of granite certainty drove the thought in his head: *I'm never going to see you again.*

Janet Grubbe FitzGerald, age 17, 1936

James and Janet, spring 1951

Wedding of George "Mac" Orr and Dorothy Benjamin, April 1946

Three generations of Georges, 1961

Jack FitzGerald (standing), James and brother Michael (centre),
and Sally (lower right), De Grassi Point, Lake Simcoe, August 1962

Sally, 1967

Sally and George, Branksome Hall formal, 1967

Sally, 30 Chestnut Park, spring 1968

Sally's graduation day with parents Jane and George, June 1968

Sally's graduation portrait

PART II

The uncanny reminds us that everything is too close to home. One's deepest wish is that there is no place like home, because one's deepest fear is that there is no place unlike home. And home is where the trouble starts.

—ADAM PHILLIPS, *Equals*

▶ X

SEVEN

Sea Change

On the afternoon of Tuesday, July 2, 1968, I was lingering in the mezzanine of Toronto's Malton Airport with a cluster of Odyssey kids, awaiting our flight to New York City. Coolly assessing two girls who were crying from homesickness even before we boarded the plane, I was struck how sick I was of home. Glancing toward the escalator, I caught sight of the familiar brown head rising into view. As Sally moved closer, I smiled hello, but she seemed distant. I was disappointed when luck failed to place us side by side on the Air Canada jet.

An hour later, we descended into the swelter of the Big Apple. As I rolled down the window of our dirty yellow cab, the clatter and heat combined with the festering stink of a garbage strike, and Real Life, terrible and beautiful, broke through.

The Italian, Naples-bound ocean liner SS *Raffaello* was parked in the harbour like a gargantuan private limousine. On the jetty, we merged with the kids from Vancouver and Halifax and were funnelled through a canopied gangplank. Coloured streamers unspooled like a scene in an old movie, and I found myself walking beside Sally, out of twenty-seven chances. Occasionally, wishing works.

Our tourist-class cabins were below the waterline. I unpacked my bag in a porthole-less space I would be sharing with three others—Sean, a co-survivor of a decade of UCC; Peter, a cheerful Vancouverite in horn-rimmed glasses; and Will, a handsome, friendly boy from UTS. I grabbed a top berth, only to find my nose a foot from the ceiling, inducing a wave of claustrophobia.

The nine-hundred-foot-long ship was only three years old and carried 2,500 passengers and crew—forty-five thousand tons of fun. The very sight of watertight doors unlocked my mental holdings of *Titanic* lore—the myth of unsinkability, the Irish rabble below and the Gilded Age plutocrats above, the iceberg. In anticipation of anything untoward happening on the trip, my mother had sewn a $20 bill into the lining of my madras jacket, as if a scrap of paper could divert any crisis. As the Statue of Liberty glided past, I was driven to tell anyone who would listen that the monument was rumoured to be modelled on the face of the sculptor's mother and the body of his mistress. Boom, boom, I was an icebreaker.

In the dining room, we were assigned to tables of four, boy-girl, boy-girl, an inspired orchestration of instant double dates. The only down side: ties and jackets and dresses were mandatory at dinner. Drifting from table to table, Nick introduced his co-leader, Tammy, a twenty-year-old former head girl from the Vancouver private school Crofton House, a live wire of near-Twiggy thinness, as steeped in art history as Nick. Together they seemed almost too good to be true.

After dinner, Sally and I gravitated to the spacious bar at the stern of the ship where a panoramic window overlooked a swimming pool and the setting sun. We knew we fell three-plus-years short of legal age, but no one demanded our ID. As we settled on stools and ordered drinks absurdly priced at a quarter apiece, Sally and I officially graduated from the childhood sandbar to the adult cocktail bar.

Sally was still Sally, only more so. I was now close enough to smell the smoke on her breath, restudy the contours of the unusual face and head. It was what she was *not* that I liked best: no pretentious egghead, no remote porcelain doll done up in eyeliner, nylons, high heels, lipstick, perfume, no idealized, prefab, painted-by-numbers head girl, no worship-me-forever film queen. She was as real and alive as they came.

Careful not to stake a claim on her, I wandered off to mingle with the rest. I made an awkward stab at dancing with Margi, a diffident Halifax girl, to a band playing antique Guy Lombardo tunes, then a sudden rush of self-consciousness drove me to bed before midnight.

First thing in the morning, I cracked my head against the ceiling of my cramped berth. Convening for the first of daily meetings in a children's playroom, we perched on yellow plastic munchkin chairs as if regressing to nursery school. We took turns standing up to give our names and schools; it would take time to pin all the names to the faces. Nick solemnly lectured us on the formation of the European Common Market and delivered a primer on the first Italian leg of the trip— Sorrento, Rome, Florence, Venice, Milan. When he forbade "fraternization" between the sexes, the room swam with nervous giggles.

That afternoon, we sunbathed in deck chairs by the pool, lulled by the hot Atlantic wind; behind the mask of my sunglasses, my eyes ravished the sirens of bikini atoll, slathered in baby oil, slithering one by one down a pink slide into the cold salt water.

After a dip, I stood by the stern railing, mesmerized by the blue-and-white wake churning into a past I longed to forget. One of my father's rare war stories, fuelled by drink, surged to mind: how he had stood on the conning tower of his frigate in the frigid North Sea, swinging one leg over the railing in anticipation of a U-boat torpedo— a confession of terror that had made me quietly proud of his honesty.

Nick appeared beside me, interrupting my daydream. "You can understand," he offered, "why some people might want to leap in."

I was so amazed that a mature male of the species had taken the time to attend to me that I was tongue-tied.

"I've noticed you tend to hang back from the group. You're a bit reticent." He made his observation in such a gentle way that I did not experience it as judgmental. But I merely nodded.

After dinner, once more we hit the bar. Moving from table to table, I deployed my categorizing mind to sort the group—thirteen girls, thirteen boys, aged seventeen to twenty. Most of us were the Protestant offspring of lawyers, physicians, businessmen, a senator, a judge, a mayor, a brigadier-general, a combat photographer, a former head of Canadian intelligence in World War II; our mothers were mainly stay-at-homers. Five of us were kids of doctors—me, Sally, Will, Liz and Annabel; only three went to public schools; only one was black, or half black. Some of us were scions of staunch Scots and Irish pioneers, founders and builders of meatpacking empires, the CBC, medical labs, exploiters of natural resources and commodities. I had trouble believing that we were in any way part of an immaculately conceived privileged class, subject to great expectations; yet that was the invisible air we had breathed since birth. The way I felt about myself, why would anyone envy *me*?

Most of the boys seemed like frogs among the princesses. Miniskirted Kat Joy, a perfect sixties name, was a gamine Vancouver free spirit who weakened my knees with a smile. Likewise her cousin Nikki—almond eyes, olive skin, jet black hair, a body off the cover of *Vogue*. A second set of cousins from Toronto, Havergal girls Annabel and Jane, turned my head. Margi, Chris, Marywinn, Barb, Robin, Liz, Kathy, Nan—redheads and blondes and brunettes, eyes of blue and brown and green, a melding mosaic of the shy and sheltered, worldly and bold, bony and fleshy, boozers and abstainers. I was learning at last that it was possible to have friends who were girls and not girlfriends.

The lack of marijuana and my aversion to beer propelled me to an intoxicant favoured by adults: Canadian Club rye, mixed with ginger ale, on the rocks. One strong, tingling sip of sweetness, then

two, then three, and then Sally pulled me onto the dance floor. I was
the rust-bound Tin Man and she the can of oil. We did not touch—
no slow dances yet. Avoiding eye contact, I fixed on her party dress,
puffed at the shoulders, a swirl of yellow, turquoise and pink, a small,
heart-shaped opening revealing a patch of slightly sunburnt skin
above her breasts.

Gimme a ticket on an aeroplane,
Ain't got time to take a fast train,
Lonely days are gone, I'm a-goin' home,
My baby, she wrote me a letter.

Back at the bar, the Italian servers, Guido and Luigi, both card-
carrying Commies, ruefully replenished drinks for the trainees of
the WASP ruling class. Sally loved to talk, but she also listened to
what I was saying, and the more she listened, the more my own
words tumbled and rolled, and we fell into our old bantering ways.
    "What sign are you?"
    "A Stop sign!"
    By the early morning hours, our group had merged into a sin-
gle organism, drinking, laughing, losing our heads, even as the
bow of the *Raffaello* sliced open a new time zone. The rigidly
enforced, all-the-live-long-day timetables of family and school,
with its unspoken program of erotic abuse, melted like the ice in
my drink and we were back on the steps of Sally's cottage, kicking
the can. Were we getting older or younger?
    Back in my berth, I pulled out my pocket travel diary and scrib-
bled, "Unbelievably fabulous time with Sally!" *Maybe someday I'll*
find the words.
    On previous trips, drunken yahoos had rolled grand pianos
overboard. In contrast we were sweetness incarnate. One night,
boosted into orbit by three rye and gingers, I was drawing a crowd

with my well-timed one-liners. By 3 a.m., the bar was nearly empty. Encouraged by Sally's laugh, I flung myself horizontally across the room, scattering tables and chairs. An overnight convert from inhibition to exhibitionism, I pounded the piano keys until the stool broke under my weight. Standing beside Sally on the open deck, I watched the rosy-fingered dawn poke through the fog.

Over a late lunch, Nick circled our tables to reprimand us. We had achieved a historic first: never in twenty years of tours had not one single person showed up for breakfast. Only in the afternoon sun did I notice the purple bruises decorating my flesh from my Superman flight. Meanwhile, word had leaked out that Nick was slinking into Tammy's cabin where they were fraternizing as if there was no tomorrow.

After five straight nights of careening around our floating pleasure palace, I decided to cool my heels for a spell and retreated alone into the womb of the ship's cinema. I was disappointed that the film, *In Cold Blood*, was dubbed into Italian—*A sangue freddo*—but I stuck it out because, by coincidence, I was reading the paperback of Truman Capote's genre-busting masterwork.

Even though I knew how the story ended, I was transfixed by the haunting black-and-white imagery and the theme of capital punishment. The actor Robert Blake plays a condemned murderer on Death Row; minutes before his hanging, he murmurs a reflective soliloquy on his horrific childhood while staring out of a barred prison window; raindrops streaking down the pane reflect back on his face as the tears he could not cry. In the near-unwatchable final scene, his head hooded and torso harnessed like a toddler's, he drops through the trap door in slow motion, the amplified sound of his heart fading, beat by beat, to a dead stop. Out of the darkness I stumbled, as if emerging from a familiar nightmare.

Back in the bar, I parked myself on a leather couch beside Sally as she held court, gushing about a guy named George. Ultra-smart, athletic, witty, handsome, he was twenty-one and sported a beard. A beard? I was lucky if a few pathetic hairs sprouted out of my chin every full moon. She babbled on and on about George, the man she was going to marry, the kids they'd have, a boy and a girl named Jason and Kimberly, and a St. Bernard dog named Petunia. Careers, house, cottage, the works.

Jesus, I thought. *All the names already picked out.*

I wanted to shut her mouth with a kiss, even as an image of George branded my brain.

Thankfully, Sean asked the question for me: "Sally, are you actually *engaged*?"

"Well, not officially," she replied, and I seized the slim opening as a sign of hope.

I was on deck, leaning on the railing, nestled between Sally and Nan, taking a breather from dancing. The ship was anchored, and in the dim moonlight we made out the famous profile of the Rock of Gibraltar. Ignited by Sally's smile, I performed my killer imitation of Skull Bassett, my lugubrious ancient-history master: "Tomorrow we will pass through the Pillars of Hercules, the nine-mile-wide pelvic portal into the Mediterranean Sea and the Pagan World." Then Peter burst through the bar door, a stray piece of shrapnel expelled by a blast of Rolling Stones. He grabbed the drink from Nan's hand, flung it overboard and hauled her onto the dance floor.

Below deck in her cabin berth, Tammy rolled over and looked Nick square in the eyes: "You know, we're never going to be this happy again."

It was official: on our delirious crossing of an epic body of water, our group was falling in love with itself.

When it came to goodbyes, the Italian stewards were messy, loud, operatic. As we gathered on deck, poised to file down the gangplank into the steaming port of Napoli, the girls were engulfed in hugs and kisses feverish enough to defrost the white eyebrows of every last WASP grandmother in the city of Toronto.

In seven days and nights, thanks to the girls, we had birthed a new world disorder free of old boyism. Though I had not surrendered my habit of anticipating impending disasters, I failed to imagine that our love boat was destined for a bad end. The Italian Line later sold the SS *Raffaello* to Iran, where it was decommissioned for use as a troop carrier for its war with Iraq. In 1983, the ship was torpedoed in the shallow waters of the Persian Gulf, and in ensuing years local divers looted the hull where Italian stewards once bussed the cheeks of teenage Canadian girls. Today, the wreck lurks just below the surface, marked by warning buoys.

189 Gordon Road
July 3, late at night

Dear Sally,

Things are in a sad state since you left me here all alone. Right now I feel like a dumb little boy who lost his best friend, but I know you're not lost, just temporarily misplaced. But if you get a convenient opportunity to break your leg, and come home, then by all means do.

Yesterday, after you were gone, I sat home and read sixteen hours straight and ended up feeling desperately sorry for myself about losing you. So this morning, I got up and decided the best thing to do to kill the next little while (exactly when do you come home?) would be to work like hell. So right now, I am writing two stories for different magazines, seeking out some department of the government to pay me $2,800 or more for the Canadian "dime" I have hanging on my wall, selling advertising for university student publications; serving as vice-president of the Rochdale Camera Club; and, as usual, cutting down the tree in front of the house. As well, I'm going to put up a notice at Glendon College, offering to type out essays and assignments at exorbitant prices.

With this much time to kill, I figure I can work fourteen to sixteen hours per day, six days a week. My newly found ambition is to clear $3,500 before the last day in July. My incentive, other than killing time and earning enough to buy a nice car for us (not ME! But US!), is that once I've got the money, I'm going to come over there, buy a motorbike and haunt you.

I'm sorry if I'm getting your hopes up only to let them down, but I've got to have something to work for and look forward to, so that's it. I just hope that if by odd chance I do make it, I won't be spoiling your holiday. If so, then let me know before I get all my vaccinations, will you?

Of the stories I'm writing, one is a short love story, or romance, or whatever, very loosely based upon certain printable experiences of ours. Once I finish it (tomorrow night), I'll mail it off by express post to *Seventeen, Redbook* and whatever other female journal of that type that I can think of. The worst they can say is no, and the best they can say is "Thank you. Please find cheque enclosed." I'll keep you posted.

The other story will be a tongue-in-cheek documentary on Yorkville, I think, and this one will go to every Canadian magazine, journal and newspaper I can think of. Again, there's not much likelihood, but then there's not much point in not trying.

I hope the boat trip over wasn't too rough, and you aren't drinking too much. They say bad wine turns your teeth purple. I'm going to steer clear of writing mushy sentimental letters soaked in tears and blood. All I ask you to do is remember I love you and I always will. I honestly hope you don't think I'm a fool for things I have said, but I'm so confused and upset right now that I don't know which end is up. So I've chewed off an almost impossible goal to work for, and even if I don't make it—I am pretty sure I won't—then at least I won't have spent all my time moping about you, which, apart from seeing you, is what I'd most like to do right now.

Keep away from those boys. Remember what I told you about me being the insanely jealous type! And if you run into Stewart, which isn't likely, give him my regards and make him take you out for lunch.

Well, angel, I've got to sack out now. Tomorrow I write, knock on doors and generally keep busy until I get back to bed where I hope to collapse in a state of exhaustion so total I won't have much time to remember when you used to lie beside me.

Don't forget (this is a threat) that I love you, and we're engaged. I haven't told anybody yet, but the temptation to shoot my mouth off is pretty strong, so hurry home and make an honest man out of me.

Think about me always, and remember how much I love you. You're my angel.

Love, George

P.S. I've now got writer's cramp, and I love you. Dream about me.

Raffaello
July 4

Dear George,

How are you? I think I'm awful. I haven't decided
whether I like the idea of going to Europe. But Nick and
Tammy are terrific. If you're feeling down in the blues, they
cheer you up.

The kids seem nice to talk to. The girls are all a lot of
fun except for one named Liz and she's in my cabin. She's
quite a child. But the other kids seem like a lot of fun.
Robin has been great. It doesn't appear she's been after
any boys. But it's the girl Barb I really get along with well.
We are so much alike. Both pinned, both getting married in
a couple of years and both very lonely.

Oh Christ, it was just awful leaving. I'll be so happy
when I get back. I cried when you left but I was OK after a
few minutes. But when I saw you in the coffee shop, that
really set me off. I think I cried until we were up in the air.
When we got to New York, I was OK. Quite lonely and
feeling lost, but OK. We got on the boat and had lunch
right away. Then some of us went out on deck to see the
Statue of Liberty. I happened to be standing alone and I
guess I must have looked awfully glum cuz Nick came up
to me and said, "What's the matter, Sal?" Well, that really
set me off again. But he stayed with me and kept talking to
me for a few minutes and then I was all right again.

Well, the first night Robin, Marywinn, Barb and I sat
in my cabin and talked. We decided to go up to the bar for
a nightcap before bed. That was good cuz it made me more
tired after my sleepless (no kidding) night before. To top
off the night, I cried myself to sleep.

Oh, it was awful. I just kept thinking about you and wondering what you were doing. As a matter of fact, I wonder what you are doing every minute of the day.

This summer is going to be so long. I think I can guarantee that it will be the last time I'm away from you. Oh, I love you so much. Please believe me when I say it. I'm going to remember what you said that when I get bored, I can start to plan our wedding. Will you start thinking about where we're going to do it?

Well, I have to go to our daily meeting now. I miss you. I love you.

Sal

P.S. I just had a long talk with Nick and he was telling me that your trip in '65 was one of the best he'd ever had.

189 Gordon Road
July 7

My Angel (I love you!)
Well, my pet, the word has leaked out through Marilyn's father, the supreme postmaster of Maple. The Canadian mail strike will be a thing of the present as of July 17, so by the time you get this thing (it's a love letter because I love you), you won't be able to reply. But they say no news is good news, so if anything terrible happens, send a telegram. Otherwise, write if you like and I'll get them all at once when the strike ends.

The last letter I sent you (also the first) might have sounded a bit confused and I guess it was. But things clouded up mentally after you left, and I figured I couldn't

last a whole two months without seeing you. I guess things
are still like that a bit: in fact I'm sure they are, so I'm
still killing several hours a day puttering around doing
unimportant things, and at present, not making any money.
But I'm not going to give up until either I have the money
and get to go abroad or I reach July 26, my final day and
don't feel I can afford to go anywhere.

But this way I've got a month killed and should be
pretty numb emotionally, a state of mind that I shall
maintain until you come home to me.

So well as all that crap (so much for ambition) in the
Rome letter, I am employed painting the house a shiny
smelly white and chopping down the tree.

I think of you always, and am just getting settled in to
being lonely and forlorn for another two months.

Don't remember if I told you or not, but CHUM-FM
plays nice music with dirty words and all, and there are
almost no commercials. But the batteries have died tonight
in "la petite radio," so I'm forced to entertain myself by playing the kazoo. I'll bet you never knew I could play a kazoo.
(Whether you know it or not, kazoo is not a dirty word).

What else is new?

Graham sold his bike for $650 and is now looking
for a car, so I've got a ride to school next year.

At school next year I will be writing a column at large,
talking about whatever I fancy, so you my pet, are going to
have to tone up your sense of humour. You shall be the
butt of countless verbal slings and arrows. But they will
all be because I love you, which I do very much.

Heard yesterday that there are 100,000 students
unemployed in Toronto so I've got company in spirit,
but not, mind you, in flesh.

Speaking of flesh, watch out! Mike was telling me about some of the boys he knows on your trip, and according to him, their idea of hand exercises would really turn you off (I hope).

Unfortunately, the tone of your boyfriend has been "I don't trust you" and that's not true. I trust you only because I love you and any obnoxious noises I make about the boys on your trip are out of loneliness.

At this point in the letter, I'm lost for words. Apart from repeating myself for the millionth time and saying I love you, and I'm GOING to marry you, I'm lost. I know nothing I can say can make you come home one second earlier. If it could, I'd write eight letters a day, each one 5,000 words long telling of my love for you, and how I feel after not having made love to you for the two or three weeks between when you left and when you read this.

While painting today, I almost fell off the house roof. Fortunately for the geraniums directly below, I had a rope tied to my waist and the chimney. But unfortunately for my waist it was a bristly rope, and unfortunately for the geraniums, I spilled a bit of paint. But no harm done. However, if anything does happen to me (which I promise it won't), I'm going to make them paint on my cast in large red letters "THIS BROKEN LIMB WAS CAUSED BY A BROKEN HEART." Then I'll telephone you and tell you I'm dying and that you had better hustle your bottom back here as fast as you can.

As near as I can make out, at this very moment it is 7:30 your time and you are somewhere on the Mediterranean Sea approaching Naples. I hope you won't think I'm cruel if I say that I like the thought of you having a rotten time, because that's pretty much what I'm having. Besides,

I'd get as jealous as hell to know that you're cavorting and screaming around with "other people."

Sorry if that last bit wasn't too nice, but that's how I feel right now. But you have found by far the most effective way of ensuring our love, if you've got any left. To take off and leave a boy hung up for two months is, these days, a sure promise that he'll be faithful in every way.

Because to live with you is to be able to laugh, neck and even blow up at you when the circumstances call. But to live without you is like living in suspended animation, where nothing happens, and where time does not move. Believe me, time has literally ceased to pass since you left. Five days since you took off. And it feels like you should be coming home tomorrow. But you're not, dammit.

During the day when there are constructive things to do to pass the time, I can see the uselessness of moping around, wishing I were with you. But at night, I sit here and actually feel my mind coming loose from its daytime point of view, and the little seeds of jealousy and self-pity come out and glow. This feeling of actually having a mental point of view becomes warped. While I can do nothing about it, it is one which I have never experienced, and is actually most uncomfortable, apart from the thoughts themselves.

I don't know if you understand, but then by going away you showed there a lot of things you don't understand.

In the second paragraph, I referred jokingly, and only that way, to my coming to Europe. I would give my left leg to do it, but apart from the money, there are many problems.

But now, forty minutes after writing the second paragraph, I can see clearly the logic of my getting a return flight ticket to London or Paris and seeing both you and Europe on my own for two weeks.

I'm sorry to keep pushing this thing of me coming there, but now you know how it is. And I'm afraid you won't know definitely until you get to Interlaken, Switzerland.

At this point, I must assume that you cannot read my writing. Hope you can.

Also at this point, I must announce that I am deeply and totally in love with you, and have written roughly one thousand, four hundred scrawly words tonight to prove it in this letter . . .

Well, darling, this little essay is now calling for my beauty sleep, so I'm going to sign off. Remember, if you can, how many times I've told you I love you. I still do, as much as ever, and I always will. I promise. Be good and write often, mail strike or not. And remember, if there's the least excuse for you to come home early, the very smallest excuse, and you don't take it, then I'll personally beat the living crap out of you, just to show you how fantastically much I love you. Answer this question in your next letter in plain words: "Will you marry me?"

I love you. I love you. I want to live with you, and make beautiful children.

Forever and forever,
Love, George

EIGHT

Eruption

On the Naples pier, I was hanging out with Sally in the infernal triple-digit heat, blasting like an open pizza oven. Our four Volkswagen minibuses from West Germany were late. Squinting at the active volcano of Mount Vesuvius rising like a purple boil five miles distant, we puffed our Viceroys until at last our four chariots pulled up, to a general cheer. To break up cliques, Czar Nick planned to rotate our bus mates and roommates as we moved from city to city.

Our baggage stacked in the back, we clambered inside, seven bodies per bus, the sexes distributed in two-three-two configurations in the front, middle and back benches. The Volkswagen, Nick reminded us, was Hitler's pre-war "car of the people" and the spin-off Type 2 minibus was conceived in 1950, the same year most of us were born. We were to travel in four boxes on smallish wheels, not terribly stable or heavy, equipped with sun roofs, sliding doors, and rear-mounted, air-cooled engines.

Together with Nick and Tammy, three of the boys—Dave, Stu and Steve—were designated as drivers, granted permission by their parents. My licence was suspended, so I didn't qualify. The previous summer, my predictably unpredictable mother had placed the keys of her Buick Skylark into my sixteen-year-old hand, smiling and waving as I drove off to cross Canada with two classmates. Too much freedom, too fast—we were lucky to escape with our lives when I smashed the car into a tractor trailer in Saskatchewan.

Nick delivered a quick primer on the free-form European driving style: "The right of way is on your right, use your horn and don't be afraid—might makes right, and they will respect you."

Designating the person riding shotgun as navigator, Nick supplied maps of the highways but not the cities; for those, he instructed us to stay in convoy, look for *Centro città* notices, then follow the hotel signs. I did not yet know that Dave had never used a stick shift and hastily practised for twenty minutes in a parking lot. Nor did I notice that the buses lacked seat belts.

I was in a bus with Sally with Stu at the wheel, our baggage blocking the view through the rear window. Witty and self-deprecating, Stu was one of our two token Catholics, adorned with snazzy aviator sunglasses, blood-red beret and buttoned driving gloves. On the road to Sorrento, a stuttering ascent up a serpentine cliffside road, he ground the gears like nervous teeth. My eyes slid from the azure sea and sky of the spectacular Amalfi coastline down to its low stone walls and the fatal drop onto the rocks below. The sputtering box powered by German hamsters was all dead weight as honking Fiats zipped past. "It's gutless!" Stu swore, afraid of stalling on a hill and rolling back, ending the lives of seven teenagers.

Our hotel, the Mediterraneo, hugged a seaside cliff just outside Sorrento, and I was rooming with Dave for the next three nights. The cracks of the shower tiles oozed ants—I imagined them pouring surrealistically out of the shower head—but I couldn't have cared less. Rushing to change into our bathing suits, we took the elevator that slid down the sheer cliff face to a narrow strip of pebble beach. Sally was wearing a flowered bikini, and together we slipped into the tepid greasy water, my first taste of the ancient salt sea of Middle Earth.

When a perfect brown turd floated between our heads, Sally cried, "Grrrrrr-oooooo-ssssss!" and we paddled back in, laughing. This wasn't the fresh water of the De Grassi sandbar, let alone the chlorinated purity of a concrete pool. This was old. This was dirty. This was real.

We gathered at an outdoor café for dinner and a silky blend of banter and wine. I figured out my lire—1,600 to the Canadian dollar—and test drove my Italian. *Buonasera. Sono canadese turista. Grazie. Prego. Magnifico.* It's a romance language.

The next morning, Nick introduced us to Rafaele, a tour guide employed by the Odyssey since the beginning, who escorted us to the base of the four-thousand-foot Mount Vesuvius. We rode chairlifts to the top of the lunar-like crater and crunched along a precarious path of pumice crust, absorbing the God-like view of the Bay of Naples. There were no guardrails. Wary of heights, I steered close to Sally on the lip of the volcano as jets of sulphur-scented steam shot up from fissures underfoot. With a scarf wrapped around her head and her sunglasses perched on top, she leaned down and lit a cigarette off a cinder, blowing a smoke ring half comically, half suggestively.

After lunch at Ristorante Vesuvio, we wandered into the mythic ruins of Pompeii under the unforgiving afternoon sun. Through the running commentary of Nick and Rafaele, we were conducted back to August AD 79 and the greatest natural catastrophe in recorded history—countless souls burned, suffocated and buried by a barrage of stones, poisonous sulphuric gas and molten lava. Only a single eyewitness account survived in two letters by Pliny the Younger, but Nick's easy erudition brought to life the town of twenty thousand thriving and suffering in the Augustan Age of Pax Romana.

Ushered into the House of the Tragic Poet, we studied the atrium famous for its elaborate frescoes in which the gods celebrated a woman's loss of virginity, her veil symbolically removed from her face as winged Cupids bore bowls of perfume. Rafaele explained that an ingenious eighteenth-century scientist made casts by injecting plaster into the cavities left by hundreds of decomposed bodies, preserved in their final postures of death, running in terror, or shielding their heads with pillows and roof tiles. Loaves of bread stood in ovens. Graffiti scratched a schoolroom wall: "If you don't enjoy Cicero, you'll get a hiding" and "Do you think I'd mind if you dropped dead tomorrow?" We came across the form of a dog twisting on a leash. But it was the figures of two young lovers locked in passionate embrace, their death throes forever tied to that fateful August day, that most riveted my attention. I felt I had crossed a threshold into an uncanny, natural museum of sex and death.

Sotto voce, Rafaele called the boys over, separating us from the girls. He explained that when a sixteenth-century architect unearthed a massive collection of erotic art and objects celebrating Priapus, the pagan god of sex and fertility, he hastily covered it over, the puritanism of Counter-Reformation Italy trumping the libertine sexual mores of the ancient Romans who celebrated the phallus as a good luck symbol that magically fended off accidents and disasters. A nineteenth-century king of Naples was so mortified by the erotica that he locked it away in a secret cabinet, accessible only to the Grand Tourists of "mature age and respected morals." The cabinet had been intermittently locked and unlocked over the past hundred years, and lucky us, it was now unlocked. Pulling out a skeleton key, Rafaele swung open the wooden cabinet door like a flasher to reveal the faded frescoes. On a weigh scale, balanced against a pile of fruit and vegetables, rested the Zeppelin-size member of Priapus; were there a caption, it would have read: Worth its weight in gold.

After two hours, I was undone by the intense heat, so Nick suggested I hold my wrists under a tap of cool running water, and it worked. As we assembled in the parking lot, word of Rafaele's revelation had leaked out to the girls; Sally did not hide her resentment at the exclusion, and I could not blame her. I felt my guts gurgling audibly and I leaned on the hood of a car, trying to suppress the dirty little secret of my Crohn's. Suddenly an explosive fart shuddered off the flat metal surface. Sally howled at the comic effect, and everyone else laughed too. "Farting is such sweet sorrow," quipped Ross, and even I had to grin. For the first time, I was mad at her. Sometimes I was not sure if she was laughing with me or at me.

That night in a café, Dave unleashed a battery of blue jokes, stoked by our immersion in the Roman fuckitorium. I was surprised when Sally suddenly left without a word; I thought she could take it.

I slept in past eleven the next day, which turned out to be a mistake. I couldn't find Sally, so five of us hiked into Sorrento to buy bread and cheese and Coke for lunch, heeding Nick's advice to avoid drinking the local water.

In the late afternoon, Dave rolled into our room drunk and collapsed on the bed. Before he passed out, he revealed that I had missed the lunch of a lifetime. As part of an annual tradition, Rafaele picked a boy and girl from the Odyssey to join Nick and Tammy at a family vineyard on the slopes of Vesuvius for a classic pasta and wine Italian lunch al fresco. Sally and I were randomly chosen from a hat with twenty-six names, but I could not be found, so Dave took my place.

"No one spoke a word of English and we didn't know a word of Italian," he explained. "It didn't really matter because everyone was laughing and joking around. They brought out a plate of spaghetti and it looked Spartan to me, very little sausage. I'm used to heavy red tomato meat sauce. But it was really good, lots of garlic and olive oil.

"Before we even started, they brought out their own wine, which was called Lacrymi Christi. By the time we finished the spaghetti, we had each drunk a bottle. It was really hot and I was getting tipsy so I asked for some more spaghetti and they brought me another bowl. I was stuffed. I thought, *That was a great lunch.* I didn't realize it was just the first course. There were eight courses and we drank ten bottles of wine. Sally and I started to get the giggles by the second bottle; by the end, we were just killing ourselves laughing. I mean, tears. What a wonderful girl. Funny as hell. I see why you like her."

How green was my envy?

Dave fell asleep but never forgot. The Vesuvian lunch would burn so strongly in his memory that years later, as a food writer with the *Toronto Star*, he would bring it back to life in words.

On our last night in Sorrento, we boarded a chartered bus for an outdoor nightclub with a live band. The cocktails were as sweet and green as we were. The MC invited the patrons to play a vaguely fetishistic game where we threw our shoes into a pile, then tried to match them with their owners; Nan easily snagged and returned my size-twelve pontoons. The game seemed like a harmless icebreaker to induce people to interact, so why did my warped mind flash images of Auschwitz?

Soon all of us were up dancing. Sally and I were both short-sighted, and we removed our geeky glasses, trading half-blindness for semi-coolness. Through the mild blur of my peripheral vision, I discerned a swarm of predatory Italians circling our girls. Robin was swooning for a swarthy, black-haired stud who thrust out a red rose, picked off the thorns and offered it to her. Asked to go for a walk, she demurred, settling for a kiss. When Will counterattacked, asking an Italian girl to dance, her bodyguard father exploded into indignant English: "You are a fool!"

Out on the street, the Italians perched on their Vespas, revving the engines. Names burst like Roman candles—Marcello! Vittorio! Armenio! I was stunned when Nan, Annabel and Kat straddled the bikes, arms ringing waists, and evaporated into the Sorrento night. "We'll never see them again," sighed Sean.

Sally resisted the call of the Vespas. But if she was being faithful, to whom? After a while, the girls returned unmolested, but an unfamiliar tension filled the big bus back to the hotel. They had left us out in the cold, and we were steamed.

In early July, shortly after Sally's departure, Toronto was trapped in a greenhouse of asphalt-melting heat. Experiencing the passing of time as an infant crawling across a desert plain, George retreated to the backyard pool of 189 Gordon Road, roasting on an air mattress, brooding over a single question: *Is this the start of my life, or the end of it?*

For months, George and Sally had danced around the subject of marriage, both waiting for George to make the engagement official. Ever since she left for Europe, he had clung to one grounding thought: *If I can make something happen with Sally, maybe I'll have something solid to build my life on.*

On the blazing afternoon of July 11, he crossed the threshold of the University of Toronto student health services on Huron Street and took the uneasy chair opposite the desk of Dr. Wodehouse. He calculated that it was only the second time he had gone for what he really wanted. But before George could speak, the doctor read his mind: "Do you intend to marry Sally?"

"Yes, sir."

Silence.

"When?"

"Not until she has finished nursing school." Then he added, "At least."

The doctor knew that an outright no might lead to an elopement; at the same time, he withheld an unequivocal yes. And so, feeling expertly managed, George carried from the office a suspended sentence: "Let's wait and see."

On the drive home, George wondered if he should delay his formal proposal until Sally's return on August 30. But the gap felt unbearable; any day now, if the dark, foreboding dream of Christmas night was real, he could lose her forever. He thought of phoning Sally in her Rome hotel, then restrained himself: she might be out, and there was no privacy in his own house that would allow him to talk freely. Worst of all, his desperation might alienate Sally; there was nothing good, nothing strong, nothing desirable to be found in the needy quaver of a young lover's voice.

He might have settled on August 18, the second anniversary of their blind date, but he was too geared up to remember. And so he targeted Monday, August 12, a full month after his meeting with the doctor, as the day he would call Sally, surprise Sally, win Sally, save Sally, once and forever after.

In his basement cave, he fed a sheet of paper into his Underwood typewriter. He addressed the letter to Sally's Venice hotel where she would arrive on July 19. As he sealed the envelope, he scribbled on the back flap, like a teasing headline: "He brought it up. I didn't."

Relaying the recent scene in her father's office, complete with dialogue, he signed off with the words, "Now that your father knows, the obstacles are starting to fall away. I truly hope that now it's only a matter of time."

On the morning of July 12, our quartet of buses tooled along the autostrada, honking as we passed and repassed one another, heads thrust out windows, thumbing noses and pulling gargoyle faces like renegades from kindergarten. Nikki was singing "Arrivederci Roma," and we hadn't even arrived yet.

A barely controlled madness drove the traffic through the stone labyrinth of the Eternal City. Misreading the signs, we navigated by dead reckoning, the passing rows of slim cypress trees reminding me of the final scene in *Spartacus* where crucified slaves lined the Via Appia like telephone poles. Near the train station we found the Hotel Nord Nuova Roma where prostitutes had picked off generations of departing soldiers. The Sorrento Vespa gang had tracked down Kathy, Kat and Nikki all the way to Rome. From her window, Kat threw her wristwatch down to Vittorio on the street and he threw his back up. Time travel.

Three days of intensive sightseeing were laid on, but first Nick urged us to "get up for the B." It was a tradition: as each of his four tours passed in succession through the city, Bernie, the silver-headed founder of the Odyssey, hosted his annual sweet vermouth party designed to impart "European sophistication" to immature colonials. As part of our class training, future leaders needed to learn how to hold their liquor, so we were told to assemble in Bernie's sweltering room in the late afternoon. Holding court like a Roman senator, Bernie forgot we were young, hot, dehydrated and exhausted, not to mention that most of us had been baptized with alcohol in the temple of the *Raffaello*.

We guzzled the vermouth like liquid candy until the room swayed and hummed. Clanking shut the wrought iron door of the lift, Sally and I weaved back to her room, passing on dinner. This was my first time alone with her in a bedroom, but even if I could have my way with her, what way would that be? I had received a letter from my mother and, on some moronic impulse, pulled it from my pants pocket; when Sal suggested I write back right then, I agreed.

It turned out I was too buzzed to write, so she produced a sheaf of blue onionskin letterhead that she had lifted from the *Raffaello*. Curled on the bed, she nibbled the tip of the ballpoint pen: "I'm ready to take dictation, Doctor FitzGerald."

My baby, she wrote me a letter.

As I confessed to the unfolding abandon of the past ten days, she scribbled it all down, editing out the slurs. What the hell, back home, my self-prescribing physician father was shooting and swallowing all known brands of narcotic, so my escapades qualified as child's play. Sally folded the letter into an envelope, rose from the bed and moved to the window. Looking down on a group of fallen women, all kohl-eyed and fish-netted, she let loose into the ochre Roman sunset: *"Quanto costa, bella?"*

Rome,
July 12

Dear George,

I was so happy to get your July 3 letter that I started to cry. It was so great to hear from you and such a sweet letter. Thank you, love.

I think maybe you'd better "shoot your mouth off" that we're engaged because everybody on the trip now knows. And it wasn't me who said it first. It was Robin. It is quite neat that all the kids know. When word first got out, a couple of the boys asked me, "Are you really engaged?" My answer was "Yes, but *not officially*." So they all have been really nice to me, and not serious.

Actually the trip is really great cuz there are only a couple of girls and a couple of guys who are after a play-mate. So most of the time as a whole we are one big happy family.

The first night on the boat was a real drag. I missed you so much. And to top things off, I couldn't sleep. Well, the second night was a bit better but by the third night things were fine. That's when I started staying up late. I've been to bed once since then at 12:30. Then the earliest was

2:30. But the average has been about 3:30. One night I
made it up till 8 a.m. That day the trip set a new record.
Nobody made it up for lunch.

The bar on the boat was great. My favourite drink was
a daiquiri. I had at least three every night. You should try
them. They're great.

The weather was fantastic. Only one day was a little
foggy. The water was really quite calm. I got such a great
tan last week. I've got freckles all down my arms, let alone
on my face and back and chest. Guess what! I burnt me
boobs again. I had a slight tan from the paper bikini but it
was not enough. One day it was really sunny but with a fair
breeze. And the sun just slipped down the top of my shirt
and I got quite a badly burned chest. I wish you were here
to help me peel it. I don't like doing it myself.

Well, anyhow, we got off the boat on Tuesday at Naples
and it was stinking hot. At least 110 degrees F. We picked
up the buses. Two are brand-new and the other two are a
couple of years old.

We just had our first meeting with Bernie. God, he
talks a lot. I had to fight to stay awake.

Well, like I was saying, the buses are okay. They have
radios and they're quite comfy, seven to a bus. So it's not
too bad.

So we left Naples and went to Sorrento. My room
was really great. I had the biggest balcony in the hotel.
But I wasn't there long enough to enjoy it. The first night
in Sorrento we went for a walk and then down to a bar for
a drink. Well, that night was kinda dull. The next day,
which was Wed., we went to Mt. Vesuvius and Pompeii.
It was really interesting but it was so hot that not much
went in after about an hour.

Oh, there was this guide up at the top of the mountain. He was a really dirty wop (please excuse the expression but it's easier to say and write than an Italiano). Well, I was among the first ten at the top of the crater. So he took people by the hips and sat them on the edge of the mountain. Then he would blow smoke in between their legs and it looked like the mountain was smoking. He did this to about 10 kids. To each one he said pull down your pants and then you can see the effect better. Well, nobody did! But he decided to try one more person and the stupid wop picked me. Fortunately I was surrounded by a couple of guys and when I said no, they protected me. I was so fed up with that damn wop I wanted to go over to the edge of the crater and kick him in the nuts. But I didn't.

So we got back to the hotel around 5 and buggered about till dinner at 8. After dinner some of us went down the street to the bar and we sat and drank until about 1. Guess what I drank. Beer! I like Italian beer better than Canadian but I'm still not too keen on it. I came back to the hotel and ended up talking to the girls till about 3. Then I hit the sack.

The next day Thursday was to be a free day. Well, it was free alright. Nick and Tammy were going out with Rafaele the guide. Ralph (I speak of him as that cuz it's easier) wanted to take the whole tour out for lunch but that was impossible. So all the girls' names were thrown in a hat and the boys' in another hat. My name was drawn along with a boy and I figured what the hell I might as well go out to lunch with them. I thought it would be a real laugh.

Well, it was not only a real laugh but a smash hit. Never in my entire life (wow, all of 18 years) have I seen so much food and vino as well as eaten and drunk so much of

it. I've got to tell you that the whole thing from the beginning cuz it's so unreal. And no kidding, all of it is true.

I started this letter at 2 p.m. and it is now 11:30 p.m.
You see, hon, I've been writing on and off whenever I had a
chance. But I have to go to bed now cuz tomorrow we are
going on the five-hour Forum tour. Ugh! So I've got to get
some sleep so I look half decent for you when I come home
on Aug. 30.

I'll dream about you. I have already a couple of times.
I'll continue writing tomorrow.

Night, hon. Be good. I love you.

Sal

Saturday night

Hi, hon, it's me again. I've got lots to tell you about
what we did today, but first of all I've got to finish what I
started yesterday. So here goes. By the way, would you
please keep all my letters and cards. I want to use them for
my diary cuz I'm too lazy to write another one.

Well, here is the lunch with Ralph and his family.
We went to his family winery near the foot of Vesuvius. It
wasn't all fancy or anything but it was nice and clean. Well,
as soon as we sat down they brought us wine. It looked just
like apple juice and it was really good. Well, the first course
was spaghetti with baby clams and sauce all over the top.
Really yummy. The next course was funny kind of fried
chicken and croquette potatoes. The chicken was the best
I've ever had in my life. Really good. The third course was
fish. It was good too. Meanwhile, our wineglasses were
never empty.

The fourth course was awful. I didn't like it. It's hard to describe, but here goes. It was really rich cheese on top of a piece of bread. Then it was coated in eggs and flour and fried like French toast. I didn't like it but I ate most of it because I would have hurt Ralph if I didn't eat it. The fifth course was a huge plate of baby clams and mussels all sautéed in butter and garlic and lemon. Really, really good. We'll have to have baby clams next time we go out for dinner. The next course, which is the sixth, was ham and cheese. Nothing too exciting. The seventh course was a kind of donut with rich rum cream filling in it. It was kind of good. The eighth course was cakey ice cream, you know, ice cream with cake around it. It wasn't bad either. Don't forget the wine that kept being poured down our throats. It was great.

Well, after the eight courses Ralph decided he needed coffee and champagne. Even it was good and you know how much I hate champagne. So that was my lunch. It took four hours to eat it. We were gone altogether for seven hours. It was the largest damn lunch I've ever had but it was great. I loved every minute of it, and I didn't eat for a day after that. I think altogether I had about three dozen clams. They were great. You know how much I eat once I get going. Well, everything that I've said is true so you can imagine what a pig I made of myself. But everyone else was stuffing themselves too so what the hell. I had fun.

We got back to the hotel at 7 and dinner was at 7:30. Well, forget dinner. I had a shower and got cleaned up instead. At 9 we all set off back to Sorrento or wherever the hell it was for this really cool nightclub. It was really nice. But the Italian boys, there were thousands. Only three girls, Barb, Jane and I, refused to dance with them. We stuck with the Canadians. The band was great and the atmosphere was supposed to be good but all the boys (ours) were so pissed off at the girls cuz they all had about three guys each and they danced with them all at once. It was really quite funny to see. Robin had a really hunky-looking guy. I don't know whether he was a wop or not but he was really tall and good-looking. She really had fun. But so did all the other girls except for the three of us who stuck with our guys. We danced and had fun but not really as much as the other girls. I found I got so depressed and lonely because I wasn't on the go. But the place was kinda a cool place to go to. Good for a laugh but that's about it.

So anyway, I think I best go now. I'll tell you about Rome in a couple of days. Please keep my letters. Don't forget, and don't forget that I love you and only you.

I'm being good and loyal. So don't worry. Please just love me when I come home on August 30.

All my love, Sal XXOO

P.S. Here is a dollar so you can buy some stamps. Please could you send me some orange and yellow pre-sweetened Kool-Aid? We don't like aqua minerale. It tastes like soda water. I love you. I always will. Don't forget.

The morning after the vermouth party, Bernie admonished Nick: "Some of the kids got drunk and missed dinner; others were late to breakfast this morning. There's a lot going wrong on this trip, but I can help you fix it."

The same scenario unfolded every summer. This was Nick's sixth trip, so he was accustomed to his role of crown prince. The owner of a robust ego, Bernie needed to be needed—a trip couldn't be a good experience without him. So Nick smiled and played along, regarding the situation as practice for when you needed to kiss the ass of your boss in your first job; to get ahead, you saluted the uniform, not the man.

Over breakfast, Nick let us have it: "It played out as I warned you. Now please toe the line. Remember to walk fast and follow the golf shirt. Don't lose him or the shit will hit the fan."

In the soaking heat, we tramped out to the Forum, the Times Square of the Roman Empire. Over the next four hours, Bernie delivered a crash course on the rise and fall of Western civilization to a herd of toxified teens.

An admirer of the military ethos that I had only recently learned to ironize, he loved repeating his favourite quotation: "If you're not the lead dog, the view is always the same." I had been told that leadership and risk had a noble, altruistic side, but countercultural counter-indoctrination was planting doubt: as working-class GIs fragged their Ivy League officers in the swamps of Vietnam, I was bowing to the deity of Dylan: "Don't follow leaders."

Bernie's ponderous lecturing style was enlivened by quirky gestures. Threading through the ruins, he held forth on the origins of the Forum, the evolution of Imperial Rome, and a litany of monuments, temples, palaces, basilicas, baths, fountains, columns, arches, amphitheatres, porticos, shrines, statues, walls, roads, bridges, mausoleums. When he lapsed into Latin verse, I thought of my battered yellow textbook *Latin for Canadian Schools*, and out of the side of my mouth, I shot puns and pig Latin in Sally's direction. Loved Ben. Hated Hur.

Bernie knew kids liked sex and gore, so he deployed the occasional vivid visual scene to cut the tedium. In 46 BC, Julius Caesar paraded the conquered Gallic barbarian Vercingetorix to the Forum and right here, right under our feet, the Big V was strangled to death. When Bernie started in on the six vestal virgins, my ears pricked up.

Hand-picked pubescent patrician girls chastely devoted themselves to pagan rites for thirty years, maintaining the sacred fire of Vesta, the goddess of hearth and home. The VVs were held in awe for their magical powers; if a man happened to see a vestal on the way to his execution, he was pardoned. On the downside, if they broke their vows of celibacy before the age of thirty—their chastity was tied directly to the health of the Roman state—it was considered an act of incest and treason, and they were buried alive, since the spilling of their blood was forbidden.

I was fascinated, but by hour four, we felt as if we were on a forced march. After we encircled the alleged spot where Big Julie was knocked off in 44 BC, I told Sally: "Time to knock off *Bernie*."

Maybe it was the marathon walking and talking in the remorseless heat mixed with my compulsive glibness and skittering imagination that finally did it. Bernie explained that over the centuries, sediments from the Tiber and eroding hills had raised the Forum floor. Citizens simply paved over the debris that was too onerous to remove, building over earlier ruins, and the city rose. Looking up, I was made to experience Rome as Freud had—the accumulating detritus of the centuries reflecting the strata of the unconscious mind.

I guessed this was the intention: sooner or later, something serious would slither through our waxy earholes. I realized that as I stood under the same sun that shone on Julius Caesar, I was nothing but an infinitesimal microbe, yet dimly tethered to the idea of the infinite. I was occupying simultaneous layers of time and space—a twentieth-century reader of an Elizabethan play of Imperial Rome even as I dreamed of the millennial future. Raw awe seeped through me.

That night, we returned to the Forum for a sound-and-light show. Like a World War II anti-aircraft battery, columns of intersecting spotlights washed over the ruins to strains of grandiose music and an

ominous, voice-of-God narration. The experience must have resonated because back at the hotel a bunch of us found ourselves sitting
around telling ghost stories.

Around midnight, Kathy burst into our room, breathless and
hysterical: at the Trevi Fountain, random Italian hands had thrust up
her miniskirt. Peter had intervened and hustled her away, but he was
nearly assassinated for his chivalry. Kathy's spontaneous entrance
quelled our ghost stories, but then out popped a crazy dare: why not
spend the night in the Forum, sleeping on the stones where mad
emperors had strutted? Only Kathy's distress made us think twice.

The next morning, Nick led a tour of the Capitoline Hill, one of
the famed seven hills of Rome. Standing in the grand piazza designed
by Michelangelo to restore Renaissance Rome to its classical gran-
deur, he performed a killer imitation of his boss, signalling that he
was on our side.

In the evening, we bused out to the third-century Baths of
Caracalla to see an outdoor performance of *Aida*. We were crammed
into a set of bleachers so far back that it was like watching a hockey
game on a six-inch TV. I had no time for the tortured story of the
doomed love of an Egyptian general for an Ethiopian princess, so I
indulged my shoulder-hunching Ed Sullivan imitation on Sally, pro-
voking Medusa glares from the avid opera fans around us. The more
they shushed me, the more they fed my juvenile brat.

On our last day in Rome, Tammy led us to Vatican City for a
tour of St. Peter's and the Sistine Chapel. Even I knew better than to
crack wise here. The prodigious Michelangelo spent five years, from
1508 to 1512, painting the chapel's forty-metre-long vaulted ceiling,
lying on his back on scaffolding, paint dripping into his eyes. The
nudes he painted in *The Last Judgment*, the monumental fresco
behind the altar, so offended counter-Reformation clergy that they
ordered drapery painted on forty of the naked figures. Shades of the
Pompeii closet.

Filing into St. Peter's Basilica, we glimpsed the majestic funeral procession of a cardinal, his confreres' crimson robes signifying readiness to spill blood in defence of the Christian faith. Robin burst into tears at the sight of the *Pietà*, the marble masterpiece of the crucified Christ draped across the lap of the Virgin Mary. I was moved to take a closer look. Twenty-five-year-old Michelangelo was about the same age as Nick when he sculpted the *Pietà*. How did such an absurdly young man conceive such a thing, let alone hew it from marble by hand?

In the afternoon, Bernie led us into the catacombs, the three-hundred-mile network of burial grounds fifty feet deep, encircling the outskirts of Rome. Originally pagan, the burial niches and sarcophagi were carved into the tunnel walls. When the Christians were persecuted, they sought out underground shelters, and their martyrs were eventually entombed here. Pagans favoured cremation, but the early Christians buried their dead in the belief that their bodies would be resurrected with the Second Coming. Forgotten in the Dark Ages, the catacombs were rediscovered in the nineteenth century by candle-bearing Grand Tourists.

Goofing around, Stu wiggled through a clammy crack and mingled with the skulls and bones, a kind of backwards birth. I felt a weird tingle. Let down by parents and teachers who poorly parented and taught, I was discovering in my happy tripsters their glorious opposites, and through them disinterring a deep secret: all knowledge is carnal.

Taking our lead from Nick and Tammy, many of us were flirting with loose forms of coupledom, chemistry experiments that sparked or fizzled. Fitz and Sally, Sean and Jane, Peter and Nan were the most visibly "together," the boys more hearts on sleeves than the girls. The second tier was more mercurial and kept the gossip mill turning: Rich and Liz? Steve and Nikki? Dave and Annabel? Will and Marywinn? Stu and Kat? John and Robin?

On our last night in Rome, a gang of us roved the backstreets on yet another let's-get-lost mission. Into a dark nightclub cellar I trailed Sally. We headed for the dance floor, ending up jammed tight to the band, the swinging guitar necks close to cracking our heads. When they ripped into "Paint It Black," I was beside myself: "I could not foresee this thing happening to you . . ."

Without a break, the mad guitars switched gears, and we were driven into "The Land of 1,000 Dances." My joints oiled, my limbs limber, I fell into a spiralling, undulating groove. Were we the first generation to invent rapture? Dave sidled up beside us: "Hey, Fitz, you're a great dancer!" He was as amazed as I was.

When the organ riff for "A Whiter Shade of Pale" softened the pace, I faced my first slow dance with Sally Wodehouse. As if planning escape, I glanced at our table crammed with wine bottles and heaping ashtrays, then turned back to gaze into her flushed face. I slipped my arm around her slowly, tentatively, resting my palm on her lower back, curving into her hip, suppressing the impulse to clutch her too tightly. As she rested her head on my shoulder, a choir of voices rose in sync with the lyric that we all knew was coming: "One of sixteen vestal virgins . . ."

Back at the hotel, Bernie was pouring another round of sweet vermouth and casting a smile toward Nick: "No question, we've turned things around. I love the leadership potential of some of these kids!"

NINE

Buried Alive

A half-day northbound drive delivered us to Florence, the cradle of the Renaissance, and with each passing moment I was soothed by the intuition that I was crawling out of my childhood in the direction of rebirth. In the lobby of the Terminus Milano hotel, Nick and Tammy fed us grand stories of the local all-stars, bright and dark—Dante, Michelangelo, Boccaccio, Galileo, Leonardo, Borgia, Savonarola, Medici, Machiavelli, Botticelli.

Since Sorrento, Sally and I had been gravitating to Sean and Jane. Sean was as enamoured of Jane as James was of Sally, an inter-lacing tension that would not have been building had the girls declared themselves boyfriend-less on the *Raffaello*. On the aimless cobblestones we four followed the falling dusk, settling in a sidewalk café on the edge of a public square, our exposed brown limbs caressed by a humid breeze. I couldn't believe my luck: how could it be that, day by day, night by night, I turned to find a three-dimen-sional flesh-and-blood "girlfriend," a girl who is a friend, constantly by my side? As my eyes drifted to the shadowed roofline of a medi-eval church, my whirling mental flywheel slowed, then stopped, and I was released into a wordless elation. Happiness, it seemed, was accidental. No one could ever steal this experience, and to myself I mouthed the words *This moment happened. It is mine alone, and I will never forget it.*

As we sipped our wine, Jane announced there was a postal strike in Canada, so the flow of letters would dry up. I glanced at Sal, but her face revealed nothing. I imagined that in her letters to George, I did not exist. Fair enough: I had been busy willing him off the planet. But ever since we started scaling the go-go boot of Italy, Sally had stopped talking about him, at least to me.

By 2 a.m., I was a goner, and Sally swung into nurse mode. Her shoulder under mine, she piloted us up to my room where we found Dave conked out like a newborn. I sprawled on the spinning bed and Sally shifted my long legs so they didn't hang over the edge. Then the moment when dread meets desire: her long fingers pulled the back of my head forward, and she pressed her lips forcefully against mine. I was surprised how guilty I felt, for wasn't this what I wanted?

When Sal disappeared, I was not sure if I was glad or sad or mad. Did she pull away or did I push her? I slid off the bed onto the floor, a wading pool of silent anguish. Longing for her to return and pick me up, all six feet three inches and 165 pounds of me, I hugged the carpet, half awake all night long.

The next morning, I found myself standing under a towering stone figure bearing the same name as my roommate. As we encircled *David*, Nick championed the genius of Michelangelo, a scant twenty-six years old when he started liberating this nude male figure from six tons of Carrara marble. Our eyes wandered over the statue's head, hands and feet, all oversize, like an awkward adolescent. I was seventeen years old, and he was seventeen feet tall; if David was the punk, I'd hate to meet the giant. He was preternaturally sexy, the epitome of narcissistic youth, beauty and strength, ageless and timeless, caught in the critical, life-threatening moment of decision, muscles tensed, veins pulsating, slingshot shouldered like a Stratocaster. This guy was a rock star. Make love *and* war.

Bernie had followed us to Florence to oversee the shooting of a 16 mm film to promote the Odyssey across Canada. He cast a handful of the wealthiest and best-looking kids boasting Family Name Recognition, and when Sally and I failed to make the cut, we pretended not to care.

Nick proposed we climb the 414 narrow stone steps of the spiral staircase to the top of the Campanile. "A piece of cake," he promised, but it was a piece of work. At the top, we were entranced by the vista of curving clay terracotta roof tiles, formed on human thighs, that seemed to undulate under the sun. Nick confessed that he had been mildly acrophobic ever since a close call atop Rouen Cathedral on his first Odyssey in 1963. While he was walking between adjoining towers, grasping a primitive iron railing, it had broken away from its rusted socket. But today, as usual, he was calm and confident, and I forgot my own fear of heights.

As my attention wandered during a tour of the massive Uffizi Gallery, Tammy pulled me back in with something that stuck: in the 1470s, the architect Brunelleschi invented three-dimensional depth perspective, revolutionizing European painting. So long, two-dimensional medieval art.

After the lecture, I followed Sally as she elbowed through the flea market. Bantering and bartering, she considered rings, gloves and sweaters before settling on a pair of leather sandals and a terrycloth dress. On the Ponte Vecchio, the closed-in arcade that spans the River Arno, she trolled jewellery shops with fervent intent, and I abandoned her to her addiction. Sally loved to shop.

Less than two years earlier, in November 1966, a flood had savaged the Ponte Vecchio and wrenched away five of the ten bronze panels of the Gates of Paradise, one of the famous doors of the Duomo cathedral, and flung them into the seething muck. Dozens of people were killed and thousands of art masterpieces and rare books damaged or destroyed. I could see the flood marks on the walls. Catastrophe, calamity, cataclysm—I couldn't get enough of it.

I was in Nick's bus bound for Venice, sitting beside Sal, obeying the unspoken rule: holding hands was uncool. We played Stump the Leader all the way to the ferry docks to the Lido, a seven-mile-long island on the Adriatic Sea. Half sandbar, the world's first beach resort was complete with a string of hotels, whitewashed huts and private villas originally designed for the nintheenth-century Grand Tourist trade. We checked into Cappelli's Hotel, not far from the Grand Hôtel des Bains immortalized in Thomas Mann's *Death in Venice*. An intrusion from a forgotten world came in the form of a letter from my brother. Mike had enclosed the box score of the Major League All-Star game, but for the first time in my life, sports didn't cut it.

After a raucous dinner, we four wandered down to the beach, trading swigs from a bottle. Tonight it was the turn of Jane and Fitz to caretake, and soon it was only my arm around Sally's waist that was holding her up. Her terrycloth dress was drunk, her purse was drunk, her flip-flops were drunk, her hair was drunk. She was bawling "Roll me oooove-rrrr in the cloooov-errrr!" as if there was no tomorrow. As I turned my mouth to hers, she belched, and I pushed her head away in the nick of time, dodging the reappearance of her pasta. Back at the hotel, I heaved her dead-weight body onto her bed, a mixed potion of lust and disgust churning my guts.

On a morning vaporetto into Venice, we threaded through striped barber poles jutting out of the water. Nick quoted Robert Benchley, a *New Yorker* writer sent to Venice, who cabled his editor, "Streets flooded. Please advise."

The legendary pigeon shit of St. Mark's Square was replenished daily with the help of vendors flogging bags of corn to tourists; when

Robin growled she'd love to brain the filthy feather dusters with a baseball bat, I was game. We were further put off when the girls were turned back from the Basilica di San Marco because their short skirts exposed columns of flesh. As we toured a glass-making factory, Sally spied a set of six florid red, blue and green Venetian goblets and urged me to buy them for my mother.

"Look, only $33 plus shipping to Toronto. What a deal. She'll love them."

"Naw, she never likes my presents."

"Come on, you won't be sorry. Trust me."

All I saw was good drinking money circling the drain, but I caved, not to please my mother but Sally.

Back on the Lido, the four of us bought two whole cooked chickens and a giant bottle of Coke and headed back to my room, where we ripped off chunks of meat with our hands and stuffed them in our gobs like the barbarians we longed to be. When I chose to stay in and do my laundry—a cover story for resting my delicate guts—Sally teased: "You're a killjoy."

The next day, ten of us headed to the beach for the afternoon. Heedless of the warnings of stinging jellyfish, I followed Sally's pink-and-green bikini bottom into the waves. The hot wind exploded her wet head into a shock of unruly curls, and as she struggled to straighten it with her palms, I wished she'd let it run wild. As I lay down on my towel, she started playfully tossing handfuls of sand on my legs. At first I liked it, but when the sand infiltrated my crotch, I didn't.

"Okay, knock it off."

"Now, don't worry your pretty little head," she teased. "Relax."

Then everyone joined in: Jane, Sean, Rich, Peter, Margi, Chris, Ross, Annabel, all grabbing and tossing fistfuls of sand. In no time I was buried alive in a tomb-like mound, neck to toe, my head poking turtle-like from a shell. Sally knelt over me, a three-dimensional art-work of flesh, her long fingers splayed on her thighs, and as I played dead in my grave, I heard the clicking of cameras. Burying my libido on the Lido. Death in Venice.

Vaporettos carried us back through the Grand Canal to the mainland. Then the buses and westward to Milan. We were booked for only one night at the Hotel Touring and Grand Turisimo, a quick stop en route to the Côte d'Azur. A gritty industrial heap not unlike Toronto, Milan was nothing to write home about, except perhaps the monastery housing *The Last Supper* by Leonardo da Vinci. The ever-feisty Robin was once more barred entry by a priest for being improperly dressed; although she was wearing a sweater and a longish skirt, she was unforgivably hatless. Denied entry to San Marco, she wouldn't take shit this time around. "Who says so?"

"The pope."

"Who told the pope? God?"

And in she strode, lobbing a parting shot: "This is my father's house."

Inside, I was disappointed by the condition of the flaking mural. But I was taken with the guide's narration: completed in 1498, the artwork captured the moment when the Twelve Apostles were reacting to the prediction that one of them would betray Christ. Symbols of the Trinity were embedded in the imagery: Jesus' head and outstretched arms form a triangle, and the Apostles sit in groups of three before three windows overlooking a landscape.

Sean, Jane and Sally returned to my room, where we idly flicked 5- and 10-lire coins out the window, no fountains below to catch our wishes. When Sal and Jane decided to hit the sack early, Sean and I fell into a heavy rap about Serious Relationships; were we ready for one of those?

I told him I'd love to find the gas station in Milan where the body of the Fascist leader Benito Mussolini, executed by Communist partisans, had been displayed in 1945. As a kid, I never forgot the newsreel footage of Il Duce and his mistress, Clara Petacci—Clara, you chose the wrong boyfriend—strung by their heels, left to rot, their faces swollen like pumpkins and their bodies bashed, shot, stoned and spat upon by a mob.

A gas station—what a place to end. I wondered if there was a plaque.

At the wheel of his bus, Stu was breezing westward over the Italian-French border, where a listless customs agent stamped our passports and waved us through. Feeling uncomfortable leading our convoy up a steep climb, Stu thrust his arm out the window and motioned Dave's bus ahead. As he pulled out to pass, Dave saw a black Ferrari blazing straight for him at Grand Prix speed. He swerved back behind Stu just in time.

With deadpan calmness, Stu declared, "I almost killed Dave."

As we crested a hill overlooking the Côte d'Azur, I was smacked in the head by the panorama of the Mediterranean and the intense luminosity of sun, sky and sea. A curving bay of palm trees saluted us into the resort town of Nice. I was disappointed that the beach was pebbled; Sally was not burying me here. As we arrived at the Grand Hôtel de la Paix, Nick told us that the main drag, the Promenade des Anglais, was named after Brit aristos who escaped their fogbound island, gambled away their inheritances, then slumped into Nice's striped beach chairs to die of TB and VD. Successive eras delivered artists like Picasso, Matisse and Chagall, attracted to the bright light and clear air; then high-voltage celebs like Brigitte Bardot and Mick Jagger; then the likes of us.

Sideswiped by a head cold, after breakfast I retreated to my bed, swallowing aspirin and wallowing in self-pity. I imagined Sally on the beach wondering, *Where's Fitz? I'm worried about him*, then materializing in her fetching bikini to fetch me out of bed, or better still, jump in. Dream on.

The next day brought redemption. For hours I splashed with Sally and the others, slipping on and off a raft like seals, stealing glances at the topless Frenchwomen, the surf whooshing over the smooth stones, which rolled and clicked like snooker balls. Although he was a poor swimmer, Ross, a white-skinned redhead, thought he could make it out to the paddleboats, but when he drew close, all had moved on. On his way back, he went under, then up, then down. In a flailing panic, he grabbed for a woman, but she pushed him off. He thought of the cartoons: if you went down a third time, lights out. Then his feet touched the pebbles, and he waded out to tell the tale.

To augment the thin hotel food, Sean and I wolfed down a second dinner in Jane and Sally's room, then we all tumbled back down to the beach. We crossed paths with some of the Vancouver Odyssey kids who'd scored some acid from a Vietnamese pusher, their dilated pupils and spaced-out stares a dead giveaway. I wanted some, but I wasn't sure how it would go down with Sally.

Still, we could fly with or without wings, and as we were engulfed by sand, sea and stars, I felt a lightness and self-acceptance that seemed entirely new. Taking turns skipping the ropes of our word play, we were hot, we were on, we were one; when the topper came, Sally tipped into hysterics of such breath-stealing force that she doubled over and collapsed on the stones. "I've pissed my fucking pants!" she cried, and a mixed mood of triumph and loss lofted us back to the hotel. Locked out, we rang the concierge and I was disappointed when he let us in.

Stopping for a picnic in the French Alps en route to Grenoble, the twenty-eight of us sprawled across an open pasture, the sky flooded with keenest blue. When Annabel, the shapely, perfectly coiffed Havergal girl bound for medical school, challenged all comers to a foot race, I sensed potential humiliation and took a pass. But the drivers, Dave, Stu and Steve, were game, and as the quartet bolted across our patch of Eden, it was no contest from the get-go. Annabel was uncatchable.

In the hotel dining room, we mingled with a tour of fifty American girls. When they started singing happy birthday to one of their own, one of our own leapt from his table to capitalize on a free kiss, and the room erupted into hooting and cackling. Hypercharged peer pressure drove the males to follow suit; when my turn came, twelfth in line, I could see she was freaked out by the serial invasions, so I affected an air kiss of the brand perfected by my mother. Returning to the table, Sally shot me a look that could kill. Was she actually jealous?

A ramble over the spectacular Swiss border led us down into the postcard-quaint town of Interlaken, population five thousand, encircled by mountains and lakes. The contrast with the sexy-violent Italian decadence was stark; all this lung-clearing fresh air and orderly hygiene looked too much like Canada.

At the hotel, we picked up our mail. Jane breathlessly relayed the news that one of her friends, also named Jane, had been knocked up by a UCC boy, scandalizing the Toronto private school set and precipitating a shotgun teen wedding. I happened to know him—athlete-scholar, born leader, the boy most likely—and wordlessly I digested the cautionary tale.

Our own in-house gossip hotline percolated non-stop. Did I know that Sean was bummed out because Jane went out with Steve? I did. Did I know that Marywinn was so pissed at Rich for carrying on with Liz that she got her ears pierced in town? I did. At Branksome, she and Sally had not been allowed to wear jewellery or makeup, so I got it.

The next morning we took the cable car up the nine-thousand-foot Schilthorn, one of a trio of peaks along with the Jungfrau and Eiger in the Bernese Alps. On the deck at the summit, turned frisky by the thin air, we swung the coin-driven binoculars on ourselves and took turns piggybacking. Talking to Sally by the railing, I was caught off guard when Margi wheeled and pointed her camera at us. Just us. Only us. I felt as if I was being framed by the four corners of a formal portrait, the eyes of the world trained on our coupledom. Why did I feel like dying? In the second before the click of the shutter, I wavered, then swung my arm around Sally's shoulder and smiled.

Disembarking from the cable car partway down the mountain, we descended on foot. Grazing sheep, open-shuttered cabins, brimming flower boxes and crystalline streams passed like a glass-lantern show, and I expected to meet a pigtailed Heidi singing songs from *The Sound of Music*. Back at the hotel, I soaked my blistered feet in an ice-filled bathtub with six pairs of all-girl feet, but I only played footsie with Sally.

Sally was rooming with Nikki. I knew Nikki believed in ghosts, so when darkness fell I hid in the closet. Bursting out, I scared her bug-eyed and instantly felt sorry. I crashed beside Sally on her bed, feeling remorseful, then sneaked back to my room at 4 a.m., dodging Nick's radar, as both girls dreamed on. I was still getting away with it, and maybe soon I would know what "it" was.

The girls had shifted into deep shopping mode: the latest craze was Swiss watches. I watched Robin parade around in a pair of leather lederhosen, her bleached-blond hair attracting a passing woman who babbled at her in German. Robin cracked, "She thinks I'm Eva Braun." Back at the hotel, a bunch of us goofed around throwing water and shoes out the window, and I was pulled into a mock slap-fight with Kat, excited by her lithe, laughing quickness.

At dinner, we were served cheese fondue, a new one on me. Some genius made up the rule that if your piece of bread dropped off your fork into the pot of melted cheese, you had to kiss your neighbour, and the meal quickly slid off the rails. All charged up, eight of us scooted, giggling, back to Jane's room, where we all rolled around on the bed like greased marbles, smooching randomly. Freud said when two people go to bed, it was more like eight, so we got the numbers right. In our dreams, we are all promiscuous. Switzerland was shifting out of neutral, and I was learning how to be "good in bed."

I followed Sally to her room and flopped on the floor. As she gave me a five-star massage, digging her long fingers into my hunched shoulders, the rules Nick chiselled on stone a thousand years ago on the *Raffaello*—don't sleep with the girls, and show up every morning for breakfast—were now down on their knees begging to be broken. But we were not alone, and once again I nuzzled up beside her in my clothes. Awakening at 5 a.m., I slinked back to my room to find Will and Kathy, Peter and Nan still awake. From the window, I sang to the Swiss dawn, "First there is a mountain, then there is no mountain, then there is . . ."

189 Gordon Road
July 14

My darling Sally,

I don't know if you'll get this letter because of the coming strike; I hope so.

Well, summer is passing, albeit very slowly. The heat is very oppressive, well over 90 today, and a hazy sun. So David, Graham, Nathan and I played tennis from 12 to 3:30. Dave kind of folded in the heat, and I'm getting in shape to take you on when you get home.

Went to the Boulevard Club for a regatta party with
Gerrie & Doug. Mrs. Grand had decided to play match-
maker, and I was introduced to a very nice kid (I guess)
named Sue Matthews. I had fun, but she didn't because
I wouldn't drink or dance. She wanted to know why, so
I told her I was engaged and went into a long song-and-
dance about you being away. So I had a lovely evening, and
she went home with her mother. So don't worry, please.
I'm still in love with you.

This mother, Mrs. Matthews, about 45–50, divorced,
now *she* was attractive. Just my type. Even had a nice boat.
So if I have to get a date for anything this summer, I'll ask
Mrs. Matthews instead of her daughter.

I presume (I don't know for sure) that you know about
your father's talk to me. As a result of that, I've gone into
some inquiry as to taking an M.A. This would involve two
more years of school after this coming one. The final year
then (your last in nursing) would be a MAKE-UP year,
and I would be a regular student.

The next year (your first at work) would be my M.A.
qualification year, and for that I would be paid between
$1,200 and $2,000. So you may have to be prepared to
work to support us for a year. But if I get an M.A., any job
I took would automatically pay me around $500 to $800 a
year more to start, and I would have a much greater scope
of choice.

So when you plan your wedding, keep that possibility
alive and in mind, and we'll talk about it later. OK?

I've thought of something to surprise you with when
you come home. But, being an unpleasant type, I'm going
to keep it as a surprise.

Next week, maybe later, I'm going to drop in on both your parents just to talk. As far as I know now, I'll be picking up both you and Robin, but if she doesn't know, then don't tell her.

I don't remember writing letters this long when you were away last summer. But this will be (has been?) the first time since I met you that I haven't (won't?) see you for two months. But I guess I'll keep, and besides today it was, and still is, too hot to do anything, including THAT (sigh!) except swim, sit and drink. But the beer stores are still closed.

I think I will start running mail for Father and some other offices in his building tomorrow, so they'll be able to function once the strike starts.

After dinner, I'm going down to Jim White's new apartment that he shares with two American newspaper reporter–draft dodger types. He phoned all excited and nervous, saying he had some pot, and was I interested tonight. He was so eager that I couldn't resist shooting him down. "No thanks, Jim. Not interested." Dead silence. "But I'll come down if you've got any beer." Which he does, so off after dinner and home early, and sober.

Hope you're getting some sun. I've been out in it for at least six hours a day all week, and plan on really embarrassing you if you come home white.

Be careful. Rumour has it here that the French student riots start in Lyon, Nantes, and Paris on or about August 10. So take care, because you're too precious to me to get squashed by a brick, or even a VW mini-bus.

Must sign off and go eat. Will try to write again, and promise to think and dream of only you. Be good (I am) and remember you are mine. Don't forget I love you, and love you very, very much.

Forever yours, George

Where will you be on the night of August 12th? Write now if you haven't already and tell me. But I'm not going to phone: I can't afford it. Just a mushy telegram. Love forever & forever, as long as you want me!

Nice, France
July 25

Dear George (my lover),
Two nights ago I sent you a telegram. I wanted to make it as mushy as possible but I couldn't because it cost 20 cents a word and I didn't have that much money. However by sending it as a night letter it only cost $4.20 altogether. That's pretty dirt cheap. I hope it didn't get there at too ungodly an hour. Please apologize to your parents if it woke them up.

But I really wanted to send it to tell you that I love you. And also I hadn't written since that beautiful letter you sent me in Venice saying that you'd asked my dad if you could marry me. I think that's a terrific idea and I'm gonna marry you and we're going to be very happy cuz we're in love.

I got your letters here in Nice. Thank you, love, they were really sweet. I loved your story for *Seventeen* magazine. I think you did an excellent job on it. And guess what, there's a girl on the trip whose name is Anne but we call her Annabel. Well, anyhow, this year she was representative at Simpson's. They have reps from each school. Well, she was the Simpson's rep for *Seventeen* magazine. She worked for them this year, you know, modelled and all that crap. Well, she read your story and so did practically every other girl on the trip and by the way they all think you're a great writer. Well, anyhow, Annabel read it and liked it and she said she could maybe get some pull and get it into *Seventeen* seeing as she worked for them. So if I forget, you remind me when I come home to talk to Annabel and she will see what she can do for you.

I'm really having fun spending money. I'll see if I can list what I bought. Nothing in Sorrento cuz it was sort of a hole. Nothing in Rome cuz it was too expensive. About $65 in Florence. Love that place. I really want to go back there with you and I want to go to the Ponte Vecchio and buy jewellery. I'm so mad I didn't have more money because I would have loved to have gotten you a good ring as well as a couple for me. But anyhow I'd already spent $65 so I didn't buy any jewellery.

Well, I'll tell you how I spent my moolah. I got a gorgeous, funny-coloured brown leather purse, hand sewn. It's just beautiful and really smart. I also got a light brown suede purse, sort of a shoulder bag. It's really quite smart, too. Then I got a cute little cheap white straw purse cuz I don't have one. I'm really mad though cuz I couldn't find a nice black one and that's what I needed the most. Oh well, I'll just have to take you out and we can pick one out. So I got three great purses. Now you'll be able to see a variety.

Also I got something for you and my dad but I'm not gonna tell you what it is. You already know about the watch so I have to have some surprises. I got a surprise: I love you. How bout that! And I bought six pairs of beautiful gloves, four of which are pour moi, one for Mum and one for Di. And I bought two pairs sandals. One pair doesn't fit anymore but I wear them anyhow. I got two great dresses in the Florence flea market. They're made out of terrycloth. One is just a straight shift and the front and the back are attached by two brass rings on the shoulder. Because there are the two rings and you can see through the rings onto my shoulder, I can't wear a bra. You know I'm really getting used to no bra. Tammy has worn one about four times since we left and now she's gotten about half the trip not wearing them. It's great but I don't wear them under turtlenecks cuz what you see through a turtleneck is for you and you only.

You know George, I'm getting sooo horny. I can't wait to get home to your arms. I think I'll just throw myself in your arms and then I'll be at your disposal. You better be able to keep up with me or you will be pretty sore the next day. I find I'm really energetic now. I can even stay up all night and drink you under the table I bet. But we'll see when I get home. So don't forget to think horny so you can keep up with me.

Well, anyhow, I got sidetracked about what I bought. I got this other neat dress. It's navy blue with a white rim around the sides and hem. It's sleeveless and has a zipper right up the front. I step into it like a coat and zip zip zip. Well, I got it with the idea that I could wear it as a sundress but to my horror (you'll love it and me too), I found the fly started right at the bottom of my crotch. From the crotch down is open space. So I have to settle for wearing it as a bathing suit cover up. But maybe for you I'll wear it as a dress. We'll see. You can tell what you think, OK, love?

Well, it was really sad leaving Florence. I thought it was a great place and I'd really love to go back but only with you. So we left Florence and went to Venice. While I think of it, here is Willy's address. I'll be there Aug. 16–20.

Miss Willy Tijs
BURGEMEESTER VAN DE MORTELPLEIN
70 TILBURG (N. Br.) THE NETHERLANDS

Sorry about the sidetrack again but I just remembered that you wanted it. Venice was quite a weird city. Venice proper was a nice place to visit but I sure wouldn't want to live there. I got kicked out of my first church there, St. Mark's. They said my dress was too short and I had on a long one. Oh well, I didn't want to see any damn church anyhow. It was really weird to go driving down the canals in a boat and look around and see the houses with their back door facing the sewage water. Could you imagine saying: "Hey, Mum, can I borrow the boat tonight? I want to take Sally out." I tell you personally I wouldn't like that set-up.

But the Lido where we were staying was really kinda neat. It was a little island, but a beautiful island. All tourists. The beach was beautiful but the sand was kind of dirty. In Venice I bought a really cute bikini, it's kinda coral pink and lime green. It sounds awful but it's really cool. The top is about normal size but the bottom is a small as I can get it. It just covers me and I mean just. Also it doesn't bag in the bum like my pink one does so I think you'll like it: oh yeah. It has a bow right in the middle of my crotch. The bow sticks out and it's very conspicuous. But it's cute. And I'll even let you pluck my bow cuz I love you. I also bought a gondola T-shirt. It's really groovy. I should have got you

one but I forgot. Sorry. So Venice was nice but I really
didn't mind leaving. Then we had one night in Milan.

We stayed in the poshest hotel in Milan. It was like the
Ritz, no kidding. Everyone had a bathtub. My tub was so
big that when I stretched out my toes wouldn't reach the
other end. But was it ever nice to lie back and relax. We
went to the zoo there. It was really neat, much better than
the Toronto zoo. It had giraffes, kangaroos, polar bears,
penguins and all kinds of great animals. I also got kicked
out of another church but I didn't want to see it anyhow.
So we left Milan and drove to Nice. What a drive, an all
dayer. It was beautiful up on top of the cliffs but the roads
were so windy. By the end of the trip which was about
eight hours I really felt sick.

I just got back from the beach and guess what, I'm
going brown. But we rented gondola kinda surfboards and
I was out on them for about two hours and I got burned in
my back and damn it I've got strap marks on my back. My
chest is getting really brown and my boobs are even getting
brown. I'll probably be all faded by the end of the summer,
damn, but I think it looks nice.

Anyhow we are now in Nice. It's very nice but very
touristy. It's kinda neat though because you can walk
around in grubs. Well, yesterday I went to the beach but
only for one and a half hours cuz I didn't want to get
burned. It was really blowy and rough. The waves were
four to five feet high. Great to swim in. I think it was the
first time I'd been swimming since the day before I left and
I was swimming at your house. I didn't think any other
place was worth swimming in but this place was out of this
world. The beach was rocky and all that but it was nice.
Nice in Nice—get it?

So I left the beach early with a couple of other girls and we came back to the hotel, showered, cleaned up and took off bikini shopping and guess what I bought—not one but two. One for me and one for Gerrie. I've learned over here that you either get a small bottom and big top or vice versa. The small bottoms are really small, so small that it covered half of me. So forget me in the small bottom. The small tops are not exactly what I thought the small top would be. It's quite like the half bra that you bought me, as low as the U goes in the bra.

Well, anyhow, the bathing suit I got for me is light green flowers on a cream-coloured base. There is a tie kinda bow but not a real bow in between the boobs and there is one at each side of the bottom. The bows are shocking pink. It's really cute and the girls say it looks OK on me. Gerrie's bathing suit is basically orange, yellow and green. Tell her the top fits me almost perfectly like I could get away with it if I had to and the bottom is about one size too big for me. It is not too, too small. The top is fairly low and the bottom covers everything that has to be covered and that's it. So that's what I did yesterday.

Today I went to the beach for about three hours. It was quite flat (the water I mean) and very, very hot. The beach just fascinates me. People make out, people get changed, people do every damn thing imaginable. I really like this Riviera, super gorgeous. This is another place I'd like to come back to but only if you came too. So that's what I've done for the last week or so since I wrote you.

I'm sorry I haven't been writing very much but it's so hard to find time. I've only written my parents two postcards and one letter. I have to write them a letter as soon as I finish this. However I did send them a telegram.

The same time as I sent you one, so at least they know I am still alive.

Hope all is well, and Spotz survived her plumbing excursion to the vet's. Give my love to your parents and Mike and I guess even to Passionflower if she's still around.

Take care of yourself, hon. I miss you but I'm being very good. Nobody has touched me yet and nobody is going to except you when I get home. So don't forget, think horny cuz I will be. I'll write you again when I can. And remember that I love you and I'm very happy that we are almost officially engaged.

Love always, Sal XXOO

On the envelope: I.M.Y.A.L.Y.A.W.Y.A.N.Y. Use your imagination and you can figure this one out.

TEN

Sleeping Together

I didn't know what I did to deserve it, but here I was, the only guy in an all-girl bus—Sally, Jane, Kat, Nikki, Barb and Tammy at the wheel. I plunked myself smack dab in the middle seat in the middle row, a girl on either side, two in front, two behind. I was a willing captive in a day-long chatterbox on wheels. Magic bus. Seventh heaven.

I flashed an English flick I'd seen only months ago, *Here We Go Round the Mulberry Bush,* in which a seventeen-year-old named Jamie struggled to lose his virginity in the dawning era of free love, yet another celluloid-dream made just for me. In the opening scene, Jamie was riding his bike and musing aloud: "I have a problem, Doctor. If the bus were to go on forever, full of birds and me the only bloke, what order would I have them in?"

We sang songs and slapped around every subject under the sunroof. I felt sunny and funny beyond words: in my next life, I was going to an all-girls school. We made frequent, dallying pit stops, stuffing coins in a jukebox, winging snowballs at each other in the July heat. When we stalled on a steep mountain pass just past the Austrian border, a flock of angel-winged American youth poured out of a tour bus ten times our size and pushed us to the side of the road.

Dusk was falling as we dawdled into Innsbruck, tucked in an alpine valley. In the Hotel Maria Theresia, Sally and I scarfed down a schnitzel as our bodies hummed with sensuous fatigue. When Nick prepped us for a full morning hike up a mountain trail—"Piece of cake, but bring your sweaters, it might be cold"—I failed to detect a set-up.

Innsbruck hosted the 1964 Winter Olympics, so Will, Sean, Dave and Steve turned the climb into a race for gold. My hard-won anti-competitive streak was hitting an all-time high, so I hung back with the girls. "Because it's there" cut no ice with me. As the Tyrolean freshness surrendered to a furnace heat, I inched up the last aching mile, sweater knotted round my waist, dehydrated by the four-hour trek. As we lolled on the summit, flies orbiting our sweating heads, I guzzled three Cokes in succession. "Young ladies do not sweat," Barb insisted. "They glisten." We were visually rewarded by the panoramic quilt of inns and towers, castles and parks, but I was still cursing Nick the Trickster and his fake promise of cake.

Ferreting out a nightclub with a killer English rock band, all leather and smoke and hair and electricity, Sally and I plumbed fresh reserves of energy, sinking into another dance-trance. When they ripped into "The Letter," she yelled, "That's my song!" We shut the place down. By the stroke of three, trying not to disturb the unconscious John in the opposite bed, I wobbled my pen over the pages of my diary: "Best night ever with S."

On the morning of August 1, we headed to Salzburg, the capital of Austria, fatherland of Hitler, Mozart and Freud. The air was cooler, the skies greyer. Why did every country have a different set of clouds?

Nick's bus was a buzzing seminar on sports and war, the pendulum swinging away from Tammy's singsong girly bus. Passing close to the German border and the Bavarian alps, I spotted a signpost to Berchtesgaden, the home of Hitler's infamous Eagle's Nest.

A World War II buff, I pulled up from my mental archive the colour films shot by the brainless Eva Braun of her beloved führer playing with a German shepherd and his equally obedient, happy gang of mass murderers.

I asked Nick if we could bend our itinerary for a quick reconnoitre, but he shot down the idea.

"Come on, a non-smoking, vegetarian teetotaller who loved kids and dogs can't be all bad," I said.

Explosive laughter. Direct hit.

In the Hotel Goldener Löwe, we celebrated John's nineteenth birthday. No one had ever seen him smashed—I think he saw the rest of us, quite rightly, as less than mature—so we enjoyed chalking up a convert to our religion. Wally told me that John earned his flying licence before his driver's licence and he was dreaming of renting a plane and flying over the fjords. He was technically qualified to drive one of the buses, but Nick felt he was not ready.

A bunch of us walked up to a castle and later settled into a bar. The trip was now a month old, halfway gone, and some of the girls were openly pining for their boyfriends back home. Sally fell quiet and I felt our connection die like a pulled plug. She seemed pissed off for no visible reason and abruptly left. She was not one for making scenes, but this qualified. Was it something I said? Or didn't say?

I was sharing with Steve, and a landslide of bodies elected our room as Party Headquarters. When the hotel manager gave us grief for the racket, we scattered into smaller groups. Nikki stayed behind, flirting with Steve. He countered with a dare of his own: come across, or get lost. Growing impatient, Steve finally turned to me: "Fitz, I'll give you 10 pfennigs if you toss Nikki out of here."

Obedient as a Hitler Youth, I scooped up Nikki like a silk purse. She meekly thrashed her arms and legs, pretending to resist, or so I thought, and as I deposited her in the hallway, the pfennig dropped. First Sally, now Nikki. Was the honeymoon finally over?

At breakfast, Nikki slapped Steve in the face. It was official: she still liked him.

Despite the steady rainfall, we headed off to the seven-thousand-year-old Hallein salt mines, first operated by Celtic tribes. But the lineup was crazy long so we drove around in circles until we were stopped dead in a traffic jam. Jumping in and out of the buses, we slapped barefoot along the autobahn in the downpour, playing Chinese Fire Drill. Forks of lightning skewered all hope of touring a Baroque church, so we holed up in the hotel for the duration. A hard rain kept falling, a vertical river of gushing and pounding, an exhilarating natural rush such as I'd never known. I saw no sign of Sally—we had been inseparable since day one—and buzzing with a full-body agitation not entirely my own, I ripped off my shirt and dashed into an open courtyard to join a half-clad Tammy in a tribal dance. At each applauding thunderclap, we cut loose with banshee screams.

When the girls decided to throw a hen party, barring the boys, I realized we were being punished for Nikki's humiliation. Stripping down to their bras and panties, the girls spent all afternoon tossing back rum and Cokes and slabs of apple strudel—Trojan women withholding the sex that they had yet to dish, at least to me. At dinner, when Margi fell off her chair not once but twice, Nick threatened to send us home. As threats went, we knew this one was idle.

After a full-day boycott, Sally casually spoiled my breakfast with too much information: several of the Rainy Day Women had overdosed on crème de menthe, with catastrophic slime-green results. Our twenty-hour stretch of cabin fever had turned our rooms into wall-to-wall dumpsters: empty bottles, cigarette butts, burned carpets, ripped pillows, stained eiderdowns, hairballs, peanut shells, dirty underwear. A hard day's night.

On the autobahn to Vienna, I finally scored the front seat as navigator. Not that I was paying attention: we ran out of gas, and Nick had to come to the rescue. The Hotel Central was a shabby, one-star dive of rock-hard mattresses, bedbugs and one can per floor; worse, the girls were stashed in another wing. I was no complainer, but five nights there seemed cruel and unusual punishment.

Breaking into small groups, we wandered the cool, overcast city randomly seeking the sights. The facades of stone and wrought iron conjured the Great War and silent film images of our grandfathers, and I wanted to surrender to a dead sleep on the pavement, laid low by High Culture. I knew Vienna was a city of avatars: here the secret of the dream was revealed to Freud; here a young Hitler trod the pavements as a tramp, dreaming of revenge. But the place made me feel as if I had been consigned to a boxcar chain of bleak, rainy, agnostic Sunday afternoons, past and future, sandbagged by mounds of incomprehensible math homework. Arrogance, rigidity, repression, repetition, suffocation, stultification. I heard the melancholic melodies of my grandmother's classical grand piano, the soundtrack of a dead-as-dust marriage; I saw my mother's stymied stab at Jazz Age rebellion; I saw the next victim in line, and he looked too much like me.

Something good followed something bad: after dinner, we drove the buses to the Prater, Europe's oldest amusement park. Sally had thawed, and we ran wild like kids at the Ex in Toronto. The sixty-five-metre-high Ferris wheel is an 1890s beauty, one of the world's oldest, taller than Niagara Falls, a luminescent *O* revolving in the night sky. Even with its secure enclosed gondolas, I was not brave enough to test my fear of heights, so we hit the go-cart track, spinning dozens of laps past midnight.

I followed Sally over to the far wing of the hotel, emanating the forbidden aura of a girls' boarding school dorm. Under a clothesline of drying bras and undies, Marywinn was asleep, or pretending to be, and as I squeezed beside Sal on her narrow single bed, it finally dawned on me why Nick rarely entrusted us with single rooms. Night after night, I'd been staying just a little bit longer, hour by hour,

2 a.m., 3 a.m., 4 a.m., 5 a.m., and here I was again, freely associating with Sally, the tops of our heads touching like jumper cables. Be on my side, I'll be on your side.

Sally was asleep. Or was she? Roving the map of her head, I connected the ski-hill contours of her brow and nose, ear and temple, cheek and chin, the strands of hair brushing the eyelids, the pores of the skin, as rhythmic breaths escaped the upturned lip. A delicate charge came in simply lying still by her side, watching, wondering, waiting, wishing. Sometimes poetry was found in the doing of nothing; even if I lost, I won.

I fell asleep, then awoke with a start, the grey light of dawn inching across our blanket, delivering that desolate, where-the-hell-am-I feeling. I dreaded early mornings as fiercely as Count Dracula: night-life birthing morning-death. Shock jolted my system: my God, it was seven o'clock. *If Nick doesn't kill me, George Orr will.*

Sally was dead to the world, so I weaved over to Jane's room where Sean was sacked out beside her: partners in crime. Sean and I took a long walk, stalked by a headaching ennui. Did we peak at the picnic in the French alps? Then, at dinner, the all-knowing Nick lost his cool for the first time.

"You and Sean left the door of your room open all night. You disturbed the other guests. You slept with the girls. I've given you guys lots of leeway but you've let me down. Enough is enough and tonight you're grounded. If you act like kids, I'll treat you like kids. If you act like adults, I'll treat you like adults."

I had no comeback. I was suffering from *esprit de l'escalier*— what I wish I'd said as I headed up the staircase to bed: Yes, Nick, but don't adults sleep together?

Two days earlier, Peter, Stanfield, Kat and Kathy had scored some visas and crossed over the Iron Curtain by train for a day and night in Budapest. A part of me hadn't expected to see them again, but now they were back, unraped and unmurdered, braver—or dumber— than me.

Passing through a militarized zone into Hungary, they saw soldiers in towers with dogs and machine guns, right out of the movies. The four of them floated romantic notions of sleeping in a park but stayed in a cheap hotel and signed up for a tour of Buda and Pest. Soviet tanks were massed on the Danube like a car show, poised to invade Czechoslovakia and crush the protesters of the Prague Spring. Bullet holes in the buildings from the 1956 Revolution. Big red stars. Nothing working right. On the train out, they were unnerved by the psychodrama of border guards harassing a young Hungarian woman whose papers were not in order. Barking dogs, pointed guns, screaming blue murder in her face.

I realized I was cowardly-glad to have stayed where I was: with Sally in an August nightclub, killing two bottles of Henkell Trocken between us, awash in a carnal maze of strobe-streaked smoke and sweat, the personal trumping the political. Even as I was scaling fresh peaks of Sally-joy—*let's never go home!*—we turned to see Margi dancing alone beside us, a third wheel, her round face a riot of tearful desolation. We pulled her off the floor and talked her down. She was homesick.

Vienna

August 6

Dearest George,

This is going to be a mushy but sad letter. I've been in a depression state for the last four days and it's just awful. It all happened in Salzburg. A whole bunch of us went out for a walk and we went to this castle and climbed to the top. It was kind of neat but damn cold. Well, we climbed down from the top and went into this bar. Well, absolutely everything got on my nerves and I just got so fed up I decided I'd better leave cuz you know that when I get bitchy absolutely anything can come out of my yap.

So it happened that another girl felt exactly the same way as I did so we stood up, said goodbye and left. George, we looked like two of the biggest bitches in the world but I just didn't care. I was so fed up.

So we walked back to the hotel and stayed in my room for a while and talked and then I went to bed. That's when Niagara Falls started to flow. It was just terrible. I was so upset. I wanted to come home to you so much. Word got around that I was really depressed and all kinds of kids came round to see me. That made it worse cuz really all I wanted was to be in my own so I could think of you. Finally I went to sleep, thank God. The next day I was kind of OK, but not normal.

Then we moved on to Vienna. God, what a drag and we have to live here for five days! The hotel is just like a pit. Not one room has a bath. We have to pay 50 cents for one so I smell this week. I'm in a double with Marywinn and it's the size of my bathroom at home. Speaking of bathrooms, we have to walk a mile to the can to take a leak. It's really bad news. And the food tastes like shit. Tonight we had the leftovers from the first night, just gross.

Vienna closes down for the weekend. We got here on Saturday p.m. and there wasn't any store or anything open. And last night it rained, so we stayed in and read. Sunday we went sightseeing. That wasn't so bad but it just looks like another city to me. That's the way I feel about Europe right now. It's terrible to admit, I know, but it's true. Christ, I've been gone five weeks today but I'm coming home three weeks Friday, thank God. I'm getting fed up and I want to come home to you. I think I can really say that I've loved Europe until about four days ago but I'm not coming back without you. So there. You're stuck with me.

Sunday night was really fun because we went to this amusement park, kind of like the CNE but a hell of a lot cheaper. They had rides like Wild Mouse, bumper cars, go-carts, a flyer. It was a lot of fun cuz we could just forget everything, almost, and just go wild like a kid in a park. It really was a lot of fun and took my mind off everything for a while.

Well, yesterday I slept till noon and then went shopping. I found a black purse and it doesn't look like a lunch pail, it's really kind of smart. I think you'll like it. Today we did nothing and tonight nothing also. Six of us girls just sat around and talked about how great it's going to be to go home. Boy, we can't wait. It's so depressing over here at times. Oh well, it's almost over, thank God.

I loved Innsbruck. Just thought I'd change the tone. I'd really like to go back there with you. We were in a really nice hotel with a great bar downstairs. The bar had this fabulous band that played mostly English songs. They played "The Letter" and I don't care if you hate it or not. I love it and it's my song for the summer. That was a cool place there.

I've decided I like Switzerland and some of Austria the best. It's just as good as it looks in the movies. So anytime you want to go over, I'll go with you. Going to bed now. Will write tomorrow.

Love, Sal XXOO

I was in Nick's bus with Tammy, Sally, Robin, Annabel and Stanfield, bound for Munich, and the topics were hot: sex, relationships, birth control, marriage, adultery.

"Males are primal like dogs," Nick offered. "They'll eat the meat put in front of them even if they're not hungry. Females are like cats—they're more discriminating."

"I can't wait to be an adult," I piped up, "so I can commit adultery."

Normally it was a cinch to get a rise out of Sally—a rolling laugh, or at least a Mona Lisa smirk—but she was too busy scribbling on a pad of paper on her lap to pay attention. Since Italy I had erased the thought of Invisible George, but now I allowed that she was probably writing him. As she whispered into the ear of Robin, who had made no secret that she was George's cousin, I stared out the window, feigning indifference. Denial had got me this far.

Munich
August 8

To My Love,

I'm afraid I missed a day when I said I'd write. But yesterday I went sightseeing for the first time in five whole damn days. The rest of the time when I was supposed to be romping around looking at old buildings I just sat around on my old fat ass and thought about you, good old you.

You will probably think I'm smashed by the way this little old letter looks and sounds but honest to God I'm not. You want to know where I am? Do ya, hon, do ya? Well, I'm in Nick's bus and Robin is right beside me and I am on my way from Vienna back through Salzburg on our way to Munich. One hell of a long drive if you ask me.

So I remembered that I hadn't finished my last
letter to you, so here I am sitting on my old fat horny ass
(how about that for description) writing to you, my love.
And also the mail strike is over tomorrow and I haven't
written to you very much because of this damn strike
so I feel I owe you many, many letters. So here comes
a long one.

I really love you, no kidding, honest to God I love you.
I think this trip has taught me a lot, not about culture but
about me. I think that I really am ready to settle down with
you in a couple of years. You know it's really funny. All the
kids know I'm unofficially engaged and they all ask when
we're getting married. But it's really hard to say right now.
I guess it all depends on when you decide what you want
to do and when I graduate. But it really doesn't matter to
me when we get married as long as it's not more than five
years from now. So if you decide to take your MA, it's OK
with me. But I guess we should start thinking about our
future plans. And three weeks tomorrow we can really talk
about that—I can hardly wait.

I bought a really nice present for me to wear but it's
actually for you. It's a flowered half bra. It's not as half as
the one you bought me but it's not like an ordinary bra
either. But it's really pretty. I think you'll like it. Hope so,
cuz I do. I've also bought some coloured bikini pants—
they're great. To hell with ordinary pants—it's bikini all
the way.

Guess what—Barb is coming to Holland with me.
Isn't that great? I'm really happy because now we can goof
around in the airport and I'll have somebody to talk to. So
now I'm not going to be all alone. We decided those four
days are going to be great cuz we need a rest. So it will be

great fun. Well, this bus is starting to get to me so I think
I'd better stop. I'll continue later on.

Lots of love, Sal XXOO

P.S. Just heard on the radio that the strike isn't over.
Damn it. Telegrams will have to do.

As if apologizing for vile Vienna, the Hotel König in the prosper-
ous, risen-from-the-ruins city of Munich boasted all the mod cons;
we had returned to our own decade. In a nightclub we were thrilled
to see the same shaggy English rock band we'd loved in Innsbruck.
What a coincidence. Sally and I once again staked out space in front
of the stage, and they remembered us with a wave. "We've got to stop
meeting like this," Sally quipped, and yet again the band delivered
"The Letter."

I was steeped in Holocaust literature, starting with reading *The
Rise and Fall of the Third Reich* at twelve. As a result, our visit the
next morning to the Dachau death camp, squatting grimly in a
Munich suburb, came as more of a shock to the girls than me. There
it was, the infamously sick, cynical slogan *Arbeit Macht Frei*—Work
Will Set You Free—arching over the gate in black wrought-iron
letters. For three hours, we shuffled and paused in sombre silence,
taking in the barbed wire, bunks and ovens. For the longest time I
studied an excruciating photograph of a prisoner in striped rags
hoisted by his hands tied behind his back, his body weight dislocat-
ing his shoulders. The act itself was evil enough, but the indifference
of the photographer seemed to lengthen its shadow.

The panels of text reminded me of what I had already extracted
from books and films: I was standing on Ground Zero, the germ of the
Holocaust. Built in 1933, the year of Hitler's election, the first Nazi
concentration camp was not an Auschwitz-scaled factory of mass

extermination but an early dumping ground for political prisoners and assorted enemies of the Reich—roughly two hundred thousand pulled from thirty countries, including one hundred thousand Germans. At Dachau, "only" thirty-two thousand deaths were documented, a far cry from more than a million at Auschwitz alone. Within the one square kilometre of the original camp, smaller than my school and its surrounding fields (Dachau grew to include more than a hundred nearby subcamps), communists, socialists, democrats, trade unionists, Christian clergy, homosexuals, criminals, German Jews, "idiots," "the work shy," "the asocial," "race polluters," all bearing coloured badges not unlike the ones I wore at summer camp, were slowly and systematically worked and starved to death.

As an enamel-skinned prep-school boy, I'd found something seductive in the Fascist state of mind, embodied in the endless rows of stiffened arms, hard-ons for Hitler, a purebred black-and-white moral universe where it was okay to unleash your inner killer and exterminate every last bastard who ever dealt you a bad hand. My brother and I had passed the occasional Sunday afternoon goose-stepping up and down our driveway, shouldering toy rifles, slapping our palms in *Sieg Heil* salutes against each other's forehead à la the Three Stooges; I was the self-appointed five-star general and he the submissive private. Even at age eight he took orders like a man.

Yet somewhere along the line, I grew a conscience. I became fascinated with the war from the enemy point of view and the drama of "the good German," identifying with the aggressor *and* the victim. Maybe it was fed by my eavesdropping on the alcohol-fuelled war stories of my aloof father and his friends, their strangely blended tones of camaraderie, terror, guilt, nostalgia and hilarity; for them, the stories were a way out, for me a way in.

I remembered how one of them had expressed regret that he had once idly aimed his artillery piece at the steeple of an Italian Renaissance church and blown it to smithereens, just for the hell of

132   DREAMING SALLY

it; another, an eighteen-year-old infantryman fighting his way across France at the time, felt guilty for shooting his unarmed German prisoners in a spasm of revenge. I didn't have to be Freud or the pope to figure out that they were seeking absolution and failing to find it in the solution in their cups. It could not be said aloud, but our fathers, the sensitive victors, felt like losers. Nobody won the war; everyone paid a price.

At sixteen, I had read and reread a nightmarish memoir, *I Survived Hitler's Ovens*, by Olga Lengyel, a Hungarian inmate of Auschwitz, amazed to learn that all the confiscated wealth of the prisoners was piled in a warehouse called Canada. One night after midnight, I put the book aside and crept downstairs in my pyjamas. I parked myself inches from the flickering TV screen, the sound low, hypnotized by a black-and-white documentary on the Nazi death camps. The camera panned over doomed Jewish women, clutching their naked breasts, pubic hair exposed, as they were driven into gas chambers; a bulldozer drove numberless naked corpses into a pit. A pornography of death.

The trance broke when I felt the groggy figure of my mother at my side. Brow knitted, she quite reasonably asked, "Why are you watching this?" But I insisted on seeing it through to the end, and she went back to bed. It was my first and only sighting of my mother in her nightgown.

Heading back to the gates with Sally, a final image burned in my mental archive: little stones, painted white, lining the exiting footpath, fringed with radiant yellow roses, a weirdly Disneyesque prettification of horror.

On the autobahn to Heidelberg, our convoy was stopped dead by a traffic jam, as if re-enacting a scene from Jean-Luc Godard's film *Weekend*. Suntanning on the roof, puffing cigarettes, snapping photos, we horsed around like the kids we still were. On her bus door Tammy drew the peace symbol with her eyeliner. Hours later we learned what caused the jam: an Innsbruck-bound British airliner had broken up in mid-air and crashed in a nearby field, killing all forty-eight people aboard.

In the Hotel Schrieder, for the first time I roomed with Wally, the only black kid on the trip, whom I knew only slightly from school. I was curious to know what it felt like wearing a dark skin in a Wonder Bread world, but I never asked. Heading out en masse to the Hockenheimring racetrack, we watched sleek silver Porsches zoom round a five-mile oval track, slipping into a dark virgin forest, then reappearing, only to do it all over again. John, a car fanatic, told me that the British world champion Jimmy Clark had crashed and died here only months earlier when a tire burst and his Formula 2 racecar skidded into a tree. The allure of the internal combustion engine was lost on me—I saw cars only as modes of transport from A to B.

To save my energy for the big bash planned for the following night in the wine village of Rüdesheim am Rhein, I was determined to hit the sack early, but Sally bounced in, ready to rock. Instead we talked for an hour, shame protecting the rough state of my guts. Finally, she took the hint and I retreated to my daily fix of homicide. I was almost finished *In Cold Blood*.

Back on July 18, the postal strike had severed George's lifeline to Sally. Through the rest of July and into August, he jabbed the Underwood with his two index fingers, saving up a stack of unsendable letters, trying to keep her alive inside him. Even when the postal strike lifted on August 9, releasing a backlog of her letters to him, he felt no relief, for between her lines he sensed an invisible rival and an effort to keep him concealed. Reading her suddenly plaintive letter from Vienna, he wrestled with his green-eyed monster: *Thank you for hating where you are. Even though I see through it, I need to hear this.*

The day he had planned to formally propose to Sally, Monday, August 12, dawned at long last. Short of telepathy, a telegram had to do. Driving downtown, he once more pictured himself surrendering to the slow walk down the long aisle, the solemn vows, the slipping of rings on fingers, and as he entered the all-too-real telegraph office, he felt as if he was already facing the altar.

Out shot the letters, all capitals:

I LOVE YOU STOP WILL YOU MARRY ME STOP

ELEVEN

August 13, 1968

On the morning of August 12, Dave and his ukulele drove our three-hour singalong ride to Rüdesheim, a wine-making village on the eastern shore of the River Rhine. Or, put another way, a tourist trap where dozens of cheap wine bars clogged a single street. Sitting beside Sally, I was feeling happily trapped.

In Rüdesheim, the local product was light but sped to the head like a bullet. The manager of our hotel, the Lindenwirt, pulled out a flat three-inch-square battery connected to a light bulb, green for boys, red for girls, that attached to your lapel.

"If you can't make it home, sit on the curb and turn on your light," he instructed. "The name of our hotel is on the light; one of the locals will phone us and we'll collect you. It's a tradition."

When he added that in two hundred years no one had ever made it upright to the end of the Drosselgasse, a narrow, pub-lined alley of non-stop music and revelry, he might as well have waved a red flag.

After dinner, I slid into Sally's room, hoping that another all-nighter was in the cards and that maybe this time we might do more than sleep together. She was perched on the bed, clutching a piece of paper. As she turned a flat face to mine, I knew something was up. Had somebody died?

"George sent me a telegram. He asked me to marry him. I just cabled back and said yes."

I was engulfed by a weird moment of blankness. Then a shot of white heat flared straight up the column of my body, flushing into my face. Six weeks of unbroken infatuation with Sally Wodehouse, all hope for our chaste but intensely promising affair shattered, and tears exploded from my eyes.

I could tell Sally was as surprised as I was by the eruption. Was our summer nothing but some kind of head game for her?

She tried to console me but did anything but: "Don't worry. We'll always be friends. I'll visit you at university this fall. I promise."

Down in the bar, I confided in Nick. I wanted to kill our night of revelry. Swinging a fraternal arm around my shoulder, he drove home the hard truth: "Fitz, you're only seventeen. You're not marrying anybody anytime soon."

His words landed like ice water in the face. He was right: I was a glib, semi-formed, pimpled preppie still wobbly on his sea legs. The corners of the triangle collapsed into the straight white line down the middle of the highway, and I felt unexpectedly free. George and Sally were the real deal, destined to go the distance, and I would have to play her friend and sidekick, maybe even his, a third wheel, trailing behind.

I joined the others on the open veranda where a hired photographer was setting up a group portrait. Nick and Tammy sat on the floor in front, and the rest of us clustered behind them in tiers, sitting, kneeling, standing, thirteen girls and thirteen boys giving one another the gears. Since kindergarten I'd usually been the tallest kid, so I perched on the railing, hanging back, and as Sally appeared at my side, I was once again hyperconscious of the imminent shaping of my future image on film. Our flurry of repartee was suspended for the click—act natural—and this time, I chose not to hook my arm around her shoulder.

Even with two weeks left on the itinerary, this moment felt like the breaking of the collective spell. Was this a class picture? A birthday? A wedding? A funeral? Was I a graduate, a pallbearer, an usher, a best man on the worst day of my life? The timing was uncanny, as if, mere minutes after the landing of George's transatlantic arrow, a photographer-spy had been charged to burn on a strip of film the lie of my smile, a smile so relaxed, so perfectly convincing, that I came to believe it myself—a sliver of time and space, labelled "The Height of Human Happiness," that I will cram into an eight-by-ten frame and hang on the wall of my study to defy the decades of gathering dust.

After the photographer promised to forward twenty-eight copies to our hotel in Paris, we poured into the night. The Drosselgasse was jammed, and we broke into roving packs of five or six, criss-crossing the cobblestones from bar to bar. I was glad there were no rock 'n' roll bands, for I had danced my last with Sally. The girls were all atwitter with the news of her engagement, but when Sean voiced his shock, I was grateful for the validation. When Sally mentioned she had organized a side trip to see a girlfriend in Amsterdam and would rejoin the Odyssey on the final leg in Paris and London, I pretended not to care, dabbing my finger with wine and circling the rim of my glass to make an eerie sound.

Hour by hour, our group shrank, not so much survival of the fittest but the foolish. Sally and I wandered off the beaten track, losing our bearings, as lit as the lamps pinned to our lapels. As we happened on Stu necking with Kat, he turned to jump a fence, crossing the railroad tracks to piss in the Rhine. Just as he cleared the fence coming back, three feet short of the tracks, a bullet train whooshed past at a murderous clip, and only blind luck stopped his obliteration.

A Good Samaritan, meanwhile, was trundling a well-greased Dave back to the hotel in a wheelbarrow. From dim mental back channels he recalled the angelic pre-dinner words of Annabel: "I've lucked into a single room. Come to my room at midnight and we'll do it." Two hours late, he knocked on her door and she appeared, smiling sweetly, in her nightie. Swaying like a hammock, he slurred, "Here I am!" The door shut in his face; Dave could not lift his head, never mind any other body part.

Sally and I barrelled in after 3 a.m. Like an invulnerable cartoon character, I tore up and down the hotel corridor, trying to gauge how fast I could sprint backwards, a last attempt to wipe George Orr from the spinning face of the earth. My back slammed into a full-length mirror, but I found no rabbit hole. The crash raised the hotel manager, but his shrieks of "*Dummkopf!*" carried no weight, for he was the guy who had set us loose.

With the help of my roommate, Ross, Sally peeled off my tie and jacket, pulled back the sheets and put me to bed. The root of my name, James, I was once told, meant "supplanter." But I dared not ask her to stay.

At dawn's light, Nurse Sally rematerialized over my bed, tapping out two aspirins into her palm and extending a glass of water. Over breakfast, the news of her engagement continued to stir waves of girly chatter. George's cousin, Robin, was over the moon, welcoming Sally to the family. Nan, who had shared a double bed with Sally, mentioned that last night a bird had flown in their open window, circled three times, then darted out—strange and beautiful, as if tied to Sally's unfolding future.

As a singing waiter poured the coffee, we heard the sound of men hosing down the cobblestones, washing away the crime scene. The unaged wine had aged us: I was suffering the Bad Mother of all hangovers, mirroring the overcast, autumn-brisk day. I made a silent vow of religious intensity: *Never again*. But words were as cheap as the wine.

As we boarded a cruise boat for a morning-long northbound trip to Koblenz, Nick, Tammy, Stu and Steve drove the four buses alongside the Rhine to meet us. The folding deck chairs were portable, so we huddled in our own group, Sally the centre of attention. As camera clicks captured the bride-to-be, Dave strummed his ukulele, crooning an improvised tune, "The Ballad of Nick and Tammy." I clowned around, as usual, pretending last night had never happened. As we headed north through the Rhine gorge, I gazed at the medieval castles on the vine-terraced hills crowning the shorelines. In sync with the current, we were gliding through history and legend and nature, along the river the Romans used as a barrier between civilization and the barbarians, through the land of the Gutenberg Bible and the Protestant Reformation, past the jutting slate cliff of the Lorelei rock and its mythic, bewitching siren singing sailors to their doom. A generation ago, the good guys had crossed these rushing waters to liberate Dachau and annihilate Hitler and returned home heroes if less-than-good fathers. Steve's own father had navigated a Sterling during the war; did one of his bombs lie under our gliding hull, unexploded?

Sally was quiet and wistful, even a touch melancholic. She was wearing her pink-turquoise dancing dress, her glasses perched atop her head, a white sweater hugging her shoulders. As she tapped ash from the tip of her cigarette, I struggled to read her thought stream. In the back of her mind, did I still hold a place?

Docking at Koblenz, the confluence of the Rhine and Mosel, I followed Sally, Jane and Nan as they descended the spiral staircase. They were singing "See You in September" in falsetto voices, and even as the words taunted and burned, I strained to forgive their cruelty:

"There is danger in the summer moon above;
Will I see you in September
Or lose you to a summer love?
Bye-bye, so long, farewell . . ."

As I watched Sally racing Jane to the buses, bitterness clogged my throat. But my family and school had drilled me well—*Thou shalt not feel.*

Sally chose Steve's red-and-cream bus while I climbed into Nick's as the navigator. We faced a short—120 kilometre—westward run to Luxembourg, meandering through wooded countryside on a narrow single-lane blacktop, hugging the twisting shoreline of the Mosel. It was our second-last day of driving; after Paris, we would take the train to Calais, then the channel crossing to London, the last stop of a trip I had never wanted to stop—until now.

As Steve's bus took the lead, a light, intermittent rain slicked the road. About an hour on, our bus passed a gas station. Nick and I swung our heads to see Steve's bus gassing up. All summer long, John, the lover of all things automotive, had been urging all five of the designated drivers to let him once, *just once,* take the wheel, but Nick had quashed the repeated requests. As Nick caught a backward glimpse of John climbing into the driver's seat instead of Steve, he muttered, "That's a mistake." But we did not turn back.

In Luxembourg's Grand Hotel Cravat, I was sharing a room with Nick for the first time on the trip. I suspected it was no accident but his plan to help me deal with my "breakup" with Sally. As we unpacked, Dave rushed in, grave faced. He glanced at me, then took Nick aside and whispered in his ear.

Nick turned to me and said, "There's been an accident. Sally is hurt." The two of them drove back down the highway and I was left hanging. Over dinner, word spread that Sally had suffered a concussion, but it was not serious. She might have to stay in hospital for a few days, then rejoin us in Paris. I felt a rush of uneasy relief, but in my diary, I didn't know what to write.

In the dead of the night, the ringing phone ripped me from my dreams. I picked up the phone and heard a man ask, "Nick? Is that you?"

It was Bernie, calling from London. He told me he was flying to Germany to see Sally, and then he'd meet us in Paris.

I couldn't fall back to sleep.

As we packed for Paris, I noticed the familiar red-and-cream bus parked in front of the hotel. My eyes fell on the dented front door on the passenger side, and it hit me: *This was her bus.* I passed my hand over a dislodged hinge. *No big deal. I've seen far worse.*

Nick and Tammy were staying with Sally in Germany, so the leader of another Odyssey trip had taken charge of us. Over half our group took the train while the rest crammed into two buses. Lost on the Champs-Élysées, we finally spotted our hotel on Rue St-Honoré in the first arrondissement, the *haut monde* heart of the city. The barricade-crashing student riots of May, igniting the mass strike that turned France inside out, had surrendered to near-empty streets, the locals mostly fled to the seaside. The tear gas, the rubber bullets, the water cannons, the truncheons splitting the heads of enraged young crying for a life of freedom—*Sous les pavés, la plage!* (Under the cobblestones, the beach!)—all gone, extinguished by the tepid August stillness.

A five-minute stroll from the Louvre, the three-storey Hotel France et Choiseul was home for the next five nights. Dave was in charge of assigning the rooms, so six of the guys—Stu, Steve, Peter, Stanfield, Dave and I—scored the suite where Franklin and Eleanor Roosevelt had spent part of their honeymoon. The sight of a pet tortoise named Caroline, crawling through the open courtyard, lent a touch of the surreal; she was old enough to have met Napoleon.

When Bernie arrived, I made nothing of it, secure in the knowledge that Sally's concussion wasn't serious. Lit by pre-dinner drinks in the courtyard, I cracked wise with a gathering circle of ten kids. Lurking in the dim foyer, Bernie began calling us over, one by one.

As each person left and returned to our table, rendered silent by whatever Bernie had said, I was still not twigging, kept spouting juvenile one-liners, fishing for laughs that never came.

Then he beckoned me over, having saved me for last.

"James, I want to update you on Sally's situation."

"I know, I heard she's fine. She's meeting us here."

Though I was slightly taller, he was still the muscular, big-boned alpha male overshadowing the rake-thin youth. He seized my hand and did not let go. He rambled on and on about the aftermath of the accident. Was this a need-to-know conversation?

"Sally was taken by ambulance to Koblenz, but the medical technology was inadequate to treat her head injury. She was moved to another hospital in Mainz. That's where she was pronounced DOA."

I had no clue what he meant.

"What's DOA?"

"Dead on arrival."

The words had a delayed effect—like those three-second gaps on radio phone-in shows designed to block spontaneous outbursts of obscenity. Then a force beyond all control tore my hand loose from his grip. Charging through the courtyard, past the staring pairs of eyes, I fled upstairs to my room, pursued by scalding shafts of shame and Steve. He didn't go to private school; he didn't know the rules about strong feelings. Sitting beside me on the bed, Steve handed me a towel, and I buried my face in it. A violent spasm, then the dead arms of an all-embracing void. A grey nothingness. Volcanic ash.

Bodies flooded the suite, a dream assuming the shape of a wake. A hand extended a glass of rye, last tasted on the *Raffaello*, and each shot restored my first blast of Sally, dancing until dawn over the surface of the sea. The invisible stage managers of my life had not lost their precision timing: my copy of our "class photo," forwarded from Rüdesheim, landed in my lap. How did it arrive so fast? Why was it black and white?

I stared at Sally at my side, our beaming, tilting, disembodied heads, floating above the bodies of the others in the back row, mere minutes after she'd stabbed me in the heart with George's telegram. At the image of her, I stared and drank, drank and stared. The smiles, those goddamn smiles.

Into the falling darkness we played cards, but games of chance only summoned scenes of De Grassi, and my mind splintered. Hearts. Crazy Eights. Kings and Little Ones. Pig. War. Cheat. Four suits, four seasons. Fifty-two cards, fifty-two weeks. Thirteen girls, thirteen boys. From the midnight street our windows glared like shark eyes, black and empty. I felt the room collapsing inward, squeezing my body down and back to its beginnings.

As I crashed on a sofa, Dave pulled from his pocket a baby oyster shell.

"Sally asked me to give you this after our epic lunch on the slopes of Vesuvius. But I forgot."

I wondered why she hadn't given it to me herself. Maybe it was his memento, his talisman, all along; was he was just trying to make me—and him—feel better?

On the afternoon of August 13, five time zones behind Paris, George Orr strode through the front door of 189 Gordon Road to find, as he hoped, a return telegram from Sally. Picking up the envelope with its cellophane window, he ripped it open and drank in the words:

YES STOP CAN'T WAIT STOP

Alive with a rapture that forgave all that had gone before, he delivered the news to his parents and was delighted by the softening of their faces. They had married young, they knew, they remembered.

Racing to his mother's Triumph, George cut through the euphoric August air down to Rosedale. Sally can't wait, and neither can he. Pressing the doorbell of 30 Chestnut Park Road, her telegram in hand, he realized he was standing on the very threshold where he had first seen Sally's face two years past.

The familiar bald head shone through the half-moon window and the oak door swung open. But when the eyes of the two Georges locked, the young man's hope vanished: only moments ago, the doctor had hung up the phone from West Germany.

Placing his hand on George's shoulder, he spoke three words: "Sally is dead."

Jane came up behind, her voice a crackling monotone in George's ears: "Her bus was barely moving when it was clipped by a car. . . . She fell from the front seat and cracked her head on the road. . . . She died a few hours ago. . . ."

George was surprised by his first thoughts: *My life has just taken a radical turn. The path I was walking stops right here. After today, these people will no longer welcome me.*

Then he was hit by that cold, granite certainty. He had been right to believe his dream when no one else would.

His mother's car carried him back up Yonge Street, robbed of all sensation. At Manor Road, he passed the florist shop where he had bought bouquets for Sally, and occasionally her mother, and he knew that when he next stepped inside the store, it would not be romance that called him.

Back home, George walked into the living room and turned to his seated parents. "Sally is dead," he said, and their two faces flattened into blankness. He stood and waited for some response, for some words of comfort and wisdom, but all his parents could do was stare.

Moving to the phone, George called his friend Graham, who lived around the corner, and soon through the door a stream of friends flowed, saying the things young men say, unrehearsed expressions of shock and sorrow and sympathy. Slumped on the sofa, George knew nothing but a vast emptiness, growing vaster by the moment. As the evening seeped into night, half-human figures hovered and flitted around him, a slide show of shifting masks, a charade of useless bromides assuming the hue of white noise, until the moment when a feeling, savage and sweet, intruded sharply: *If I die, I will welcome the release.*

The phone rang. George's father picked up the receiver, listened and passed it to his son; it was Stewart, his closest friend, the one who had introduced him to Sally. All summer Stewart had been rumbling alone across Italy and France on a motorcycle, ending up in Ireland, where he intended to explore his Celtic roots. The two had not spoken since Stewart left in early June. Why was Stewart calling him at this of all possible moments?

From the earpiece, he heard, "George! What the fuck is going on?"

"Sally is dead."

Absorbing the words, Stewart was swamped by the force of the uncanny. He told George he'd been sitting in an apartment he'd rented near St. Stephen's Green in Dublin, when out of nowhere he was hit with the irresistible conviction that he needed to fly home immediately because something was terribly wrong with George. He didn't even think to telephone; he simply headed to the airport and caught the next available plane. But fog prevented the landing in Toronto, so his plane was turned back to Montreal. Stranded in the airport, Stewart found the nearest phone booth; he had to call George right that minute and had no idea why.

Only now did it all make sense, and he told George he would be there as soon as the plane landed.

———

In and out of the courtyard of our Paris hotel, the members of the Odyssey wandered, as if sharing a mass concussion. I picked up fragments of eyewitness accounts of the accident. After John took over as driver, he'd nosed the bus out of the gas station, stalled, then reversed to try to avoid the flow of traffic. A car nicked the edge of the passenger door, somehow pitching Sally backwards onto the road. I averted my eyes from the faces of drifting girls, Jane and Barb and Kat and Robin, and could not speak.

Over the night and into the morning, Bernie sought out the ones who did not yet know. I wondered why he did not tell us all at once and together, why he separated us into units of Protestant isolation. He sat down with Stanfield and John in a Wimpy Bar and said, "Sally didn't make it." Stanfield thought he meant she didn't make it to Paris, but John instantly understood and turned white. When Kat told her cousin Nikki, she unleashed a long laugh of unearthly weirdness, its intensity shocking them both. Later, anxiety robbing her of sleep, Nikki made out a black human figure at the foot of her bed. She closed her eyes, hoping it would disappear, but when she dared to peek, it was still there. Without waking her roommate, Nan, she fled downstairs to the courtyard and into the streets, shaking with fright. She changed rooms with Nan to be with her cousin. For years, she would tell no one of the quasi-human apparition that haunted her that night.

The days and nights bled one into the other, and all of us killed time in our own restless ways. With Dave and Stu I hiked to the Eiffel Tower. Funnelled into a suffocating elevator full of tourists, we endured a three-hour ascent and descent. When Nick and Tammy arrived from Germany late in the evening, I was glad to see them, but we said little. I wandered the halls of the hotel, but Sally's voice and face kept following me; she wouldn't leave me alone. In the dark corner of the courtyard where Bernie had taken me aside, I made the mistake of taking a seat, for when Sally caught up, I broke down. Kathy and Kat came to sit quietly with the two of us, but when I lifted my head from my hands, Sally had disappeared into the night.

A morning excursion to Notre-Dame Cathedral felt like a funeral without a body. When Tammy suggested we light a candle and say a prayer for Sally, something in me protested: *No, this is not good enough.*

Everywhere we turned, my eyes fell on monuments and memorials to the dead. In the Place Vendôme, round the corner from the hotel, I read a plaque marking the apartment where Chopin had died mysteriously at thirty-nine. In the Conciergerie on the Île de la Cité, I studied the prison table and chair where Marie Antoinette spent her last hours before losing her head.

When I bumped into John, I noticed he was hobbled by a bruised thigh, which he'd jammed against the gearshift of the bus as Sally fell out the door. We said next to nothing. Decades would pass before I would learn that he and Walter had wandered haphazardly through the rainy, midnight streets of Paris, replaying over and over the scene of horror.

In the Louvre, I stood before the *Mona Lisa*, disappointed by its smallness. Back at the hotel, I returned a phone call from my mother, handling her awkwardness with a practised reflex: "I'm fine, I'm fine." She'd heard the news of Sally when my brother read a squib in the newspaper; other parents heard via CFRB Radio when the host, Gordon Sinclair, had ranted about the recklessness of teenagers spoiled by the permissiveness of the times. Bernie had been beaten by the speed of the media.

Passing up a tour of Versailles, I spent most of an afternoon composing a letter to Sally's parents, crossing out words, tearing up paper, starting again, struggling to nail down an honest feeling. As I sealed the envelope, I packed away Sally's death as ruthlessly as I had her devotion to another, and in my diary I wrote, "Enough eulogizing."

Our five nights in Paris climaxed in the nightclub of the Folies Bergère. I couldn't believe they let a seventeen-year-old through the door. Sitting with Nick and Tammy, I longed to exchange them for my real parents. A string of acts unfolded across the stage. As if spewn from the Delacroix painting *Liberty Leading the People*, with its bare-breasted allegorical figure, a brace of topless, figure-skating Gallic goddesses glided over a pad of ice. I cracked Tammy up with my inevitable Ed Sullivan imitation—"And now, for all you youngsters out there!"—and plugged back into the electric thrill of moving a woman to tears of laughter. Ringed with flutes of champagne, our table tipped into infectious hysteria. For the first time ever, I saw a row of perfectly formed breasts, and for a time Sally was forgotten.

S.S. *Raffaello*, Sally and Robin

S.S. *Raffaello*, Sally, Tammy, Nick, Stu, Barb

Mount Vesuvius, Italy, James and Sally

James and Sally, Rome

Sally, Rome

James buried on the Lido, Venice: Sally, Rich,
Jane, Sean, Chris, Peter, Annabel, Ross

James and Sally, Lido, Venice, July 1968

Sally, Nice, France

Tammy

Sally and James, summit of the Schilthorn, Switzerland

James, Innsbruck, Austria

Annabel and Stu

Jane, Stu and Sally

Nick and Stu

Dave, Jane, James, Paul, Sally, Sean

Annabel, Steve, James, Barb, West Germany

Group portrait, Rüdesheim, West Germany, August 12, 1968;
James and Sally, top left

Barb, Sean, Kathy, Stan, Wally, Sally, Rhine steamer, August 13, 1968

Sally's last photo, Rhine steamer, August 13, 1968

Rich, James, John, Robin, Nan, Paris, France

Be careful. Rumour has it here that the French student riots start in Lyon, Nantes, and Paris on or about August 10. So take care, because you're too precious to me to get squashed by a brick, or even a U.W. micro-bus.

Must sign off and go eat. Will try to write again, and promise to think and dream of only you. Be good (I am) and remember you're mine. Don't forget I love you, and love you very very much.

Forever yours

George

— When will you be on night of August 15th? Write now, if you haven't already and tell me. But I'm not going to phone: I can't afford it. Just a mushy telegram.   Love forever + forever, as long as you want me!

George

Ending of George's letter to Sally, July 14, 1968

PART III

When we do not have bodies in front of us, we hallu-
cinate them, and when we do, we try to control them
by covering them with words.

—JAMES ELKINS, *The Object Stares Back*

TWELVE

I Told You So

On Monday, August 19, as the hands of the clock swept toward 1 p.m., a host of mourners filed into the chapel of Trinity College on Hoskin Avenue in Toronto. The Odyssey was scheduled to return home on August 30, eleven days later, but Sally's parents had decided that her funeral would proceed without her summer companions.

In the neo-Gothic enclave of grey sandstone, George and Sally had intended to be married. But never again, even for one last time, would George gaze into the universe that was her face, for when Dr. Wodehouse flew to West Germany, red tape had delayed shipment of his daughter's body to Toronto, and he was compelled to order her cremation. He bore the ashes on the homeward flight, a father alone in his quiet devastation — all alone, for he had refused George's request to accompany him on the trip.

In the austere oak pews in the rear of the chapel, in Stewart-green kilts, dozens of Branksome Hall students clustered. The four-year-old girls that Dr. Wodehouse, the Branksome physician, had once bade not to cry as he jabbed them with their vaccination needles were all teenagers now, and now all were crying.

Together with Sally's father, mother and sister, George sleep-walked down the centre aisle, accompanied by moaning bagpipes. Through the overflowing congregation of 150, he glanced neither left nor right, not even into the faces of his parents. Feeling everything, feeling nothing, he followed Dr. Wodehouse, his face stoic as his wife shed tears for them both.

George moved past familiar figures: Gerrie, Sally's best friend and last-minute dropout from the Odyssey; Eve, regretting her enthusiastic endorsement of the trip to Sally and destined to one day adopt the two children of close friends killed in a car crash; and Nancy, feeling she was reliving the shocks of the King and Kennedy assassinations.

Over the past six days and nights, George had dwelt on the pounding cruelties and compounding coincidences. The postal strike had lifted on August 9, and just two days short of the second anniversary of their blind date, her last letter had arrived, postmarked Munich, a letter he could not bear to open, for on the back of the envelope she had jotted the last words she would ever write him:

"Don't forget August 18!"

He could not bear the fulfillment of his premonition, nor the thought of his last unspoken words as she'd left him at the airport: *I'm never going to see you again.* It was not his bride but her remains, raked from a German crematorium, placed in an urn and encased in a polished mahogany box, that now stood before the altar, alone amid the wreaths of brilliant flowers.

George stepped close and placed a single yellow rose on the box. He would not remember a word of the biblical consolations that followed.

His dread of the wake at Sally's house was justified: nothing but an assembly line of clichés, akin to slow-drip water torture. From the familiar murmuring voices, gin and cigar smoke, George escaped into the open air of the front veranda, a blinding pain in his eyes. Loosening his tie and fumbling for a cigarette, he contemplated the branches of the maple tree rooted in the front lawn, the grace and beauty of the curving street, the small, triangle-shaped traffic island of grass where Cluny Drive met Chestnut Park, the erect lines of wrought-iron lamps stretching down the sidewalk of interlocking red bricks, reaching inexorably into a dark, mad place. Glancing at the self-winding Bucherer wristwatch that Sally had bought him as a present in Switzerland, retrieved by her father from her luggage, George was unsure whether to faint or vomit or scream.

Then, the thought, most terrible of all, rose up, the unforgiving voice of accusation married to the force of perfect logic: *If Sally is dead, then it must have been I who killed her. If I am responsible, I am guilty, and I deserve to die.*

The thought was written on his face, at least for those with eyes to see. But it was only Stewart who knew what to do. "Get into my car," he commanded. "Right now."

George sprawled across the back seat of the 1965 canary yellow Skylark—the back seat of his first date with Sally two years past—as Stewart drove due north on Highway 11. Fifty miles out, they passed the De Grassi Point turnoff, but this time they did not stop. They pressed through the Sudbury nickel belt toward New Liskeard in the rough Northern Ontario bush. On the lip of Fairy Lake, nudging the Quebec border, they settled into a crude box of a cabin built during the war by Stewart's parents—Fred, the most non-judgmental man George had ever known, and his wife, Mary, the kindest of mothers he had ever met.

The cabin provided the basics: food, beer, bunk beds, outhouse, wood stove, oil lamps, sunsets promising sunrise. George was barely able to move or form a sentence, but there was comfort in knowing that no one knew where he was. Filling the void left by Sally, Stewart let George feel what he needed to feel, and it felt like losing everyone, everything, his very self.

Day upon day the two friends drank, swam, fished, raged, wept. Struggling to make sense of the nightmare, they backtracked through events and determined that Stewart's impulsive decision to quit Ireland and contact George closely coincided with the moment on August 13 when Sally's head cracked on the German asphalt. But the realization only deepened George's torment: why had no one listened to his premonition, his pleas, especially Sally? And for all his hating, why must he hate her most of all? But he did, because it was Sally who had abandoned him to this place, this firepit of intolerable loss and guilt.

Ten days later they returned to Toronto. All childhoods must die, and in the sudden death of his own, George grasped for a thread, a hidden meaning, a larger pattern and purpose. All he could find was Stewart, the natural, intuitive young man disdained by Dorothy Orr as a bad influence, yet who had saved his life. But for what?

In his absence, the Wodehouses had buried Sally's ashes in Mount Pleasant Cemetery in a family-only ceremony. In his mailbox, among many notes of condolence, George found one from Sally's mother:

> *Your flowers for Sally were simply beautiful and all the*
> *colours she adored. You were a tower of strength to us all*
> *and a great comfort to me. I know why she fell in love with*
> *you, dear, because you are as fine a man as I fell in love*
> *with 30 years ago. Come and see us often and look to the*
> *future where you will find happiness.*
>
> > *Affectionately, Jane Wodehouse*

But George doubted the sincerity of the last sentence. He was now only a reminder of their loss, possibly its cause, for had they not urged the Odyssey on Sally to break her tie to him?

Our group was scheduled to spend six nights in London, then return to Toronto on August 25, but a labour dispute delayed our charter flight an extra five days. With formal tours and lectures over, we were left to wander the city on our own. Instead of going to a funeral, we must keep having fun.

Icons of the UK—helmeted bobbies, red double-decker buses, black cabs, brolly-bearing businessmen—passed me on the streets. The moon faces of Big Ben both echoed and dwarfed the UCC clock tower that had dominated the days of my childhood. In the Imperial War Museum, I touched a sleek Nazi V2 rocket; in Madame Tussauds I came upon a perfect life-sized mannequin of JFK lacking a bloody head wound. Wandering alone through Westminster Abbey, I found rows of chiselled heads in Poets' Corner—Chaucer, Shakespeare, Blake, Keats, Shelley, Wordsworth, the Brontë sisters, Dickens, Hardy. The storytellers.

I felt like an unsupported idea of a potential person drifting through space. Could I extract a pinch of solace or self from fragments of cultural bric-a-brac? I might be marooned on the original island dedicated to the emotional strangulation of children, but I knew the antidote lived here too—the Beatles, the Stones, the Who, artists who embodied primal feelings—passion, anger, love.

In the womb of a cinema, I swam in the images of *Yellow Submarine*, the Beatles' psychedelic cartoon of Pepperland and its Sea of Holes. As the credits rolled, the four faces of John, Paul, George and Ringo popped onto the screen, and I was overwhelmed by the shaggy heads, fifteen feet tall, more than alive, more than real. John declared that a gang of music-hating Blue Meanies had been sighted near our theatre, and we must join with them singing "All Together Now." But everything was falling apart.

A heavy downpour confined us to the hotel for a full day. Wild world events meshed with my mental haze: the youth of the Prague Spring raining Molotov cocktails on Soviet tanks, Chicago police clubs cracking random heads in a political riot. Wandering from room to room in an agitated torpor, I sucked on a bottle of vermouth, the taste guaranteed to revive Sally and Rome; I craved a purging act of violence to make me feel I had not misplaced my body for good. Cash-poor Kathy pleaded for a pound to buy "Hey Jude," the Beatles new single, released that day. I cut open the lining of my madras jacket and handed over the $20 Canadian note my mother had planted there in case of emergency.

Opening a letter from my mother, I read the news that Millie, my friend Mike's mother, had drowned in a backyard pool around the time Sally died. Mike was the one who had taken a sledgehammer to the walls of his parents' bedroom during the crazy Dunvegan Road Destructorama, and now this. Why did my mother think I needed to know about another sudden death *now*?

On our last night, we merged with kids from the other Odyssey trips, thundering through the halls, overturning beds, raising the dead. An uncanny moment came when I heard a Simon and Garfunkel song, "April Come She Will," and was seized by the line "August, die she must." I couldn't believe my ears. I gushed recklessly about Sally into the faces of strange girls, then fell silent. When John crashed on the floor at the foot of my bed, I tried not to imagine his nightmares.

On August 30, we crammed into a double-decker bus to Heathrow terminal, trailed by the cameraman, last seen in Florence, who was shooting the last scenes of Bernie's promotional film of the Odyssey. The show must go on. Several of the group had undergone Carnaby Street makeovers—Dave was in a bowler hat, Stu in a deer-stalker, Robin in a flowing cape, Stanfield in a blue Nehru jacket, white turtleneck, grey stovepipe pants and black Beatle boots. In sync with the unrelenting unreality, I turned to face the camera and gave Bernie what he wanted: the idiot grin of the happy-go-lucky.

The whole world is watching. As we checked our baggage, Marywinn dropped the souvenir wicker-wrapped Chianti bottle she had been toting since Italy, the smash of the glass on the terminal floor flushing shards of anguish. Keep calm and carry on.

As the wheels of the BOAC jet touched down in Toronto, clapping and crying engulfed the cabin. I sat in defiant silence.

At the baggage carousel, everyone was poised to scatter on divergent paths, some out west, some back east. Out of self-protection I slipped away, dodging the hugs that might jolt my body into unthinkable emotion. Passing through the sliding doors into the din of the terminal, I scanned the faces of the crowd scanning me, until I spotted my mother and brother. From the back seat of the car, I blathered with nervous tension, sensing my mother's unease. No FitzGerald knew how to transmit or receive an atom of sensitive concern, and it was far too late to start now.

I had changed while away, but nothing had changed at home. Hovering on the threshold of the TV room, I watched my father watching the coverage of the Chicago riots, and we exchanged a few terse words. He was there but not there, stalled in the mad traffic in his head. Her marriage dead, my mother was reinvesting her energy in me. But I was too young, too blind, too stunned to notice the raising of the emotional stakes.

When she wordlessly slipped into my hand a folded sheet of baby blue onionskin paper, I realized I was holding the effusive, vermouth-stained letter I had dictated to Sally in Rome. In my mother's face I detected no feeling, but I needed to believe that this was her way of acknowledging the catastrophe.

The sight of Sally's delicate handwriting restored her to life, and a thin fissure cracked the concrete of my chest. I bolted up the stairs to the third-floor bathroom and behind the door I smothered the deluge. Perching on the toilet seat, I realized I was back where I started: out in the cold. The fever dream of Italy rewound at hyperspeed, image after image: Volkswagens, Vesuvius, Vespas, vermouth, Vercingetorix, vestal virgins, Venetian vaporettos, in vino veritas. My thoughts ricocheted from the Atlantic salt spray to the mouth of the volcano, the mosaics of Pompeii to the dance of the Roman nightclub, the orange roof tiles of Florence to the sands of the Lido, the sublime Swiss pasture to the peak of the Schilthorn, the ovens of Dachau to the dream castles lining the Rhine, our six-week path marked by Sally's bent smile. How could the loss of a single body and soul make me feel this way? I was thrown back to the solitary confinement of the infant crib, longing and fearing to be heard. But if I knew anything for certain, I knew that no one would climb the stairs, or open the door, or extend a word or a hand, for no one could give what they did not have.

On September 1, the Sunday of the Labour Day long weekend, two weeks before my eighteenth birthday, my mother drove me up to De Grassi Point. After receiving my letter from Paris, the Wodehouses had invited me to their cottage, hungry for first-hand details of Sally's last summer.

They had also invited George Orr.

My mother and I were staying with friends on the other side of the point. After dinner I set off alone. Six summers had passed since I had seen the place, and I deliberately took my time in the late-summer dusk, hugging the shoreline, marking the way, cottage by cottage, dock by dock, tree by tree. As I passed the sandbar of the baby beach, the gentle lapping of the waves seemed strangely drained of their original enchantment. I expected to come upon the acre of wild waist-high grass near the Wodehouse place where Sally and I had moved barefoot, single file. When I saw that the grass had been cut down, forming an open commons, something about the tidy flatness thickened the pang in my throat.

Approaching the familiar worn steps and the double screen doors, I recognized the home base of our blissed-out games of Kick the Can, and a voice was released inside me: *"Don't worry. We'll always be friends. I'll visit you at university this fall. I promise."*

Dr. and Mrs. Wodehouse ushered me into the familiar two-storey-tall living room, its open atrium a reminder of the Paris hotel. I greeted Diana, so different from her sister, and a neighbour, John Harrison. I had not seen either of them since 1962, and I was relieved that they remembered I existed. When my eyes fell on the black-bearded face of a stranger, the doctor asked, "Do you know George Orr?" I thought I had quietly assassinated him in Rome, but as my hand rose to meet his, he turned as real as the flesh on our bones.

As Dr. Wodehouse rolled out a trolley of liquor, Mrs. Wodehouse invited me to the sofa where I had watched TV with Sally. They urged me to speak freely of the trip, holding back nothing, a prospect both exciting and dangerous. They were playing to my strength— memory—so I conducted an animated six-week travelogue, from Sally's first day on the *Raffaello* right through to the last hours on the Rhine steamer. I reported that the boys voted Sally the most popular girl on the trip, as if such a simple, happy fact might miraculously set all to rights. I did not think to ask why they held the funeral before we returned home. Why did they not wait for us?

I filled myself with alcohol as I emptied myself of stories. One last all-nighter with Sally. Then I realized that the more I was holding up the parents, the more I was dropping George, who had withdrawn into a corner in silence and now stared at me with unnerving intensity. I could not say aloud what he needed to know: *Yes, I slept with her, but I only slept with her.*

I could guess his thoughts: *Did she actually fall for this shallow asshole?*

No one wept.

Standing to leave, I shook George's hand and glimpsed the void in his eyes. I did not know that Dr. Wodehouse had been treating his sleep deprivation with doses of thorazine; drugs, the young man was learning, were a blessing, for they killed the dreaming state.

Declining Mrs. Wodehouse's offer of a flashlight, I headed back to our friends' cottage as pink glimmers of the rising sun streamed through the arms of the pines and reflected off the still face of the lake. Mercifully I was spared the execution-at-dawn feeling that never ceased to haunt my early mornings. Passing our old rental cottage fronting the baby beach, I remembered the salamander that as an eleven-year-old I buried in a glass jar back in that ancient August when Marilyn Monroe died. I knew exactly where it was, but I kept moving.

Days later, Gerrie Grand entered nursing school at the University of Toronto, where she and Sally had planned to share a room in residence.

At a small gathering one September night, two student nurses pulled out a Ouija board. Gerrie's fingers were not touching the heart-shaped planchette, but the board was emitting a compelling energy. Gerrie watched as the girls posed question upon question:

"Are you female?"

YES.

"Did you die under age twenty?"

YES.

"Do you know anyone in the room?"

YES.

"What is your name?"

The planchette slowly spelled out SALLY.

Gerrie felt the hair on the back of her neck rising. "Do you have a message for us?"

Letter by letter, the planchette spelled out TELL GEORGE I'M OK.

Despite her fear, Gerrie believed she had connected with Sally and bought a Ouija board. She tried to duplicate the experience with George, but nothing happened. George told her that he had burned all of Sally's letters, the ones she had asked him to save. But, in fact, he had stored them in a box.

If Sally was OK, George was not.

THIRTEEN

George Orpheus

A s the dying summer of 1968 seeped into fall, George was learning there was no value in room-clearing displays of emotion, no audience for his grief and guilt over the loss of Sally. His friends, save for Stewart, were sick of it; new people he met at school were made uncomfortable by it. His mother kept repeating, "He'll be fine." In the eyes of his war veteran father, George could see the question, Why lose sleep over one girl?

Sally's parents remained gracious and welcoming, until the day Diana spoke the words that while echoing George's own suspicions, he did not need to hear: "You probably shouldn't be coming around much anymore. You remind them of Sally."

One day from the radio the lyrics of "On the Way Home," the new Buffalo Springfield song, seemed to witness his agony, and for a moment they served as a salve:

When the dream came
I held my breath
with my eyes closed.
I went insane,
like a smoke ring day

when the wind blows.
Now I won't be back
till later on
if I do come back at all.

On a chill afternoon in late October, he drove alone through the Yonge Street gate of Mount Pleasant Cemetery, pushed open the door of the administration building and asked directions to the grave of Sally Wodehouse. A map was produced, a red circle marking the spot. Down the asphalt lanes he rolled, through the two-hundred-acre arboretum of rare and exotic species, past the serene autumnal lawns and tufts of orange leaves clogging the moribund flower beds, past the still fountains and statues. Arriving at plot Y, he stopped the car and moved among the waves of graves, compelled forward by a mix of longing and dread, until at last he found the upright granite slab, its flat, cold face meeting his own:

IN LOVING MEMORY OF SALLY LYN WODEHOUSE
MAY 25, 1950 – AUG. 13, 1968

He averted his gaze, then turned back, staring. Wreathed in crumbling roses, the monument was divided into quadrants, the three blank spaces awaiting the inevitable appearance of the names and dates of her father, mother and sister. Flushed, nauseated, he felt worse than the moment of the funeral when he'd stood before the wooden box containing her ashes, flower in hand, for now the truth was carved in stone: she was never coming back.

George could talk only to himself, not to Sally. And so he retraced his footsteps through the Toronto dead, returning to his mother's car and the underworld of the undergraduate and the forgiveness promised by music and drugs.

———

Stewart had planned to remain in Dublin and attend Trinity College, but Sally's death changed everything. Quitting Ireland, he entered his first year of York University specifically to take care of George. In the figure of the stocky, bearded, blue-eyed "psychic Viking," George would find in Stewart a sturdy post to lean on.

Incapable of tolerating stillness or silence, George craved constant stimulation, yet parties weren't working for him and nothing academic was sticking: psychology, philosophy, English and history all reeked of the rote data-cram of high school. In the works of Thomas Hardy and their gloomy skein of outlandish coincidences, he gazed into the mirror of his own life. He felt more real playing contact sports. Then, one Friday afternoon, he and Stewart passed six hours in the embryonic radio club, high on magic mushrooms, spinning records and driving each other into spasms of hilarity; from such small beginnings a campus radio station was born.

They also discovered the student newspaper, *Excalibur*, affectionately nicknamed *Low Calibre*. Under the editor, Ross Howard, George typed out articles on the plight of the environment and the legalization of pot. When Stewart, the sports editor, organized a contest to name the inept football team, a stern Anglo moniker emerged: the Yeomen. At last, George felt he was tapping into the potent world of storytelling.

Lacking fraternities, York University was an undeveloped nine-year-old bereft of a sense of community, and George set about enlivening the remote, soulless cow pasture, if only to enliven himself. The campus had no Homecoming Weekend, so that fall George and Stewart started an arts festival. Students were invited to attack an old Volkswagen with sledgehammers, scope a twenty-four-hour marathon of Roadrunner, Bugs Bunny and Rocky and Bullwinkle cartoons and razz the abysmal football team as it worked on a record-breaking losing streak.

For the Saturday-night headline act, George and Stewart signed

Gordon Lightfoot, but when Canada's premier folkie inspected the condition of the makeshift stage, he snarled, "You're a bunch of fucking amateurs. I'm not performing on that!" Charm and persuasion prevailed, and he did go on: the show sold out at $5 a head, and the next day the budding impresarios threw $8,000 in cash into the air. They paid themselves $200 each for their trouble and gave the remainder to the student council. Heading downtown to Sam the Record Man, George blew the entire wad on dozens of rock 'n' roll albums. Stunned by the success of the festival, the university president told George and Stewart, "You guys will take over the world!"

That same fall of 1968, a bright, vivacious, second-year arts student strolled into the *Excalibur* office. Valerie was amused by the sight of Stewart, a hulking, hirsute character in granny glasses, white jeans, fringed leather jacket and cowboy boots. Although Stewart was entranced by Val, he tried to manoeuvre her into George's orbit. But soon Stewart realized that in this young woman he had found the meaning of his life.

When she learned the Sally story, Val tacitly understood not to wade too deeply into the dark pool of George's shifting moods. She also knew, uncomfortably, that if not for Sally's death, she would never have met Stewart because he would have stayed in Ireland. A girl Val never knew had set the course of her life.

On Saturday, May 24, 1969, nine months after they met, Stewart and Valerie were married in her hometown of Delhi, nestled in the tobacco belt of Southwestern Ontario. Stewart shaved off his beard to please a father who didn't need pleasing. As best man, George did his best to transform himself from slouching hippie into well-mannered, upright gentleman, dancing with rural grandmothers who cooed, "Such a nice young man!"

At the wedding, George found himself taken with Val's cousin, Katherine Grant. One day in June, not long past his twenty-second birthday, he drove his mother's Triumph two hours westward to Katherine's hometown of Aylmer. With Val as a bridge between them, he anticipated a romance. George and his date passed a balmy evening strolling the sand dunes on the north shore of Lake Erie, but when he extended a single yellow rose, the young woman returned nothing but a tepid brand of Canadian politeness.

By eleven that night, he resigned himself to the long drive back to the city. Puttering along a deserted two-lane road, he drifted past silent farmhouses in the pitch-blackness. Then headlights flashed in his rearview mirror, and he watched a hulking, Detroit-made car scorching up from behind at twice his own speed. Cresting a small hill, pushing 80 mph as it passed George, the yellow car seemed to lift off the road a second before it smashed head-on into an oncoming Volkswagen bug.

Skidding to the brink of the ditch, George sprinted back to find the two cars welded together like a grotesque sculpture, gasoline spewing from the fuel line. Low moans from the drivers fused with the ominous ticking of hot metal. A sick terror flooded his stomach as a spark ignited the gas and a deafening fireball exploded the moonless night. Then came the wail of a police car.

Stopping shy of the inferno, a cop got out of the cruiser and ran up to George: he had been pursuing the speeding yellow car. Bringing George back to his car, he opened his trunk and pulled out an extinguisher, blanket, flashlight and axe, and together they dashed back. They doused the flames, pulled the driver of the yellow car out and laid him on the side of the road. He was bleeding heavily but still breathing.

Inside the wreckage of the VW bug, the driver was pinned by the steering column. The cop forced the door open with the axe, releasing a stench of roasting flesh. The spray of the extinguisher reduced the flames enough for the pair of rescuers to move in. But as George reached for the driver's arm, he felt strips of flesh melt in his hands, and the limb detached. The cop kept hacking away, but George was certain the young man was past saving, and soon the cop gave up, dropping the bloody axe on the asphalt.

More police cars, more swirling red lights. The driver who caused the carnage was loaded into an ambulance; cops murmured that he had been drinking. Miraculously George had suffered only a surface singeing of his hair and eyebrows. But three hours of cigarettes, coffee and police interviews gradually eased the blur of shock sheathing his nervous system.

At dawn, George headed home, arriving as Mac and Dorothy Orr were rising. Ten months earlier, he had walked into this same house, this same living room, and told these same parents that Sally was dead, and their reaction had been only to stare at him wordlessly. But this time, as her son crossed the threshold, Dorothy Orr lifted her hands to her face and screamed: George was covered in blood from head to foot. For the next two days, he managed his distraught mother; to manage himself, he scribbled an account of the experience, another chapter for the melodrama of his life so far.

Two days after the accident, George was charged with manslaughter. The drunk driver, the son of the local mayor, claimed that George—the man who had helped save his life—had forced him into the oncoming lane. A court date was set; if he failed to appear, he would be arrested. Two weeks later, George and his father drove back to the scene of the accident; their dread of a cover-up evaporated when the judge asked George a few questions, apologized for his trouble and told him he was free to go.

For years to come, passengers in George's car would tease him about driving like an old lady. But it was okay with him: he wanted to reach the end of the road.

———

After four years of university and still no degree, George drifted through the summer of '69 in a jobless fog. When the newlyweds Stewart and Val moved into an apartment building south of the university, George moved into the bachelor unit next door. Although the move freed him from his parents' basement, he was more than ever prone to melancholy. He fed his head with a mix of narcotics and the daily news cycle—John and Yoko's bed-in, the moon landing, the Manson Family murders. Even as he wallowed in endless replays of the double concept album, *Odessa*, and the quavering voices of the Bee Gees ("You'll Never See My Face Again")—he could not shake an amorphous physical pain and struggled to find its precise location in his body so he could make it stop.

Hoping to divert his floundering friend, Stewart talked up a trip to the Woodstock Festival, to be held from August 15 to 18 in upstate New York. But the dates meshed with the third anniversary of the blind date with Sally, and the first anniversary of her death, so George passed up a defining moment in the history of his generation because a different moment was defining him.

On an idyllic stretch of a Lake Erie beach, a gang of fast friends gathered outside a cottage for a day-long picnic. The gas-fired water heater had lost its pilot light, and as George crawled under on his back to reignite it, a burst of flame singed his eyebrows. His mind snapped back to the burning Volkswagen, hard on the heels of his failed wooing of Katherine. He rejoined the free-flowing game of Frisbee on the sand, and then . . . nothing. His chaotic inside conversation stopped cold, as if an audio jack was pulled. The dead-letter office of the mind.

For a full year, his failure to control his feelings had shamed his nice, normal family who wanted nothing more than a nice, normal son. But now something new, something else, something darker, was upon him, as if he were a floating astronaut leaking oxygen from his space suit. The more he dreaded the white whale of emptiness, the deeper it seeped under his skin.

———

As told by the poet Ovid in the two-thousand-year-old *Metamorphoses*, Orpheus was a legendary semi-divine augur and seer of royal blood venerated by the Greeks and Romans of the Classical Age. A charming and gifted player of the lyre, he made spellbinding music capable of calming savage beasts, coaxing trees and rocks into dance and diverting the course of rivers.

He led a simple, sheltered life until the day he met the nymph Eurydice, and they fell deeply in love. On their wedding day, a satyr saw Eurydice and wanted to possess her. Fleeing in terror through a field of tall grass, she fell into a nest of vipers and suffered a fatal bite on her heel. Overcome with grief, Orpheus played mournful songs that made all the nymphs weep.

Upon their urging, he slipped through the cleft of a cave and followed Eurydice's ghost on her downward path deep into the Underworld. Crossing the Styx, the river of death, he confronted Cerebus, the three-headed dog guarding death's door, who fawningly let him pass. Singing sweetly among the ranks of the dead, Orpheus suspended the repetitive tortures they were condemned to suffer: fetching water from cracked vessels, tantalized by luscious fruit hanging out of reach, sunk neck-deep in water but unable to drink, rolling boulders up hills. Softening the bloodless ghosts with the magic of his music, Orpheus came upon the implacable King Pluto and his consort Persephone.

"How did you make it here?" demanded Pluto.

"Love," Orpheus responded, "had greater strength than I."

Then he sang for the return of Eurydice to earth: "If you deny me, I cannot return alone; you shall triumph in the death of us both." Persephone was the first to be moved; Sisyphus himself ceased his labours, sitting on his rock to listen, and the faces of the wild Furies dampened with tears.

Then the stern Pluto himself fell to weeping. He agreed to release Eurydice to Orpheus on one condition. As they silently surfaced to the sunlight, Orpheus must cover his eyes with his hand—symbolically blind to the reality of her death—and not look back at his beloved; if he did, she must dwell in the Underworld for eternity.

Orpheus said he understood and headed through the fog toward the light of day. Trailing behind him, a limping Eurydice begged him to acknowledge her; did he not still love her as madly as she did him? Approaching the threshold to the upper world, he could no longer bear the anxiety of losing her a second time. The instant he turned around, she disappeared into the darkness, fulfilling his worst nightmare. As Eurydice cried a final farewell, his longing arms swept the empty air.

Orpheus tried to re-enter the Underworld but this time he was denied by the ferryman. For seven years he lingered at the brink, singing his pain to the rocks and mountains, uprooting oak trees and melting the hearts of tigers. Devastated, he vowed to never love another woman. Enraged by Orpheus's failure to be a true lover and die for Eurydice, the god of wine, Bacchus, released the Maenads, a swarm of wild Furies. When Orpheus repulsed their lustful advances, the Furies tore the body of the musician to shreds.

The pieces of Orpheus's body were collected by the Muses, who buried them at the foot of Mount Olympus, except for his head, which was carried by a river to the sea, then buried in Lesbos. Jupiter fixed his lyre among the stars; shrines containing relics of Orpheus were regarded as oracles. Orpheus was allowed to rejoin his beloved Eurydice as a flitting ghost in the Underworld, gazing upon her as much as he desired. But the Upper World was now deaf to his music.

In the North York General psychiatric ward, confined to a white room with black curtains, George Orr sat slumped in a circle of human forms he could only perceive as lost in space. The impersonal rotations of white-coated psychiatrists seemed to make no distinction between schizophrenia and a unique case of personal loss and attacked his natural grief with anti-psychotic drugs. Nothing worked.

To the huddle of inert bodies, the twenty-two-year-old patient told his near-supernatural story of a dead lover, but he knew no one was sharing the same reality. The day he heard the word "electroshock" was the day his experience of the inside of a locked mental ward unwittingly conferred a blessing: after two weeks, he realized he was not a terminal head case, merely a smouldering blanket amid three-alarm fires, and he found the door. Where else might a Nowhere Man go but a fifth year of university?

When George and Stewart sought volunteers for the second annual York arts festival, among the first to appear was Sandy, a sunny and athletic twenty-year-old blonde. A science and phys ed student who had organized the cheerleading team for the hapless York Yeomen, she had for weeks been circling George, and when she finally introduced herself wearing a royal-blue-and-white jumpsuit, he jumped.

In the spring of 1970, Sandy was poised to enter the workforce, but George remained adrift on his own not entirely unpleasant carpet of confusion. They were reaching a crossroads: Should we move in together? Parked with her cross-legged on a floor in an empty York classroom, George for the first and last time opened up to her about Sally, ending with a warning: "I am bad news."

Blinded by love, Sandy dismissed the Sally baggage: Why burden a new relationship with a previous one? If people are fine on the surface, she was cool. Although she regarded George's parents as proper, private-school types, never saying what they felt—"Don't you guys ever argue?" she wondered aloud at a family dinner—she was optimistic that George would evolve under her influence. Her father was a plain-spoken Nova Scotian jack of all trades; in her family, blow-ups were quickly forgotten.

George's reflexive reaction was that if he dared to love someone, that someone would disappear. But here stood a strong, flesh-and-blood young woman, willing to risk it. The least he could do was try.

FOURTEEN

Alma Mater

I n September 1968, I headed off to first year at Queen's University in Kingston. I was innocent enough to hope that the stone mother of limestone slabs might offer sanctuary, but my residence, Leonard Hall, was irredeemably male, a facsimile of the UCC boarding house; visitors of the opposite sex were compelled to sign out by 2 a.m. and return to the aptly named Victoria Hall. From a coed summer romp in Europe I was back in the Presbyterian arms of God's Frozen People. At the same time, I was disarmed to discover that most of my floor mates were not privately schooled, poison–Ivy League snobs, but small-town Ontario egalitarians from places like Port Hope, Barrie, Smiths Falls and Red Lake.

In English class, I met Mark, a confident, witty character raised by his Polish Catholic immigrant parents in a humble suburban bungalow. Mark was everything I was not—quarterback of his high school football team, a junior hockey player, a provincial wrestling champion, brilliant yet comfortable in his own skin. I was amazed he stooped to befriend a self-effacer such as me.

On my first weekend, I gained entry to my first porn movie—*that* bit really does go *there*—and my loss of innocence came cheap for the price of a blue five note. In French class, meanwhile, I was the sole male of the species, encircled by twenty razor-smart teenage girls. I had not shared a class with girls since Grade 2. I tried to disappear in the back row, but my long-lankiness was hiding in plain sight. One day the female prof asked with a smirk, "Monsieur FitzGerald, what is your masculine opinion?" Paralyzed by the rush of tittering, I could not muster the will to answer, or transfer out. The same went for psych class: hoping to find solace for Sally's death in the wisdom of the sages, I was bitten by Pavlov's dog and tuned out.

Happily, Nan, one of the Odyssey girls, was installed in Victoria Hall, and together we organized reunions nearly every weekend. In late September, all the Torontonian tripsters—nearly half the original twenty-eight—convened in my parents' house. Pulling back the dining room furniture to screen slides of the trip, we sprawled on the carpet in the dark, the intermittent figure of Sally riding the shafts of shifting light. I was startled when Jane disentangled herself from Sean, nuzzled up beside me and leaned her head on my shoulder. Convinced that I had stolen her, Sean retreated upstairs to the unsympathetic company of my parents. The next day my mother told me that she had found Sean's display of distress "funny."

When, days later, a package arrived from Venice addressed to my mother, it took a moment to remember I had sent it. I explained that in a glass-making factory, Sally convinced me that a set of goblets would improve the rosewood sideboard. As my mother opened the box, I allowed myself to believe that finally, this time, she would be touched. But her expression of revulsion was unmistakable, and Sally's glassware disappeared, never to be seen again. Like Sally herself.

The following weekend, a group of us visited Mrs. Wodehouse in Rosedale to pass on an album of the best snapshots of Sally we had gathered from our collective cameras. I had never set foot inside Sally's home and I felt a new layer of sadness, laced with guilt, for I was parked on the sofa beside the newly won Jane. Even as we attended to the grieving mother, my eyes fell on Jane's crossed legs, where curving thigh nudged hem of dress.

When some of the girls visited Sally's grave in Mount Pleasant Cemetery, I was not invited. Nan reported back that they placed a vase of flowers on the headstone and stood for a moment in silence. When the flowers suddenly toppled over, it released a cloudburst of laughter.

"We took it as a sign," Nan said. "Sally was saying lighten up."

Easy for her to say.

During the week of her eighteenth birthday, three weeks after my own, Jane threw the next Odyssey party at her house in North Toronto. She was in Grade 13 at Havergal, and her high school sweetheart was away at university. As she opened the front door, I hovered over her like a construction crane—I was a full foot taller. I breathed in the smile, the perfume, the party dress. This felt different from Sally; I couldn't yet bring myself to say better than.

For thirty seconds, a minute, I lingered like a delivery boy waiting for a tip. Exasperated, Jane finally grabbed my wrist and pulled me across the threshold. As the party unfolded in the basement rec room, Robin appeared with her cousin, George Orr. I was sliding down into the velvet womb of my third drink and his haunted face failed to snap the trance. We exchanged awkward words—he seemed older, so much older, than the rest of us—and before long our brainless pleasures banished him into the night.

Week by week, Jane and I exchanged phone calls and letters. In one, she wrote in French that she liked me because I had *"bonnes intentions"*; I did not think to ask myself if she did. One weekend, our happy gang travelled down to Kingston for a bash in my residence; as the slide show flooded the white wall of my bedroom with Sally's face, Marywinn, who had sat with her dying friend in the German ambulance, broke down. But I didn't.

By November, my academic progress was subverted by the arrival of *The White Album*. I stopped cutting my hair and started artfully dodging classes; I was now majoring in the Beatles with a minor in Hendrix and Cream, finding delicious masochism in the unfinished, undelivered essay. I was neglecting my higher education for a lower one; virginity was something to lose, and I wanted to join the losers. "Mustang Sally" was now supplanted by "Gotta See Jane." One night four of us were parked in the dark lot of an elementary school and the song—"red light, green light"—was blasting from the radio. As Will and Marywinn thrashed in the front seat of our bedroom on wheels, Jane and I rolled around in the back, my long legs stretched stork-like out the window. As I came up for air, Jane whispered, "I want to have lots and lots of babies." But weren't we still babies ourselves?

On a weekend in late November, I took the bus to Toronto where Jane, resplendent in black leather boots and a full-length coonskin coat, met me at the terminal. The Queen's Golden Gaels were playing for the national football championship at Varsity Stadium, a night game, and I was staying over at Jane's house. Before the game, I shot a game of snooker in the basement with her father, a charmer who put me so completely at ease that I let him win. I must have passed the audition, for I detected no hint of "Hands off my daughter."

The scene was set: Saturday night in her living room, her parents out, a December frost dusting the windows. Margi was visiting from Halifax, and on a nearby sofa Dave was conducting a clinic on how to separate a girl from her bra. I carried Jane up the stairs to her bedroom, buttons and zippers popping and sliding, no birth control, no control at all. At the moment of truth, her older sister stormed through the front door to find Dave and Margi, if not in flagrante, then almost. From the foot of the stairs, she bellowed, "What the hell is this? A bordello?"

As Jane scrambled downstairs, I flashed on the voice of Sally, yelling from a Roman window, *"Quanto costa, bella?"*

The next day, my mother asked me in a tone of accusation, "Are you going steady?" I felt like a stammering drunk caught in a radar trap. I couldn't mount a simple defence—Why aren't you happy for me? I was long past wondering why she had never talked to me about Sally, but now she was making me feel I must apologize for liking a girl. Any girl.

On New Year's Eve, Sean hosted the latest in our chain of post-Odyssey revels. It was a testament to the strength of our boyhood friendship that while Sean might be nursing thoughts of homicide, he seemed resigned to the sight of Jane nestled on *my* lap on *his* sofa. Playtime turned real when, embracing Tammy, Nick broke the news: they were officially engaged. The room exploded into squeals of delight, and the love-in began anew, pushing us through the dying moments of 1968.

As midnight passed, the taste of the white wine shot me back to Rüdesheim, and abruptly an invisible hand pulled the circuit breaker. I pushed Jane off my lap and exploded: "I can't stand it any longer!"

Jane was blindsided, and the sight of her shock shocked me. Who could explain it? Was I making her feel what I felt when I lost Sally? Even as I scrambled to take the words back, I knew a body thrown from a bus stayed thrown.

At three in the morning, Stu piloted me home past deep banks of snow. Shedding my shoes, I skulked up the stairs past my parents' bedroom door, but I guess the creaks betrayed me, because at dawn, my father, a stranger to my bedroom and my life, charged through the door and yanked back the curtains of the dormer window.

"Your mother and I have had enough. Get the hell out of this house right now!"

Knowing it was my mother who had sent him, I felt immune: I had never *lived* here, and neither had he. A threat of eviction meant nothing to a squatter like me.

Before heading back to school, I tried to reverse my suicidal split with Jane on the phone, but we both sensed something had snapped. Unwisely fishing for sympathy from my mother, I unpacked my distress on the sunroom sofa. Days past her fiftieth birthday, she was still as stunning as an arctic glacier, and she did not bother to conceal the look of glee in her eyes over the news of my breakup. No one usurps the queen.

When Jane returned to her high school sweetheart, I wrote her a wounded letter accusing her of using me as a ploy to make her old boyfriend jealous. The moment I slipped it into the mailbox, I regretted it, for I knew none of it was true; our feelings had been genuine. Much time would pass before I began to see how I was playing an integral part in my own downfalls.

In the concrete bunker of Leonard Hall, I burrowed into a winter of discontent. Guys were dropping out and other guys were digging in, the grasshoppers vs. the ants. I could not imagine following any of these future leaders into the future. A frosh in the adjoining residence tried to kill himself by swallowing five bottles of aspirin, setting his bloodstream ablaze but surviving. Others succeeded where he failed.

One day in philosophy class, I was impressed when the prof remarked that we, a class of privileged whites, were "emotional eunuchs." Repelling the daily maid service with a Do Not Disturb sign, I often slept till noon and continued to devote my waking affections to books, films and music bearing no relation to the curriculum. My Tuesday-afternoon economics class had come to signify all that was wrong with the world, and in my moody blueness I dropped the needle into the vein of *Days of Future Passed* and stretched across the unmade bed, awash in the Moog-synthesized fugue state of "Tuesday Afternoon." Seeking a pattern, I realized that we had boarded the *Raffaello* on a Tuesday afternoon and Sally died on a Tuesday afternoon.

On a weekend trip to Toronto, I waded through the hemp-and-hair haze of Rochdale College, the anarchic eighteen-storey free university and student co-op at Bloor and Huron Streets, then infiltrated a raucous frat house jungle on St. George Street. Through the strobe-lit blasts of acid rock and billows of pot smoke, I made out the bearded glare of George Orr. We exchanged wordless nods.

By spring, a fledgling rock band, Led Zeppelin, was assaulting the halls and the walls of Leonard Hall. Night after night, roving packs of engineers burned off exam pressure by flinging "arts fags" into bathtubs of ice-cold water and inflicting thousands of dollars' worth of property damage. The exhilarating violence released me, for a time, from my passive-aggressive funk. It now made sense to me why for millennia armies have recruited eighteen-year-old males lacking fully formed brains—at that age, we're all potential killers.

I acquiesced to my mother's wish that I work the summer of 1969 as a trainee at a Royal Bank branch at Oakwood and St. Clair. Her father, Talbot, had been a banker, and my mother pictured me stepping into his giant rubber galoshes. As part of a four-year summer program designed to speed undergrads up the corporate ladder to their executive destinies, I was paid far more than the female tellers with twenty years' experience, and I was not yet nineteen.

One June day, my mother called me at work to ask if she could open my marks, which had arrived in the mail. At least she'd asked. A paper-cutting sound, a long silence, then the mother of all sighs. I felt a deep rush of pride that, given I rarely darkened a classroom after Christmas, I was worth as much as 31 in French, 38 in economics, 40 in psychology, 50 in philosophy, and 70 in English. My whole life I had tried my best, to no avail; time to do my worst.

The following week, Dr. and Mrs. Wodehouse appeared at our door for evening cocktails. They had never visited our house, nor would they again. I assumed their sudden appearance was my parents' way of acknowledging that Sally had once walked the earth. I was struck by the doctor's loud red sports jacket and the buoyant bonhomie of the two couples as they greeted one another. As I shook the firm hand of the university's birth control expert, I recognized traces of his dead daughter in the lines on his face. As he lingered over the liquor cabinet, I fished for a conversation that I hoped would extend beyond three sentences. I revealed that I flunked my first year of university but withheld what I was feeling: *I've been having a bad time, too, you know*. Letting out a short laugh, he headed outside to the patio by the pool, and I realized with a jolt that Sally was not invited to this party, and neither was I. *Watch and learn—this is how it's done.*

In the summer of 1970, my brother toured Europe in an Odyssey group led by Nick and Tammy. On the Lido, where Sally had buried my body in the sand, Mike watched as a drowned man was pulled from the waves and could not be revived. The Odyssey itself expired later that year, capitulating to backpacking baby boomers and the rebuking ghost of an eighteen-year-old girl.

The serial sieges of stomach, school, Sally, the breakup with Jane, my mother's coldness, my father's madness were flooding the projection booth in my head. I wondered if my parents' toxic *folie à deux* had entailed a silent trade-off of mania and depression—you take the high road and I'll take the low road—and I was the cyclothymic monkey in the middle. The fist clenching my guts was finally pegged as Crohn's disease. When the medication failed to eradicate the pain, I took it in stride (only much later would I understand, if not fully eliminate, my need to be punished).

For my twentieth birthday, my mother gave me a Super 8 camera. Film, that magical, time-travelling escape hatch, had often saved me, and maybe she knew that better than I did. She'd always been capable of sporadic gestures of lukewarm support when it came to my artistic aspirations, though she undermined them with a subtle, unsettling, sibling-like competiveness. Her own early aesthetic impulses had been quashed by her father, and I sensed she both admired and envied my potential. When I showed early promise with watercolours, she framed two of my Georgian Bay landscapes, but in a strange imitation of her self-thwarting bent, never again would I pick up a brush. I would not be framed by my mother.

But if I could paint or shoot a portrait of my own life so far, how would it look? *Love Story*, a box-office hit about a Harvard preppie and his dying working-class girlfriend, not only left me cold but with the conviction I could do much better myself. Short of turning the camera on my parents, I wrote and directed a political satire, *The Assassination of Alderman Alderman*, complete with a mock newscast voiceover, recruiting my brother and a close friend, Jay, as actors. The rebellious son of a Rosedale lawyer whose stutter had led to his early exit from UCC, Jay played a deranged populist demagogue campaigning for mayor of Toronto. Speechifying atop the Peter Pan statue at Avenue Road and St. Clair, haranguing bewildered passersby, he was gunned down by a black-hatted assassin, played by my brother, the ketchup-stained body rushed to the door of the UCC infirmary where no one received him. Jay was the kind of one-off character who spontaneously scat-sang the solemn Anglo hymn "And Did Those Feet in Ancient Times" on kazoo, sending us into paroxysms of laughter. We were the assassination generation; this was how we handled it.

In the spring of 1971, while I was away at school, my mother sprang the news that she had sold our house on Dunvegan Road. The roof, floors and walls that had contained my body for the past fourteen years simply dematerialized, as if it, or we ourselves, had never existed in the first place. I knew, but did not allow myself to know, that six months earlier, my father had made a second try at suicide by morphine, this time in my brother's bedroom, and that our sister had saved his life, in body if not in mind. I was left to imagine my mother emptying my bedroom of its contents without my knowledge or consent, as if disposing of the evidence.

Simultaneously, my rock star narco-gods were dying for our sins, one by one: Brian Jones, Jimi Hendrix, Janis Joplin, Jim Morrison, all crashing the Peter Pan barrier of age twenty-seven into sweet oblivion.

In my final year of Queen's, my roommate Hal rocked my world when he erupted into a weeks-long jag of scattershot paranoid schizophrenic hallucinations. I was crying into the lap of a girl I knew from film class, hoping she'd take pity and deliver me from my twenty-one-year-old virginity when Hal burst purple-faced through the bedroom door waving a condom—"Do you need some protection?" With this latest in a long line of bizarre teaching moments, lust died a quick death. When I committed Hal to the psych hospital and a barrage of electric shock, I was unaware that my father was suffering a similar fate in Toronto.

A dismal Christmas was redeemed by the fact that I'd at last formed a bond with my brother, Mike, who had followed me to Queen's. Falling in with a pair of teenage prodigies, we stayed up all night, aping the Dadaists of Cabaret Voltaire by taking turns at a typewriter composing lines of a marathon group poem—a surrealist parlour game known as "the exquisite corpse." As we feverishly discoursed on Dylan, Zen, Yeats, transmigration of souls, precognition and Sufi mysticism, we spun the avant-garde "music from outer space" of Sun Ra and Frank Zappa's *Weasels Ripped My Flesh*. We compiled a cast of characters, live and dead, historic and fictional, to invite to a massive dinner party in heaven, seated at tables of four: Cathy and Heathcliff, meet Stanley Kubrick and Mae West. Gregor Samsa and Grace Slick, meet Timothy Leary and Mary Magdalene. And why not include the immigrant maid who made our beds every morning? If we were going to crack the Mystery, we needed help.

It never crossed my mind to invite Sally.

FIFTEEN

Communing

I n the spring of 1970, George and Sandy, together with Stewart and Val, moved into 7 Inkerman Street, a two-storey semi-detached Toronto house built in 1837. The foursome was joined by three others: George's childhood friend David, the one who had cheated death in a motorcycle accident in the summer of 1967; Glenn, a friend of Stewart's; and the intuitive prodigy, Graham, the only person who had really listened to George when he reported his premonitory dream of Sally's death.

A ten-minute walk south of the countercultural vortices of Yorkville Village and Rochdale College, Inkerman flowed westward a short distance into Bay Street, where it met St. Michael's College, home of the mass media guru Marshall McLuhan. Southward loomed the despised canyon of rapacious stockbrokers; eastward stood quaint peak-roofed working-class cottages. Global villages within a global village.

Each side of the semi—ground-floor living room, hallway, dining room and kitchen—was a mirror image of the other, joined like brain hemispheres by an open archway. Upstairs, three bedrooms and a bathroom occupied each side. Before moving in the furniture, seven bodies slapped coats of paint on the walls, then crashed on the floor to finish the job the next day. The landlords had warned of the presence of a female ghost who wandered the house by night, and sure enough, when Sandy rose at 2 a.m. to visit the bathroom, she saw a young blond woman in a white nightgown glide out of Stewart and Valerie's bedroom and pause at the doorway. Taking her for Val—a petite woman in her early twenties with shoulder-length blond hair—Sandy rejoined George without a second thought.

Over breakfast, she was puzzled to find Val clad in dark pyjamas. "Why did you change out of your white nightgown?"

Val revealed that not only did she not own one, but she had not gotten up during the night.

In the months ahead, whenever the sound of unknown footsteps emanated from the staircase, Stewart's two dogs hovered and snarled. David scoffed at the suggestion of apparitions, but then he too saw a young woman with shoulder-length blond hair in a white nightie in the hallway. From then on, whenever anything in the house went awry, the ghost was blamed.

Though George considered himself lucky to have five friends and a lover, only Stewart remained intimately acquainted with his bedrock sadness. Most weekdays after class, the tribe routinely beamed itself upstairs into the tiny TV den, where the ugly psychedelic wallpaper overlaid the ugly Victorian wallpaper, to watch reruns of Captain Kirk going boldly where no one had gone before. For one two-week period, a harried Vietnam deserter and his girlfriend crashed on their floor, the young man unfurling heart-rending tales of war trauma, exile in this northern backwater and pining for home. The Canadians listened, horrified and sympathetic; for them, dodging the draft meant stepping out of the winter wind.

To replenish his $10-an-ounce stash of cannabis, George shuffled over to nearby Rochdale College, the hippie utopia fast turning into a biker dystopia. Convinced of their ability to defy gravity, two acid heads had recently plunged from the top floor to their death, leaving George Wodehouse, the beleaguered U of T public health doctor working out of his office on nearby Huron Street, straining to grasp the social pathologies of his daughters' generation.

Rochdale, Yorkville, Cinecity, the El Mocambo, the Planetarium— all were within a half-mile radius of Inkerman. On a fateful Friday night in the basement of the Embassy Tavern, the gang encountered a young doctor who extended his palm bearing a cellophane packet of fifty tabs of acid, the pure, original stuff straight from the Sandoz lab in Switzerland. And so it was that at 2 a.m. on a Saturday morning, bloated with draft beer, George and friends began an hallucinatory, twelve-hour, Ken Kesey-esque bus ride.

George knew that acid favoured the prepared mind; if a magic mushroom was a nine-volt battery, acid was a tongue thrust into an electrical socket. Bad trips were born of excessive dosing and fighting the experience; a safe-as-milk holding environment forestalled tipping off the cliff into psychosis and never coming back. If not exactly dropping out, George was tuning in and turning on to the message: just the right dosage, set and setting, soft lighting and music and a relaxed brain—"You have to be out of your mind to use your head"— were the keys to a wild-yet-safe cortex-clearing trip through the waking dream.

Splayed under the black ceiling of the living room, decorated with the orbs of the earth and moon cut from glossy posters, the Inkerman Seven settled into their makeshift planetarium, their wows and far-outs relaying the shared synaptic overload. George stared at random objects hour upon regressive hour, ingesting a reverberating flood of patterns and visual metaphors, the usual surfaces made unusual: beads, mirrors, drapes, fingernails, a mote of dust, a mole on Sandy's skin, the candlewax coating the flickering wine bottle, the whorls in the crown of Stewart's shaggy head.

Emerging clear-headed from the underworld on Sunday afternoon, George observed, "Amazing how you can sober up on LSD."

A genial, long-haired draft dodger from New York regularly rang the front doors of the houses on Inkerman Street and environs, an Avon Lady in combat boots, pushing his wares from pot, hashish, mushrooms and LSD to mescaline, opium and peyote—even the banana skins suggested by the Warholian art decorating the album cover *The Velvet Underground*. Taste tests around the kitchen table, littered with roach clips, rolling papers and bongs, kept Inkerman up to everything but speed.

Into routine all-night parties over a hundred bodies crammed, rock 'n' roll cranked to raise the dead. All embraced the sacred tenets of Timothy Leary, the renegade Harvard prof and politician of ecstasy, and Aldous Huxley, the English intellectual and opener of *The Doors of Perception* who dropped acid on his deathbed, the same day in November 1963 as JFK was murdered. After a McLuhan-themed, the medium-is-the-message party, George penned a hundred-page paper, "Media Self-Validation," about how we defined ourselves in multiple ways through media images. Bottom line: You were only real if you existed in print, photograph, narrative or some external construction. Then he lost the paper. He was, like the house itself, semi-detached.

George came to favour the fast, smash-in-the-face rush over the trickle-down-the-spine hash-brownie experience. His tastes were not subtle. One Saturday afternoon, as Sandy stood on the front porch enjoying a mushroom-clouded yet intelligible conversation with a black squirrel, George perched on the can waiting for the windowpane acid to kick in, when suddenly it did: an entire side of the bathroom wall bulged like a Nietzschean forehead, rocketing out with such force that he was blown clean off his porcelain throne. He was delighted. "Reality is a crutch for those who can't face acid."

On a dual-track, reel-to-reel tape recorder, George assembled audio collages out of random lyrics pulled from his album collection married to snatches of the Firesign Theatre, *Monty Python's Flying Circus*, *National Lampoon* and the Bonzo Dog Band. With a razor blade, he cut and pasted stream-of-consciousness word-association images and soundscapes, a promiscuous pastiche of puns, alliteration, onomatopoeia, neologisms, synesthesia—the found art of the unconscious, with juxtapositions pleasing and jarring. *Suite Judy Blue Eyes/ These Eyes/Brown-Eyed Girl.* He buried a small tape recorder behind a wall in an alcove, playing an endless loop of his own voice: "Really moist brownies come from Duncan Hines!" His exasperated associates bought him a set of headphones to keep his stoned humour to himself.

But the shared ideals of the Inkerman Seven, unchained from social convention, inevitably crashed on the hard kitchen floor of the domestic economy. As the women tired of handling the shopping, cooking, dishwashing and money management—"Where's your share of the rent? The food?"—emotional hand grenades burst the socialist-utopian-psychedelic bubble. On the day the place was burglarized, the women insisted on amending the hippie constitution and locking the front door; in such ways the female invited the male to grow up.

When it could no longer be denied that the house needed a dining room table, George and Stewart drove up to Rio Lumber on Merton Street, overlooking Mount Pleasant Cemetery where Sally's ashes were buried. They loaded up their old Chevy with nails and glue and strapped two-by-fours to the roof. Undeterred by a shared ignorance of the art of woodworking, they headed down to the basement of 7 Inkerman and cobbled together a rough beast of a table.

George knew that working with your hands failed to qualify as an Upper Canadian pursuit, but still, he borrowed his father's hammer with one of the prongs broken off, dipped his nose into a manual and shed his ignorance one step at a time. Healing himself was not a conscious intention, but as particles of sawdust settled into the black grooves of the spinning albums, George Orr was falling in love with pine.

Clunky pieces of furniture found their way into the homes of family and friends. Form and function rarely agreed, but they got along. The hippie cottage industry with an 1837 soul grew, scoring a contract to build shelves for a health food store on nearby Yonge Street. With each delivery, the refrains of the customers remained constant in their Canadian politeness: "That's nice." A name was born: the Nice Furniture Company. Stewart was in; if they'd never make it as cabinet ministers, why not cabinetmakers?

Glenn quit the commune and was replaced by Jane, the tall, self-confident girlfriend of Ted, a talented musician who was often drawn into the basement workshop. Refugees from Establishment Toronto families, Ted and Jane slid seamlessly into the Inkerman scene.

One day an idea, germinating for months in the collective boomer psyche, popped out of George's mouth: "Let's split from the city and grow things in the country! Vegetables and livestock! Back to the land, man! Weekend hippies to full-time hippies!"

Over the summer months of 1970, George and Stewart drove the battered Chevy back and forth between Toronto and Barrie, Port Hope and Niagara Falls, checking out three thousand miles of rural Ontario to find a place where they could set up a self-sustaining organic farm and a furniture shop to which they would devote their lives.

Nearing summer's end, they happened on a property five miles east of Lindsay, outside the hamlet of Downeyville. The narrow hundred-acre strip of pasture land and hayfields held a pond and grove of reforested pine; a classic Ontario working barn faced a dilapidated wood-frame farmhouse. The village of Omemee, where Neil Young grew up, was a short drive distant, as was Rochdale's own rural commune, Golden Lake Farm, on the edge of Algonquin Park. Irish Protestant pioneer farmland wrested from the natives was being reclaimed by a tribe of white brats who identified with the natives.

Each kicking in enough to cover the down payment and the $35,000 mortgage, the group of seven baptized their sylvan utopia Never-Neverland. Patrick, the precocious UCC old boy turned Yorkville pianist and part-time studio session man, replaced Jane as the seventh tenant, and all helped heave his piano into the farmhouse. Patrick was the only permanent resident, while the others drove up from Inkerman on the weekends.

One warm September evening, everyone clambered into George's Chevy and zigzagged all over the moonlit fields. The entire county was abuzz over the arrival of the first outsiders in years; were these the scandalous hippie sex-and-drug fiends so demonized by the media?

Heeding the advice of the Department of Agriculture, the novice farmers fixed on strawberries as a healthy cash crop and granted the neighbouring farmer permission to keep his forty-three head of beef cows in their barn over the winter. In the spring, the grazing livestock scuttled the plans for Strawberry Fields Forever.

That fall, stoned out of his skull, George stumbled into the gymnasium of Upper Canada College for a five-year reunion of the Class of '65, seeking he knew not what. Narcotics had served as a salve, but not his salvation, and in his recurring dreams he never ceased aching for a place that had never existed and a time that never was. Sally's fingers pulling back the velvet curtains of his nocturnal amphitheatre, she emerged incandescent from the fortified Rosedale sally port, moving as only she moved, speaking only as she spoke, laughing as only she laughed.

He started to seriously believe that Sally had never died, that her parents had hidden her from him. Because he had never seen her body, there was room for reasonable doubt. It was no more far-fetched an idea than the moon landing was staged, or that Paul McCartney was replaced by an impersonator after he died in a 1966 car crash. A corpse lying cold and motionless in a coffin was the clos-est thing to certain truth, but inside him Sally remained warm and moving and promising and real. Rarely did a morning pass when he did not expect her to appear in the flesh at the table. Was not Orpheus, charmer of the Gods, granted a second chance?

In the spring of 1971, after six years of undergraduate work had failed to materialize into a BA, George gave up on school.

With his father's pull, George was hired as the Canadian sales rep for the Ecclesiastical Insurance Office of the Church of England, insurers of nearly every church in the world, including the Vatican. He quit within a week, telling his father he refused to live in a cage.

He landed a job as the sole sales rep for House of Anansi Press on Jarvis Street, a seedbed of Canadian cultural nationalism, founded in the Centennial Year of 1967, where the poets Dennis Lee and Margaret Atwood were emerging with seminal works. Loading his trunk with books, George covered a route of assorted bookstores, filling a steady demand; *The Circle Game*, a book of Atwood's poetry, had sold five thousand copies, the mark of a Canadian bestseller. One day, assigned the task of keeping Atwood busy, George repaired with her to the Red Lion pub, where she drank him under the table.

In high school, Sandy had dreamed of becoming a newscaster, but she was now tapping into a gift for working with fabrics and textiles. In the spring of 1972, when a mentor figure invited her to work in the Muskoka Lakes resort town of Gravenhurst, George was thrown into a panic, afraid that he would lose her if she left. They argued and bick-ered constantly—a reprise of the intense days four years earlier when

Sally had announced her trip to Europe and George had revealed his terrible dream and failed to divert her fate. Or maybe caused it.

The shadows of August 1968 reinvaded his nervous system. No one was more shocked than he to find himself on his knees, wheedling, crying and pleading, Sandy suddenly Sally. She hesitated, then agreed to marry him, pushing down the inexpressible feeling that although she loved George, she was giving in out of pity.

On April 21, 1972, George and Sandy, ages twenty-four and twenty-two, exchanged vows before a small circle of family and friends at Toronto City Hall, Stewart standing as best man. For the civil ceremony, George wore a full-length Little Lord Fauntleroy tunic, handcrafted by his bride, while she wore a gingham gown. The traditional phrase "Till death do us part" did not form part of the ritual, but four parental smiles telegraphed relief: their children no longer lived in sin.

Two years of communal living had made George feel neither better nor worse, and he knew a magical, weird time of indulging not entirely stupid/not entirely bright enterprises was running its course. None of his tribal brothers and sisters had helped him metabolize anything emotionally deep or lasting, but critically, a string of warm, alive bodies had been consistently present, containing his half-deadness in their sweetness and generosity. With Stewart he had reached a point where they no longer needed to talk; they just understood.

When George's waterbed sprang a leak—sudden screams, a scramble for a siphoning hose—he took it as a sign. Somebody in a fit of rage hurled the last chunk of hashish into the compost bucket; multiple copies of John and Yoko's "War Is Over If You Want It" posters were ripped from the walls and the Inkerman collective dissolved into a memory. Living up to its name but not its promise, the Never-Neverland farm was sold back to its original owner for the original $35,000. One by one, the communal bodies scattered. A sixties bust-up.

The original quartet, George and Sandy, Stewart and Val, regrouped and rented 48 Summerhill Gardens, tucked in a quiet cul-de-sac near the Yonge Street liquor store. Val took on an administrative job at York; like George before him, Stewart was inching across the rope bridge from school to work. Because degrees were rare in his family, he persisted.

As George struggled to conjure a career path with a pinch of personal meaning, Sandy knew, as Sally had before her, exactly where she was going. That summer, she learned that a former boyfriend was setting up an art gallery with his wife in Barrie, a town of twenty-five thousand an hour's drive north of Toronto, buying and renovating a two-storey, three-bedroom semi-detached 1890s Victorian with gingerbread trim and twelve-foot ceilings. Numbers 1 and 3 Berczy Street shared a main floor kitchen, with bedrooms upstairs and separate store spaces below. How would George like to help Sandy run a semi-rural crafts business in the smaller, adjoining space of number 3 for a dirt-cheap rent?

In August, that black dog of a month, they packed up and headed north. Stewart and Val elected to stay in Toronto until Stewart found his feet. Four years had passed since Sally's death, and while Stewart was not cutting his soul brother loose, he was negotiating the right distance.

With a neatly timed $10,000 legacy from his late unlamented insurance-broker grandfather—the one who once inflicted emotional blackmail on George's father by threatening to jump from the Bayview Bridge if he deviated from the family business—George splurged on an AMC Gremlin and pieces of utilitarian antique furniture. He and Sandy gathered store inventory of jewellery, pottery, weaving, hand-blown glass, woodwork, dolls, quilts and crocheted bedspreads. Until they could build a business, Sandy taught at Georgian College while George toiled in the basement fashioning cabinets and a pedestal desk. When the store, Artifact, finally opened in March 1973, Sandy could never have imagined that it would thrive for the next thirty-six years.

By summer's end, after a year of separation interrupted by occasional visits, Stewart and Val moved from Toronto to the town of Bradford, twenty-five miles south of Barrie; the emotional bond between Stewart and George would not be severed. Now seven months pregnant, Valerie blessed the revival of the Nice Furniture Company, prodding aimless hippie hobbyism into a sustainable enterprise; together with the birth of the crafts store and a child, maybe the foursome could actually make real the sixties artisanal dream. When Stewart bought a used Volkswagen van from a York professor, he was not immediately aware that when he rumbled into Barrie to reunite with George on a late August morning, he was delivering a mixed message of help and horror: George was elated to see his soul brother, but the very sight of the vehicle drove him back five years to an overcast West German highway.

Directly across from the store, George and Stewart discovered a vacant, long and narrow nineteenth-century, four-floor shoe factory, standing on the edge of Kempenfelt Bay with a vista of shimmering Lake Simcoe. Stewart set to work on a butternut wood cradle, finishing it just before the birth of Jessica on October 11; the young parents were delighted that their daughter, a future Crown attorney, possessed ten fingers and ten toes, clear refutation of right-wing propaganda that LSD invariably fried human chromosomes.

Within weeks, three friends, Brad, Ted and Bill, expanded the manpower of the Nice Furniture Company to five. They worked hard and harmoniously, building maple boardroom tables, kitchen cupboards in laminated pine, a cherry dining room set. The task at hand filled George's head, driving his moods into high and low and sideways places, hammering down sudden half-unwelcome thoughts of Sally. When they hit their stride, the quintet pumped out a table a day. Having removed the middle seat from the VW van to make space for their wares, they delivered orders across town, together with the feeling that they were improving one small corner of the world.

Over the summer of 1973, George's attention was riveted to the televised U.S. Senate Watergate hearings and the promise of executive criminality brought to heel; making the lying, devious bastards squirm and come clean served him as a kind of narcotic. Engrossed by the serial, what-will-happen-next political drama, he rediscovered his passion for journalism, driven darkly underground by parental disapproval and a lover's death. Having amassed boxes of newspaper clippings on the scandal, he now had a place to hang them—the 150-foot-long walls of the furniture shop—and so they were covered, from floor to ceiling. He had never lost his fascination with the way that dedicated reporters could drive the story they were covering, influencing the direction of history.

Commuting from Bradford, Stewart remained George's daily anchor. In December, George was surprised and delighted when Stewart and Val decided to move to Barrie, a few blocks from his and Sandy's place with a view of the lake, three-month-old Jessica in tow. Val landed a job with the Children's Aid Society, and the Inkerman originals were reunited.

But to Sandy's growing bewilderment, the once-aggressive rock promoter she'd married was turning into a passive furniture maker. A self-admitted Type A, Sandy was frustrated by George's phlegmatic want of motivation; he was a thinker, she a doer, and together they were failing to forge a combined vision of their future.

Relying on occasional cash bailouts from his parents, George lacked drive and may even have suffered from depression in a time and place when such labels remained unspoken. His virtues—he was quiet, thoughtful, charming, funny, handsome and good company—had counted for much, but something essential felt unplugged, no doubt sustained by the smokescreen of pot that veiled truer feelings. In the car, their petty carping and backbiting often escalated into all-out gloves-off fights, shocking backseat passengers into grim silence.

Feeling like a balloon trapped under an umbrella, Sandy struggled to break free, but George reeled her back. The moment she learned she was pregnant was the moment she fell into a rage. The weight of Sally's six-year-old ghost had failed to lift off the shoulders of her husband, and so, on a brisk autumn day, after the couple agreed on an abortion—the only option, as both were too self-involved to raise a child, too close to childhood itself—George moved into Stewart's basement. As he drove the hour south to the Wellesley Hospital in Toronto, the unrevivable relationship lodged between the couple like an invisible corpse; although a lapsed Catholic, Sandy felt the brute sting of conscience, then laid responsibility for the debacle at the feet of George. Marking their mutual capitualiation, Sandy stitched an eight-foot square wall tapestry, complete with horse and mounted knight wielding a spear, embroidered with the words, "St. George and the Dragon."

Renting a shabby one-bedroom apartment on Bayfield Street, George upped his narco-alcohol intake, lived in restaurants and crashed on the couches of friends, becoming worse and worse company. One night, barging in on Stewart and Val, he insisted on playing *Apostrophe*, the new album by Frank Zappa. The music woke up the baby, evoking such a rush of anger from loyal friends that not even his fabled charm could defuse it.

A pivotal moment came when Ted and Stewart, who were putting in eighteen-hour days working at a Toronto furniture show, happened to catch sight of the truant George, his head nestled on the shoulder of a beaming beauty behind the wheel of her red convertible. The bottom of the bucket was leaking; no amount of drugs, music or casual sex could fill him.

One night, as a passenger on a drunken joyride, George rolled toward the open back end of the speeding station wagon, a young man of unsound mind long past making love or money or war. Stewart grabbed him a split second before he fell out. It was the second time Stewart had saved his friend's life, and for the moment at least, all were spared the shock of a cracked skull reddening the black asphalt, George merging with a dead girl in the underworld.

One morning, a car pulled into the driveway to deliver something like a reprieve. Standing before George was Alison Lay, the giver of his first electric kiss on the sandy shores of Shanty Bay. She had matured into a striking brunette, seemingly unaware of the spell of her own kind gaze, and they spent the next hour catching up.

Noticing his pickup truck, Alison asked for a favour. Her late grandmother was the youngest sister of William Lyon Mackenzie King, Canada's longest-serving prime minister. His ancient Montreal estate was being broken up by his descendants. Would George drive Alison and her mother to Montreal and help with the heavy lifting? When he agreed, she produced her mother's address in Toronto. George was stunned: the Lay family home stood on Chestnut Park Road, eight houses east of Sally's place.

On the appointed morning, George appeared at their front door on a Rosedale street that had never left his memory. Mrs. Lay climbed in beside her daughter, and they headed east, straight into the teeth of a blizzard. When they reached Kingston, halfway to Montreal, police waved them off the highway. Needing to make it to Montreal that evening, the mother decided to take the train from Kingston, suggesting that Alison and George follow the next day when the roads were clear. Producing just enough cash for a single hotel room, Mrs. Lay, as if dispensing a blessing, bussed the cheek of her daughter, then George's, and caught the train.

The two found themselves occupying the front seat of a steamed-up pickup, holding hands, fourteen again, simultaneously realizing what they needed to do next.

Still, in the days to follow, George knew he was not prepared to follow Alison to Quebec, and the thought only deepened his post-Sally, post-Sandy angst. It had been six years since Sally died, but he knew that growing back the charred tendrils of human feeling obeyed no timetable.

Bleeding money from the moment of its birth, the Nice Furniture Company lacked a hard-headed business manager to staunch the flow; if David the Born Entrepreneur had stuck around, factories would be dotting South Korea by now. The five partners realized too late that Niceness Was Not Enough: they had consistently under-priced their products, unable to ask for more money.

Just as George sensed his carpentry days were history, a galvanizing figure stepped into his path. A shapely, jeans-clad, brown-eyed young woman with shoulder-length brown hair, Ronda radiated a robust sensual energy. When George looked at her, he thought, *She's out of my league*. But she looked back.

Recently split from her husband, Ronda was a talented potter who had decided to relocate in Barrie to take courses at Georgian College. As they got to know each other, she was intrigued to hear the story of George's uncanny dream presaging Sally's death. In turn, George was interested to learn that Ronda came from an affluent but brutal family where her unhinged father fired guns in random directions. She became a teenage hellion, and her parents packed her off to board at Branksome Hall for a year, two grades ahead of Sally. But she remained hard-wired to boys, booze and fast cars, hot clay refusing to conform to the shape of cool porcelain.

In late June 1975, Ronda told George she was heading for

Vancouver, en route to Australia: she wanted to see the world. When she invited him to join her, George vacillated. She scribbled down a phone number in Calgary where she would be staying with friends for a spell, and her eyes said it all: *Do come.* He told Ronda what he had told Sandy: "You need to understand that I'm still emotionally involved with a dead person."

But it proved hard to let Ronda disappear down the road. He started to construct a wooden camper, complete with bunk bed and bookshelves, for the back of his Chevy pickup truck. On Canada Day, July 1, 1975, he laid down his tools, and although he was first tempted to disappear without a word, he told Stewart and his other friends that he was heading west—dropping everything, leaving for good, splitting the scene, burning the bridges holding him up.

When he turned the key in the ignition and drove away, he suspected his loyal yet exhausted second family felt as massively relieved as he did. Since Sally's death, George had been the magnet holding them together longer than needed, most of all himself. George knew the move would make or break him, but he chose to imagine that when he hit B.C., he would clean the slate and recast himself.

In the original myth, after losing Eurydice a second time, Orpheus lingered at the brink of the Underworld for seven years. As George rumbled down the Trans-Canada Highway curving over the north shore of Lake Superior, pressing across the dead flatness of the prairies, chasing the sun falling behind the spiked wall of the Rockies, he declared his personal Seven Years War over. *Third time lucky*, he allowed himself to dream. Still, only a fool believed in the foolproof, and we are all guilty until proven innocent.

SIXTEEN

"Some Things You Will Never Know"

I n September 1972, I headed to journalism school, a one-year post-grad diploma course at the University of Western Ontario, a default position given that I could find no career listings for poets, dreamers or nihilists-in-progress. Although I admired investigative reporters who nailed the bad guys to the wall, I felt no drive to join their ranks; if anything prodded me forward, it was an aimless romance with words.

I had not lost my fear of speaking up in class, although in my off-hours I was drawn to the noisy voices of the New Journalism: Wolfe, Capote, Mailer, Talese and the Nixon-shredding gonzo madman Hunter S. Thompson. Their intensely personal authorial slant was outlawed by the traditional third-person journalism taught at Western; no wonder my essay on the sixties underground press failed to enthuse the prof. When I did not pass his course—falling precisely one point short of 50 per cent—I took it as a sign and a point of pride. I left diploma-less.

I returned home to my collapsed father and prickly, shape-shifting mother. Over the summer of 1973, while seeking a newspaper job, I was wired to the televised Senate Watergate hearings. Evasion, denial, deceit, duplicity, dissembling, whitewashing, cover-up—let us make the lies we are telling perfectly clear. Journalists must ask hard questions of Authority, but I was nowhere near up to the task. As I tentatively edged into the hurly-burly of the real world, I sensed something large and low, dark and unfinished, the mother of all untold stories, sealed inside my own nuclear family. But when I tentatively pushed on the family secrets, my mother, the ex-spy and frustrated artist, cast out a one-liner of impeccable smugness: "Some things you will never know." Perhaps one day I would muster the emotional muscle to expose the secrets of the two strangers who never wanted to have children but had us all the same.

That same summer, my brother was earning his university tuition by mowing the lawns of Mount Pleasant Cemetery, circling the tombs of famous establishment Canadians from Fred Banting to William Lyon Mackenzie King to Egerton Ryerson. Every day after work, my friend Jay and I met Mike to shoot scenes of our latest Super 8 production, titled *Fear*, set among the vaults and headstones of the century-old city of the dead that I had dubbed "the Granite Club."

We loved collecting comic names carved on the grandiose crypts—"Captain Fluke" took the cake. But one August day, our mood abruptly deepened. Mike reported that as he was clipping the edges of a knee-high headstone, one among random thousands, he glanced at the chiselled capital letters:

SALLY LYN WODEHOUSE

Over the past five years, a mix of inertia and semi-amnesia had stopped me from visiting her grave, so I experienced the coincidence as a slap. Of all the sleepers underfoot, Sally was the only one I knew.

When Mike said she was buried in plot Y, I thought he'd said, plot why? Criss-crossing the serene tree-shaded lawns, dodging the sputtering sprinklers, I moved from monument to monument until I found her. Standing before the stone, I experienced that familiar backing-up on myself, that blankness, as if I were as much an object as the stone itself. My gaze deflected off her birth and death dates, and with a suddenness that seemed involuntary, I turned and walked away.

We abandoned our film half finished.

In the fall of 1973 I started my first full-time job as a "minimum-rage" cub reporter with the *Scarborough Herald*, a family-run weekly newspaper lodged in a dingy suburban mall. On my first assignment, I was dispatched to photograph and interview a group of indigenous teenagers arriving in Union Station from the North. As my flash camera popped, they huddled together against the tiled wall, heads turned away in fear, and I had a flash of my own: maybe this wasn't the life for me.

I had no stomach for hypercompetitive, story-breaking, front-line journalism. Facing a deadline felt like marching to my execution. Unlike my peers, I thrilled not at the sight of a front-page byline. Realizing I preferred reading newspaper stories to writing them, I quit my job in the spring of 1974 and set off with Andy, a fellow reporter, to travel the world. The plan was to pick up odd jobs on the fly, imposing no limits of time or space.

Our first stop was Halifax, where I worked for several months as an assistant manager of the Odeon Casino Theatre on Gottingen Street that served the city's angry black underclass in the shadow of the Citadel. The casual references of my co-workers to "niggers" opened my eyes to Canadian racism; had I landed in a northern Alabama? The theatre manager, a pugnacious Cape Bretoner with a Grade 9 education, taught me how to befriend and disarm the black gang leaders; in exchange for not throwing rocks through our marquee window, we issued them free passes to the movies and all-you-can-eat popcorn.

My days were enlivened by ejecting glue sniffers and chasing purse snatchers. Once a month, the theatre hosted dusk-to-dawn horror movie marathons and blaxploitation flicks when eight hundred stoned, Shaft-worshipping, "kill-whitey" patrons carved up the seats with switchblades as a pair of timid beat cops failed to keep the peace.

When we'd earned enough for passage across the ocean, Andy and I pressed on to Yorkshire, the birthplace of the Industrial Revolution, where in the town of Huddersfield, I worked first as a milkman, then a warehouseman. When I slipped off the back of a lorry while unloading forty-pound sacks of sugar, I nearly pulverized my skull into jam on the concrete floor.

Andy and I slept in a grotty vermin-infested boarding house, five bunks a room, mingling with coal miners who blew their pay packets every night at the pub. One night before falling snoring-drunk into bed, his brow laced with stitches like Frankenstein's monster, my neighbour relished reporting his savage encounter with a "bottle merchant"—the generations-old practice of thrusting of a smashed pint glass into the face of the adversary. He ended with the boast, "You should see the other guy."

Andy and I bought a used Bedford van, dreaming of permanent mobility, but then he fell ill and returned home. I sold the van, bought a bicycle and moved into a smaller boarding house run by a tough-sweet socialist landlady and single mother named after the martyred revolutionary Rosa Luxemburg. She taught me how to play mah-jong, and I was adopted. Her fifteen-year-old flirt of a daughter, Sally, pretended an interest in my swelling stack of paperbacks. One evening when her mother was out, Sally invited me into her bedroom on the pretext of needing help to locate a lost school book. As she bent over the bed, even I picked up the signal. Days later in my local pub, the barkeep inquired, "So, have ye had a go at Sally yet?" In a flash I realized that others had, and I never would.

On a drizzling December Sunday, I threaded through the Yorkshire dales to the Brontë family parsonage in the time-stilled village of Haworth. I found the place deserted, and as I communed with the mossy headstones in the adjacent graveyard, I sank into my memories of *Jane Eyre* and *Wuthering Heights*.

In the empty rooms, I merged with the exquisite haunted quality, redolent of my grandfather's house. Pausing over the sofa where thirty-year-old Emily, all four feet eleven inches of her, succumbed to tuberculosis, I studied the teeth of the comb that fell from her hand with her last breath. On the nursery wallpaper, surviving from the 1820s, the four motherless genius-waifs had scribbled stories in miniscule script, birthing intense micro-worlds of fact and fantasy, Gondal and Angria, their words driving up and down the wall and into tiny books. I identified like mad with these emotionally starved children of Irish blood and felt a dark thrill as I scanned the embryonic scratchings of the masterpieces to come. How did Emily Brontë, a girl who never ventured outside of her parochial village, conceive of such a magisterial piece of art as *Wuthering Heights*, driven by the immortal character of Heathcliff, clawing obsessively at the grave of Cathy, the betrayer who chose class comfort over the wildness of the moors?

Over the spring and summer of 1975, I cycled the back roads of England, Wales and Ireland, paying homage to the literary shrines of Wordsworth, Byron, Shakespeare, Dickens, Hardy and Austen, the storytellers who had filled the empty spaces. One late afternoon after a strenuous day of pedalling, I drifted into Winchester Cathedral, once again astonished to find that I was alone. The sublime strains of evensong emerged from an unseen place, a choir of incarnate angels delivering a concert for one; dehydrated and exhausted, I gazed up into the vaulted ceiling and fell into a monkish swoon.

Cycling in the rainy wilds of County Kerry in southwestern Ireland, I was unaware I was deep in FitzGerald country, for my father had never told me where we came from. One morning, I emerged from a youth hostel to chat with a vivacious Australian of my age. As we unlocked and mounted our bikes, she complimented my 1940s brown fedora—a cast-off of my father's—and cast me a smile magnetic in its naturalness.

"I'm heading west. Which way are you going?" she wondered.

The other way, of course. But instead of shifting gears and spending a day by her side, I turned my bike in the opposite direction. I derived a subtle pleasure from her disappointment, but coasting down the hill I felt a puzzled regret. What was it with me?

For eighteen months I had survived on thick beer and greasy food, shunning the medication I needed to treat my Crohn's disease. My gut was not my friend. In a burst of loneliness under one too many Irish downpours, I realized that I could no longer sustain the vagabond life. But I also realized I would miss the milkmen, miners and forklift drivers who had accepted me into their circles as an equal, a scenario that would doubtless find no reciprocity in the dens of Rosedale and Forest Hill.

Back in Toronto, I felt I had caved in and sold out; in the words of Pablo Neruda: "He who returns has never left."

In my absence, my parents had split up. Finding work at the University of Toronto, my mother was now busy fending off assorted suitors while my father had retreated to a rented one-bedroom high-rise apartment and a full-time regimen of TV and psychiatric drugs. I viewed his choice as a sit-down strike against the expectations that had killed him in everything but body; on my infrequent visits, he regarded me like just another channel on the remote control.

I started work as a reporter for the *Port Hope Evening Guide*, the smallest daily newspaper in Canada, an hour east of Toronto. In a local bar, I was drawn to Claire, a kind school teacher. On New Year's Eve 1975, amid the debris of a party in her house, she whispered into my delighted ear, "Let's be wicked." I was twenty-five and she was thirty-two. Generously and patiently she tolerated my immature fumblings; over the winter, I felt like a long-starving Irish immigrant gratefully docking in a port of hope.

In time I would take solace from the historical roster of genius-virgins and near-genius near-virgins: Goethe failed to bed a woman till age forty, and Freud stayed celibate after age forty; T.S. Eliot was asexual when he married at twenty-six, and maybe thereafter; G.B. Shaw lived with his mother until forty-two, then lived an unconsummated marriage. A pioneering expert on sex, Havelock Ellis likely never had any; a passel of brainiacs from Immanuel Kant and Isaac Newton to Henry James and John Ruskin were all virgins and celibates, or so it was said. When I eventually learned that even Pierre Trudeau and John Cleese did not lose it till the age of twenty-five, I counted myself in good company.

One night, as Claire sat up reading in bed, she risked a moment of deeper intimacy. "I think you really do like me," she said. I did, but I could not bring myself to say it aloud and, cut off from my own terror, I did not realize my unconscious mind was now plotting the beginning of the end. To me, liking, lusting and loving formed a confusing trio, and sadly, even two out of three was more than I could handle, even with a warm, open-hearted woman like Claire. I quit the paper.

Back in Toronto, I drove a cab, then worked half-heartedly on a medical journal. I binge drank and committed regular acts of parapraxis: fender benders, knocking over drinks in bars, blurting cringeworthy faux pas. I pretended I was not receding into the darkness.

With my brother and Jay, I rented Elmbank, a stone farmhouse on a semi-rural branch of the Humber River built by my pioneering maternal Scots ancestors in 1834 that survived as one of the oldest houses in Toronto. The family had sold the property in the 1890s during an economic depression, and my grandmother—the one who paid for the Odyssey—had recently bought it back. We threw dance parties so energetic that the planks of the original hardwood floors, the fireplaces and sash windows vibrated under our feet, even as the voice of Eric Clapton courted the Victorian and contemporary ghosts:

> *Lay down, Sally, no need to leave so soon.*
> *I've been trying all night long just to talk to you.*

We threw a one-day, $10-a-head, jazz and blues festival on the grounds, complete with bleachers, tents, kegs of beer and pots of hot dogs. Scouting out talent at Grossman's Tavern on Spadina Avenue, we hired bands with names like the Original Sloth Band and Kid Bastien's Happy Pals to perform. Jammed into the pie-shaped acre-and-a-half property, three hundred people danced and drank and toked and shagged in the woods in a mini-Woodstock we captured on our Super 8 cameras. Because her father was born in the house in 1882, our mother felt entitled to crash our parties. One minute she longed to join the revelry, trolling for a hit of a passing joint; the next minute she turned gorgon, quoting Old Testament scripture— "Honour thy mother and father."

The dance floor of my young life was more crowded than I knew.

George and Sandy, 7 Inkerman Street, Toronto, 1971

Stewart, 7 Inkerman Street, 1971

George, 7 Inkerman Street, 1971

PART IV

We are all geniuses when we dream, the butcher's
the poet's equal there.

—EMIL CIORAN, *The Temptation to Exist*

 X

SEVENTEEN

The Long Goodbye

After parking his green Chevy truck beside a gas station phone booth in Calgary, Alberta, George dialled the number Ronda had given him. Through the Plexiglas, he scanned the cloud-capped teeth of the Rocky Mountains, eighty miles distant, as on the other end of the line Ronda told him how glad she was that he had come.

Moving on to Vancouver together, they merged with the shaggy influx: the refugees and refuseniks, the dreamers and the disgruntled, the gentle and the bold, the deadbeats and the live wires, the draft dodgers and the ban the bombers, the charismatic and crazy, naïfs and desperados, nudists and Buddhists, vegans and dopers, tree huggers and whale watchers, each in his or her own way splitting from bad families, bad scenes, bad vibes, bad winters, bad news. The population of the city had recently topped a million, a growth spurt driven by the sixties boom. In their restless, homeless drivenness, they were not so much running away, they told themselves, but running toward.

British Columbia. Before Christ. Before the Crash.

Dropping her plans for Australia, Ronda shacked up with George at 1274 Barclay Street, an old lumber-baron mansion that had been broken up into apartments, and together they started to assemble something half-resembling an adult life. Staring into the mirror one morning, George found streaks of silver in his brown hair; within days, his entire twenty-eight-year-old head and beard turned grey as a winter sky. George was unfazed, even pleased, by the sudden skipping of an entire developmental stage.

Sally had remained a fitful, murky presence in his dreams. Then one night she burst before him spectacularly alive, real, radiant. He gazed into her eyes, and as she opened her mouth to speak, instead of words a rainbow of erotic, psychedelic colours gushed out, the arc seeming to connect heaven and earth. Waking, he wondered, *If this is a sign, what does it mean?*

Ronda enrolled in the pottery program in the Emily Carr Institute of Art and Design, and George found a job at the new CBC-TV building on Hamilton Street, employed not as a journalist but a carpenter by the institution he had worshipped as a kid. In workshops three floors below ground level, George steeped himself in the art of scenic carpentry for various shows and specials featuring Juliette or Blood, Sweat and Tears.

On the set of Canada's first late-night TV talk show, *90 Minutes Live*, temporarily imported from Toronto, George built the desk for the host, Peter Gzowski, a radio star whose transition to the tube failed to divert Canadians from their habitually early bedtimes. Still, as George lingered backstage, he thought, *I could do that*. But he wasn't ready yet.

George and Ronda began to buy, renovate and flip a series of houses as a path to early retirement. Scrounging money from various sources, they acquired a fixer-upper in Kitsilano, living in the gutted shell while they worked. One day George noticed an ad for a six-hundred-square-foot cabin with a wood stove in the wilds of West Vancouver, two blocks from the ocean and twenty minutes from downtown. Racing out to 5410 Keith Road, he snared the place on the spot for $45,000 without consulting his partner. Fortunately, Ronda loved it as much as he did.

Built in 1918 on a dead-end survey road by a free-spirited young war widow named Lillian, the cabin sat on a triangle-shaped half-acre lot near Lighthouse Park; with its stands of one-hundred-and-fifty-foot cedars and Douglas fir and a set of rolling terraces shaded by an eight-hundred-foot cliff, the place was a lost-in-the-woods oasis where they caught glimpses of deer and bear. In the garage, George built a gas-fired pottery kiln for Ronda, where she made and sold her wares. The property was overgrown with blackberry bushes, and they would spend the next two years hacking it all back, like a bad childhood, gradually revealing Lillian's 1920s English garden of roses and lilies.

At Christmas, the two flew to Toronto for the holidays. George's worldly possessions—books, records, handmade furniture—were still stored in his parents' garage, so he built a ten-foot shipping crate to pack them all in. On the January morning in 1976 when the crate landed like a giant coffin on his B.C. driveway, he knew he was never moving back east.

After two years in a permanent part-time position, George approached his boss, Gilbert Mitchell, an Alberta cowboy who could pass for a Hollywood character actor, and asked to work full-time. Gilbert responded with a blunt challenge that George would later acknowledge as pivotal: "Don't settle for this life, George. Use your brains."

Feeling like a child standing outside his parents' bedroom door, George teetered on the threshold of the newsroom: dare he set foot in there? Two days later, he was allowed to edit Canadian Press wire copy and type it into the teleprompter for the on-air newsreader. For two months, he juggled two jobs, moving up from the windowless production studios underground into the sunlit main floor news-room; descending and ascending, he hammered sets by day, copy by night. Then the news editor gave George a second push: "You've got talent. Go to journalism school."

On June 2, 1977, his thirtieth birthday, parked on a barstool in the Sandman Inn across the street from the CBC, George drank beer and wondered, *Do I coast or climb? Pass and surpass my father? Become more than an engaging nobody? Can I be somebody and still be myself?* When at sixteen he'd told his parents that he wanted to break the fourth-generational chain of Upper Canadian Georges, quit school after Grade 12 and study journalism, their response—"You are disgrace to the family!"—stopped him like a bullet to the head.

Slamming his fist on bar, he resolved to catch up to his younger, wiser self. Changing his life, his death. Sigmund Freud believed true happiness sprang from the adult fulfillment of a forgotten or deferred childhood wish; that's why money did not ensure true happiness, for children did not wish for money. When they jumped, it was for joy.

Enrolling in a two-year broadcast journalism program at the British Columbia Institute of Technology, George discovered he was eas-ily the oldest student. Grizzled, bottle-in-the-desk-drawer veterans of radio and TV were not born teachers, but they drilled him use-fully, if tediously, in the technological pragmatics of deadline-driven newsgathering.

Graduating in 1979, he lucked into a job as a stringer with CKNW Radio; the station had never hired anybody out of school, but George's grey-haired gravitas created a precedent. The largest station in western Canada, it ran a dynamic, imaginative news operation, a rotation of thirty editors and reporters churning out newscasts every half hour, twenty-four hours a day. At first, George fell back into his cell of self-doubt. Then the news director, Warren Barker, delivered the advice he would never forget: "Don't ever confess your rookie incapacities to anyone. Keep your cards close to the vest; you're bright and you'll figure it out."

Jumping into a white Ford sedan equipped with a two-way radio and the bold block letters NEWS painted on the doors, George cruised the streets of the city. Fake it until you make it. Traffic accidents, forest fires, shipwrecks, typhoons, strikes, toxic spills, holdups, rapes, homicides, suicides, parricides, political scandal, human interest—he sweated out twelve-hour days, six days a week, often not returning home till breakfast. Typically putting in several hours to create a single, forty-second, hundred-word spot on-air, he pared his sentences to the bone, choosing nouns as pictures, verbs as actions, presenting the facts as visual poetry, speaking directly to the gut of his listeners.

Unlike most cub reporters, he had been gored by the world. But he loved the fact that no one knew who he was, or where he came from, nor cared. He crafted a sardonic, on-air James Bond persona that made him feel invulnerable. He disinterred his buried competitive streak, and it was a beast. It turned out that he loved winning, and hard news was a measurable, competitive, goal-scoring enterprise. At the same time, he was never rude or abrasive, falling back on his mother-trained politeness, his lending of a sympathetic ear broadening the dimensions of the story.

He felt as if he was on a mission to tell the story first. It was not unlike war, long stretches of boredom punctuated by sudden detonations: staking out numbingly protracted labour negotiations in a hotel room, then jolted by the wail of a passing ambulance. One morning, he interviewed Miss America, an adorable little ice princess; that afternoon, he met the activist Elie Wiesel, author of *Night*, his memoir of surviving Auschwitz, and as George listened to the warm soul with the engaging smile and tattooed forearm, destined for a Nobel Peace

Prize, he thought, *I'm in the right business.* As a teenager, Wiesel had endured one of the most unspeakable experiences of the century, yet emerged an exemplary man. *That's a story*, George realized, *and there are stories everywhere.*

It was a dream job.

After a frenetic workday infused with acidic cups of coffee and drags of Camel cigarettes, George needed a counteracting bring-down that he found in booze. Sometimes, driving home across the Lions Gate Bridge, he saw three swaying bridges and threaded slowly through the middle one. On the hangover-hating return trip the next morning, he worried he was becoming his father. But he told himself he was different: he could handle the stress and control the drinking.

Still, George felt that he was not fully part of the world but parked off to the side, watching from a safe place. He managed his emotions, for he knew what devastation felt like. The journalist-observer was a predatory, parasitic creature, but how else to function? A feeling of invincibility came with the job—the ability to build a brick wall, putty the cracks and distance the pain.

Within such a frame he could place Sally, and he found a pinch of solace there. In 1968, he tried to capture his teenage passion in an article for *Seventeen* magazine and had mailed her a draft when she was in Europe; the most powerful story in his life, the mother of all stories, was the one he could not bear or dare finish, for the ending never changed. He could never forget how Sally's cremation denied him a last sight of her body, and for the longest time he awoke from dreams in a trickling sweat, believing he was the victim of a horribly elaborate conspiracy, that on July 2, 1968, the Wodehouses had plotted to spirit Sally away from him, that her Odyssey trip was a cover story, that her death was staged, that she was living a secret life in a secret place where he would never, ever find her.

For over a decade, he'd lugged from place to place the Sally Archives—letters, photos, mementos—contained in a cardboard box. In an idle moment, he might pick up a letter, scan the traces of her moving hand, then drop the pages as if he'd scalded his fingers on a stove. One day, his eyes fell on the photograph of his twenty-year-old tuxedoed self, standing beside Sally, slim and glowing and promising in her white gloves and formal gown, and a lost "what-if" world pierced his chest like a flung dart. He wanted to burn the box as passionately as he wanted to preserve it.

EIGHTEEN

The Cold Black Yonder

I n August 1978, the tenth anniversary of our Odyssey, I was the prime mover behind a reunion party. What compelled me to capture a block of time under the heading of a rounded numeral? Maybe it was a simple equation: if I don't remember, I don't exist.

I'd lost contact with most of the out-of-towners, and I failed to unearth many of their new addresses and phone numbers. Only ten of the twenty-six showed—Sean, Dave, Ross, Marywinn, Barb, John, Nan, Robin and Annabel. A decade on, I remained more enamoured with a body of people than a single body.

Many of the group had married, were starting families and heading down dedicated career paths. Even as I was touched by the sight of Nan cradling a baby daughter in her arms, the thought of "settling down" was beyond imagining. As we assembled for the obligatory group photograph, I was conscious that I was forcing something.

I had recently been transfixed by *21 Up*, the latest instalment of Michael Apted's Seven Up documentary film series in which he was tracking the lives of fourteen English schoolchildren drawn from across the spectrum of the class system. He started in 1964, when they were seven, and was recording their progress every seventh year. One scene had taken up permanent residence in my mind: the trajectory of a Latin-quoting upper-class toff had been so seamlessly shaped by the parental board of control that in a clipped prep-school accent the boy politely declined to participate in the remainder of the series. What was the point when life was preordained?

Over the years I had stayed in touch with Nick, now running his own European travel business, the Upper Canada Study Society, founded after the demise of the Odyssey in 1970. In a freak snow-storm on April 7, 1977, numbing our hams on aluminum bleachers, he and I witnessed the inaugural game of the nascent Toronto Blue Jays baseball franchise, and occasionally I would pinch-hit on Nick's champion pub-quiz league team, his fluid erudition leaving me in the dust. He remained the same witty, wide-awake, protective older brother figure in my life, but we had never opened the cellar door marked "Sally." Even as I tried to bottle the Odyssey vibe, a strange brew of the exultant and the catastrophic, I knew I was straining for an unrepeatable experience. The sixties were never coming back, and neither was Sally. But if I kept the magic bus rolling, could I orches-trate a different ending?

Maggie, my boss on the medical journal, correctly perceived that I was a twenty-seven-year-old overburdened by the past, strangling his potential by slow degrees. Through her influence I began cautiously prospecting Therafields, a therapeutic community born in the early 1960s, its core composed of groups living in Edwardian brick houses in the Annex neighbourhood of the city.

I learned that many of its therapists were brilliant apostate Catholic priests and nuns busy breaking their vows of celibacy while wedding liberation theology to depth psychology. They believed the overly rigid institutions of family, school and church no longer served the welfare of the young and sought to tap the energy of the collective to restore a balance. In addition to its houses in the city, the community ran marathon group therapy weekends that unfolded on an organic farm in the Hockley Valley north of the city. One weekend, Maggie invited me to a literary event at the farm. Although I was drawn to the concentration of long-haired poets, teachers and artists, the sixties anti-psychiatry sensibility espoused by the Scottish psychiatrist R.D. Laing, the respect for the restorative power of dreams and the unconscious mind, a cultish "us and them" vibe turned me off.

On May 24, 1979, Queen Victoria's birthday and a week before our fourth annual Elmbank Jazz festival, Jay died in his sleep. That he disappeared at the axial age of twenty-seven, as he often predicted, as we so often laughed off, doubled the shock. The autopsy found no trace of a drug overdose, although that's how most chose to explain his mysterious exit; we invent answers when none are present.

Days after the funeral, three hundred people gathered for our backyard festival, and I was spirited back eleven years to the courtyard of the Paris hotel and the surreal hours after Sally's death. As we chattered and drank and danced to the trumpets and clarinets, drums and guitars, an elephant lumbered across the grass: Jay now slept under a small stone in Mount Pleasant Cemetery, not far from Sally, the place where we abandoned *Fear*, our irreverent, death-defying film.

Months later, my maternal grandmother, Mabel, died at ninety-three. Despite her annual doling out of birthday cheques, her bankrolling of my private education and the Odyssey, I failed to summon the sadness, love and gratitude I was made to feel I should. Strange to realize her part in my destiny: without her money, I would never have fallen for Sally.

My routine Sunday visits to my grandparents' three-storey redbrick house at 21 Delisle Avenue had given me something else: a free pass into the museum of my mother's childhood and the chance to solve the Rubik's Cube that was her character. How was it possible that my dynamic, protean, thoroughly modern mother—aesthete, world traveller, interior decorator, gardener, photographer, book-keeper, fashion plate, sophisticate, wit, spy—had incubated in this stifling mausoleum?

My head recorded like a silent-film camera the rooms and objects of my mother's 1920s childhood: the giant sack of birdseed in the dank basement, the hand-carved, lion-headed arms of the Edwardian sofa set against the sickly yellow wallpaper, the elevator door of the dumb waiter, the foot-buzzer concealed under the dining room carpet to summon the kitchen help, the spooky third floor straight out of a Brontë novel.

I pictured my mother as an exotic bird of a little girl, flying into precocious puberty and adolescence, boobs and gams busting out all over, attracting envy, male and female alike, for her beauty and intelligence. Her fervent wish to attend the Slade School of Art was stopped dead by paternal command; her acquiescence, her failure to honour her own rebel heart, spelled the beginning of the end.

When my mother's mother solemnly pressed a Bible into my hands on my fourteenth birthday, the message was clear: in this stilted, TV-less tomb of mothballs and lace curtains, Jesus outranked the Beatles. Yet neither here nor at home did I ever hear the word "love" passing through human lips, no gestures, no hugs, no kisses, no tender touch to give language flesh or meaning.

The hatchet face of my imposing maternal grandfather gave even less away; all I knew was that he spared no time for me beyond occasional random, scalding scoldings. Only my precocious sister could find the feather to enliven that cadaver, and I could almost hear the face of Mount Rushmore crack when he surrendered to a fleeting smile. When his youngest daughter married my father—the young doctor from an eminent medical family—the groom was made to feel he was not good enough for her, and he refused to set foot in the house of his in-laws again. For this boycott, my father eventually earned my sidelong respect.

One day, my mother let slip a story that cast a ribbon of light on the dark seams of a childhood she had idealized. Except for a stint in the army, her middle-aged bachelor brother, Dave, my godfather, had lived under his parents' roof for his entire life. On an early Saturday morning visit, my mother revealed, she found her silver-bearded brother in the living room, astride his childhood rocking horse.

In 1979 I backed out of journalism altogether and joined the less-stressful promotion department of the book publishing firm of Holt, Rinehart & Winston, an American-owned branch plant. My mother made it clear that she thought my change of course into a more feminized world rendered me unfit for the grit of a real man's job. Yet even in publishing, the macho men dominated the executive positions and reverence for books as precious cultural objects seemed nowhere to be found. "As long as the dogs are eating the dog food," pronounced our Darth Vaderesque sales manager. Executives and secretaries, editors and sales staff, married and single, coupled and decoupled with the checkmating moves of a chessboard. I confined myself to a tight box of a cubicle where I ground out even tighter promotional squibs for the company catalogue; escorting touring authors to radio and TV stations to pontificate on their new books, I allowed myself a brief thought: *I could do that*. But I didn't.

One night at a party, catching the eye of a tall, unknown woman across the dance floor, I resolved to seduce her. I was struck by how readily I assumed the role of Casanova for the first time, as if flicking a light switch. The next morning, as I turned a cold shoulder to my disillusioned prey, she scribbled in red ink on a piece of news-print, like a headline: "A woman is like a bus." If her intention was to induce guilt and shame, it worked.

At a pre-wedding stag party for a UCC old boy in a penthouse suite of a downtown hotel, my moral education deepened. Anticipating booze, stud poker and sports banter, I was not prepared for the entrance of two prostitutes, no older than twenty, hired to inflict public acts of sex on the unsuspecting groom.

I was struck by the equanimity of the naked women, the agitation of the clothed men, and I felt for the visibly mortified victim, forced by the intoxicated chants of his "mates" to strip down and submit to his humiliation. Under the leering gaze of twenty suits and ties, the rite of passage mercifully expired within seconds.

I should have left on the spot, but I stayed put, disgusted by my own voyeurism. Over the next two hours, the women took on a receiving line of old boys in an adjoining bedroom at $50 a head, likely unaware of how they served as a homosexual bridge among and between the brotherhood. As the two women prepared to leave, one realized that the heel of her pump had been broken off and she erupted into a rage. Several of the men returned a blitzkrieg of a verbal gang rape—"Fucking bitch! Whore!"—and I took my cue to split.

In the morning, I picked up the phone to hear the voice of the groom: "James, you were the sanest man there last night. What did I do?" I was amazed that he noticed I was noticing. Under the sewer grate of my continuing Upper Canadian upbringing, I tucked yet another Lesson Learned: in their collusive, camouflaged terror of the Big Bad Mother, old boys will be old boys.

Standing on first base during a company softball game, I met Linda, a brown-eyed, curly-haired single mother of two sweet-tempered kids, ages seven and five. I was charmed by the combination of her relaxed ways and the sexy gap between her front teeth; maybe I could resolve my triangle drama by going for a quadrangle.

But when, months later, Linda and I moved into a townhouse in the suburb of Mississauga, I was blindsided by the magnitude of what I was taking on. Over a nine-month stretch, the kids grew to accept and love me as their new father. One night I made an unprecedented leap of intimacy when I whispered into Linda's ear, "I adore you." A look of alarm crossed her face, or so I imagined, and a Sally-like kiss of death slipped into the bedroom.

A short time later, smelling blood, my mother moved in for the kill. As Linda and I drove home from a Sunday family gathering, Linda looked as if she had been hit by a bus. After a long silence, she turned and asked, "Do you know what your mother just said to me?"

I cringed in anticipation.

"'You've done a nice job with James, but he's a dreamer and a loser.'"

My first impulse was to defend my mother.

Over a hellish Christmas, Linda revealed that she was warming to the advances of her boss, and I surrendered to a feeling of inevitability. Sitting on one of the kids' bunk beds for the last time, I tried to soften the blow: "I'm not going to see you for a long time."

"You mean ten years?" the boy wondered aloud, stretching his arms to the imagined length of a decade, and I felt my heart blaze, then freeze, with guilt. Giving them each a last kiss, I turned off the lights, and closed the door. In the chill of the January night, I glanced back at the window of the children's bedroom, and I was hit with an ancient agony, a buried memory of a boy lost in the cold black yonder, beyond stark, beyond bleak, beyond desolation, beyond abandonment, beyond all beyonds. If I hoped to keep breathing, I had to once again muster the will to kill that unbearable feeling. As I turned the ignition of the car, I welcomed the rescue of the neutralizing voice—*Cut your losses and drive on; no one will ever know*—and I retreated to the familiar well-lit surfaces where no sensation lived.

On the rebound from Linda and the kids, at a party I met Ann, a palliative care nurse of Scots blood and waist-length black hair who wore her abundant passion on her sleeve. Sally, of course, had been destined for nursing, and in the moment when Ann and I fell into bed in my downtown bachelor apartment, lust turned to stone.

We continued dating, broke off, then reunited. As we returned on a city bus from a day trip to the Toronto Islands, the sight of a shuffling, balding passenger with glasses, fumbling to deposit his fare, conjured my father, hibernating in his cave, plugged into the boob tube.

"Oh, God, that's me not too far down the road. Losing my hair—then my mind."

"I'll still love you," murmured Ann.

I shot back: "Don't!"

She buried her face in her hands and wept. I had not grasped it yet, but I was playing the Dickensian role of Estella in reverse, revenging myself on the female sex.

Ann knitted me a red-and-blue wool sweater with the *S* of Superman on the chest, which I took as a Lois Lane slap to the "Clark Can't" side of my face. As with Linda only months earlier, I penned Ann a eulogy to our relationship in the form of a letter and left her. It was still easier to write than speak.

Something was happening here, but I didn't know what it was. Only in the days to come, as I tasted an acidic edge to my daily interactions with others, did I sense something much larger, deeper, something altogether else, something I had not yet dared to attach to a name: blind rage.

NINETEEN

TV Dreams

The best years of George's life were spent at CKNW. But once he'd mastered the hot medium of radio, he felt it was time to tackle the cool visuals of television. In the spring of 1982, he joined Channel 13, a private TV station with 100,000 viewers. Standing on street corners in wind and rain, he fashioned a live-to-air face, catching the countdown of the studio voice in his earpiece, determined not to flub his lines, for now he was being heard *and* seen.

At a jammed press conference, he encountered a federal Liberal cabinet minister, Robert Kaplan, the man for whom he'd cast his first vote as a twenty-one-year-old in June 1968. Within the scrum of reporters, there was a tendency to play it safe: let the competitor ask the difficult question, risk appearing wrong or stupid and suffer the flip putdown of the smug politician. But George figured that if journalists served the public trust, they must never be cowed. As Kaplan skirted an issue of cable TV regulations, George shouted, "Excuse me, that's a lie!" As the politician mumbled to his handlers and left, the phalanx of cameras turned on George, and for a moment he was the story. He was forging an existential code: never let the powerful, from parents to teachers to politicians, control the narrative. Only God was unavailable for comment.

Now seven years into their relationship, George and Ronda, each burned by a divorce, continued to embrace a mutual disdain of matrimony. But then an unexpected pregnancy changed everything, and that spring of 1982 he stood with Ronda before the altar of St. Francis-in-the-Wood, an Anglican church in West Vancouver. Stewart and Valerie flew in from Ontario for the wedding. When he left Barrie in 1975, George had waited a year before contacting them, ashamed of how he had abused the good graces of his old friends who for seven years stood as emotional substitutes for Sally. But the old bond ran too deep to be permanently broken.

Ronda's pregnancy was arduous, their son born prematurely at four pounds on August 8, 1982. After spending two months in an incubator, George Nicholas Orr happily emerged as a robust, healthy boy, a strength that would play out in his insistence that although he was the fifth-generation male Orr to bear the name of George, he would answer only to Nick. Their daughter, Lily, born on May 25, 1984, was named in homage to Lillian, the widowed builder of the Keith Road cabin.

As the father of a growing family, George felt his ambitions intensify. When CBC-TV cleaned house in the wake of a lawsuit over an erroneously reported story on an influence-peddling politician, he was hired as an assignment editor and forged a new skill: deploying troops into battle. He closely eyed the competition, BCTV, which pulled in an astonishing 700,000 viewers in a province of two million, the largest single audience share in North America. How did they do it?

One day in 1985, he called his direct competitor: "If I can beat you every day for a month, will you hire me?" George delivered and moved over to take a job as an assignment editor in the CTV building on Enterprise Avenue in Burnaby. He was scaling the money-and-status beanstalk.

His one-year stint at CTV skidded to a halt in 1986 when his boss, driven by a blend of heartlessness and a peerless news instinct, crossed a line. In pursuit of a story, a helicopter was hovering over a man pinned under a tree in the mountains, and the newsman on board radioed George for permission to land and help the victim. When George relayed the message to his boss, he replied, "Our job is to cover the news, not save people. Tell him to shoot it and get back here pronto." George had been thinking of quitting, and now his moral idiot of a superior had provided a pretext.

Returning to the CBC, he was quickly promoted to producer of the nightly six o'clock news. Sent on a marathon forty-two-day training course in Toronto led by Donald Brittain, the legendary National Film Board documentary director and producer, he felt inspired and galvanized, a dissonant experience in a city he had long linked to slow suffocation.

A few days before flying home, George was driving down Mount Pleasant, the avenue of bottomless dreams. At his side sat Ronda, who had been vacationing with the kids in cottage country; Nick and Lily, now four and two, were safely belted in the back seat. Impulsively George swerved through the cemetery gates and pulled up to plot Y, last seen in the fall of 1968, eighteen years earlier. He stepped out, but Ronda stayed in the car. She knew where he was going.

As a producer, George embraced each morning with the words, "I have no idea what's going to happen today." Dispersing news trucks and helicopters across the Lower Mainland, he "juggled the Jell-O," as the raw material flowed in over the morning and afternoon, chopping stories into tight segments in the race toward the immovable deadline. The job demanded the multi-tasking instant-response skills of an air-traffic controller: fluidity, dynamism, decisiveness, adaptability, stamina.

On the morning when he learned that a stricken 747 airliner was flying in from China with a broken undercarriage, dumping fuel over the Pacific, he didn't waste a second. Deploying seven cameramen to the airport, he savoured a twisted thought: *If it crashes, I can sell the tape and retire.* In his head he brilliantly directed from every conceivable angle a perfectly framed, giving-the-people-what-they-want film spectacular: the slow, doom-shadowed descent onto the foam-covered bed of the concrete runway, the apocalyptic Hollywood crash, the livid fireball, the crushed fuselage and severed wings, the screaming crimson fire trucks and ambulances, the riveting chain of master shots and close-ups, the whole hypnotic theatre of total human disaster and its aftermath, an award-winning blockbuster that, alas, failed to deliver: "Fuck, they landed!"

In a moment of serendipity, George one day caught a news item that the Calgary city council had received as a gift the bell of the HMCS *Calgary*, the corvette on which his father had served in the North Atlantic. George knew it was a mistake because his father possessed the real bell. He phoned the mayor of Calgary to set him straight, then called the CBC *National* newsroom in Toronto. When a camera crew appeared in the living room of 189 Gordon Road, Mac Orr was thrilled to authenticate his ownership of the bell and spread his war stories across Canada, his first and last time on TV.

For George, the real story turned on an emerging moment of truth. For decades his parents had tagged him as "poor George," the unrealized lawyer/politician/businessman who had settled for the apostate life of a hippie carpenter, a lowly tradesman who worked with his hands, giving the finger to the Upper Canadian gentry. But with the appearance of a national news team in the place where he lived, Commander Orr saw his son in a new light: a maker of waves, a man of influence, a force, a big wheel. For George, the bell rang cleanly in his head. The son who had once looked up to his war-hero father now looked down; the father who had once looked down on his disappointment of a son now looked up. If there was a moment when they saw eye to eye, it lasted but a blink.

When Mac retired from the family firm in 1987, he visited his newly respected son in Vancouver. He was much taken with the soft green climate, the winter-blooming flowers, the over-the-rainbow independent utopia of "Cascadia" filled with ex-Easterners freed of the freight of their eastern-ness. While driving drunk in an elite neighbourhood of West Vancouver, Mac was pulled over by a policeman. When he mouthed the magic words, "Be careful, my son is a CBC producer," the cop let him off with a warning.

Back in Toronto, Mac and Dorothy asked George to shoot a video of a house in Horseshoe Bay, only five minutes away from George's Copper Cove Road home: they were thinking of leaving Toronto and relocating not only to Vancouver but to their son's very own neighbourhood. When they bought the house, George experienced serial rushes of shock, bewilderment and anger, but he could not bring himself to forbid the gross intrusion.

Naturally, he felt compassion too. Childhood sweethearts, his parents had passed their entire lives in Lawrence Park and York Mills, prisoners of social convention. They had finally got it: maybe the sky will not fall if we do what we want. At first, his mother needed persuading: uprooting from a lifelong network of friends was no small feat. But George thought it was the bravest thing she had ever done, and so, weirdly, he realized that years after striking out west, he had liberated his parents too.

Buying a second-hand cabin cruiser with a smoke-leaking engine, Mac ploughed up and down Howe Sound reliving the myth of his naval days. On the occasions when George joined his father on board for drinks, he was struck by a familiar feeling of detachment: Who is this guy? Why am I here? Why is he here? He sensed his father's loneliness, made plain by his parents' refusal to babysit their young grandchildren, Nick and Lily. Children remained messy, noisy little

creatures, best unseen and unheard. Over Christmas dinner, when
Dorothy was vexed by the rambunctious play of the kids, Ronda
confronted her mother-in-law. Caught in the crossfire between an
outlaw hippie wife and a Victorian-stiff mother of equal willfulness,
George swivelled from one face to the other, beached in the middle
of nowhere.

In April 1989, George was fired by the CBC, one of many casualties
of cost-cutting. When he returned to his office, he found his possessions stuffed in a cardboard carton, but one was lined with silver: he
figured that if he had not been shown the door, alcoholism would
have dropped him into a larger body-fitting box. He soon landed a
job teaching journalism, starting in September, and the buyout package included 120 days of unused paid vacation that allowed him to
dry out over the summer.

But now he was at home all day, face to face with Ronda, and his
presence struck them both as worse than his absence: George's
intense, decade-long affair with current affairs had stolen his passion for his partner. One evening, Ronda waved a magazine article
on the adult children of alcoholics in his face: as if awakened from a
spell, she recognized herself and the scars of her father's booze-
fuelled oppression. She began to attend meetings, which in George's
eyes made her a better mother but a worse partner. She'd resented
his overworking and overdrinking and the intrusion of his parents;
he resented her accusation that he in any way resembled her father.

When Ronda proposed couples' therapy, George thought she
was plotting an exit strategy, assuming that he, like most men, would
resist help. In fact, he wanted to save the union. When, after two
months of one-way anger, the female therapist tactfully invited more
give and take, Ronda threw in the towel. George stayed on; when the
therapist confronted him over the fact that he was an alcoholic,

the-man-who-will-not-be-told-what-to-do retorted, "No I'm not."
After a time, he quit therapy—and drinking.

The coming-apart of the marriage was horrible. In the Greek
myth transplanted to British Columbia, Orpheus, tied to the dead
Eurydice by his prolonged grief, was torn to pieces by the enraged
Furies, and Ronda was nothing if not furious. When it seemed she
might move away with the kids, George panicked and gave her
everything she asked for. More than anything, he could not bear
losing the children.

Ronda went back to school while George moved into a rented
apartment; flung back to ground zero, he found much to contemplate. The parental invasion, followed by the sudden firing and the
family breakup, threatened to rekindle the crisis that had nearly
killed him in 1968, when Sally died. When you were a silver-haired
forty-two-year-old man encircled by aging, clinging parents, an
angry ex, needy kids of seven and five whose normal developmental
tantrums you overcontrolled as if your own; when you were once
a humble carpenter who dreamed his way westward to stake out a
patch of freedom on Easy Street, living life his own way, only to find
his shoulder harnessed to the wheel; when you were ashamed to be
still haunted by the ghost of a long-dead girl; when you were all of
these things, all at once, you were a man at risk.

In his compulsion to get it right at work, he got it wrong at home.
But wasn't he dead right when he'd dreamed the fate of Sally? If her
ghost killed his first marriage outright, she was at least a guilty co-
conspirator in the demise of his second. But in the ashes of his life, he
discerned a seed.

TWENTY

Something Has Got to Give

My denial of my situation had grown so all-consuming that even I could no longer deny it. The bodies were piling up, the back-to-back losses of Linda and Ann heading back down the highway to Sally; I was the unconfessed serial killer of the ones I loved, a failed idealist, a chronic cynic, blocked writer, and it was a toss-up whether I would ever again find value in human effort or desire.

Awakening one morning, I recalled the loving face of Linda's son, confused by my abrupt departure from his world, and felt a spike of honest pain. I was living three feet north of my body and it was time to move back in; time to confront myself; time to give myself the time of day.

The damage inflicted on my hapless father by the drug-and-shock troops of conventional psychiatry had made me wary of seeking help. But now I saw a shaft of daylight: Therafields, the grassroots lay therapeutic communal experiment that I had cased five years earlier had recently disbanded and planned to open a formal training school on Dupont Street devoted to individual and group work. No self-serving cult would have packed it in.

The community took the soundest thinking of the sixties and ran with it. Unbound by dogma or ideology, their unorthodox philosophy drew on an eclectic Canadian-style synthesis of Freud, Jung, Klein, Winnicott, Reich, Laing, Sullivan, Bowlby, Kohut, Fairbairn, Bion et al. From the trenches of a long collective experiment, they had developed a working method that was psychodynamic, bioenergetic, nutritional, interactive, humanistic and non-medical. They respected the power of dreams, transference and resistance. I decided if talk therapy was good enough for John Cleese, it was good enough for me. The spawn of a spineless father and a monstrously manipulative mother, Cleese once said that what he most derived from his therapy was that he no longer feared the intensity of his own feelings.

In my screening interview in the fall of 1983, I was asked if I wanted to work with a man or woman. *A man, give me a real man; I don't know who I am.* On the night before my first session, I dreamed I was sitting on a hill in a leather swivel chair of the talk-show variety, facing my mother and Peter, my assigned, still-unmet therapist. Turning to him, I pointed to my mother: "Tell her to leave me alone." My mother was right about my being a dreamer but not in the way she meant.

We met in the basement office of Peter's home, and I basked in his wise tough-tender regard. For the first time I began to feel safe in the presence of a male elder, a paradoxical safety that would, in time, allow me to take risks. Built like a linebacker, Peter emanated a calm intuitiveness and a cast-iron integrity; his benign, bear-like presence made me feel that if I did my best, I could potentially bear the worst. He became an actual mentor, not a tormentor; if there were answers, if there were more questions, they were camping out inside me.

In my third session, I reported a seismic nightmare that would serve as a template for the hard work to come. A five-year-old, I was standing in the cinder playground of Brown Public School on a moonless winter night, staring over the fence at the rear of my grand-father's grey Edwardian Gothic house, all squinting dormers and slanted slate roof—the cauldron of the first seven years of my life. Heaving into view was an image of a small boy impaled on a stake. My throat burning, I screamed a stomach-emptying, silent scream. The original cold black yonder.

For years, my family had lived with a secret, known but never voiced: as a toddler, my younger brother was routinely sexually molested by Hank Besselar, a Dutch carpenter who was the husband of the live-in help; the couple occupied the third-floor apartment in our house. Even when three-year-old Mike ran away on two separate occasions and was returned by the police each time, our parents remained oblivious—isn't that what parents did?—and the abuse rolled on for two more years. Peter helped me see that the dream was like a movie trailer of a real event I could only now bear to view: that as a boy of kindergarten age, witnessing the quiet exploitation of my younger brother and identifying like mad, my nervous system had been fried like an egg on a skillet.

Through Peter, and the dreams to follow, I realized that the resurrection of my own disowned voice was the only way out. Had I been naive enough to relate my dreams to a psychiatrist, he would likely have reached for his prescription pad and sentenced me to the fate of my drugged-to-the-gills father—a slow, silent, cotton-batten death-in-life pinioned to the haunted house of his, and my, childhood. I'd rather feel bad than feel nothing at all, since what you can't feel you can't heal.

Session to session, I moved three steps forward, two steps back, one step forward, pulled by hope and fear. Though our parents had separated in 1975, my sister insisted on bringing them together every Christmas, complete with gift exchanges, the struggle to make-nice breeding migraine-inducing tensions. A clean break seemed impossible.

That Christmas of 1983, one month into my therapy, a full-blown psychotic break landed my father in the psych ward. Days later, I landed in hospital myself after fainting from intestinal bleeding, but the baffled psychologically impaired GI specialist could find no pathology in my bowel. I was opening myself up in ways I did not anticipate.

Eventually I found myself recollecting to Peter the scene, from some years earlier, when the family was discussing the fate of the family dog, a decrepit seventeen-year-old poodle then staggering blindly into the furniture. Our mother could not bring herself to have her put down, nor could our father. He had given the dog the attention and affection he denied us—a put-down all its own—and when the issue reached a head at a family meeting in a restaurant, my sister Shelagh's vulnerability tripped the family alarms against feeling. Our father needled her cruelly and I piled on, our callous, scapegoating laughter chasing her from the table in tears. I failed to twig to the link—how my mother, knowing our father was suicidal, had heartlessly set up my sister to save our father's life when he injected himself with a lethal dose of morphine. Madness, I had yet to see, wore many masks.

Listening intently to my confession, Peter responded with only four words—"I get the picture"—and instantly, of course, so did I. The next day, I walked over to Shelagh's apartment to apologize and make amends. With the expression of her relief, mine followed. For the first time, I hugged my sister. I was breaking the dead branches of the family trance, one snap at a time.

When Peter suggested I join his group of fourteen people, which he ran with a woman partner, at first I flatly refused. Then I realized: why am I here if not to confront my worst nightmare—talking and responding freely within a group? I was sick of the straitjacket of my lifelong reticence. When I agreed to join, Peter explained the two basic rules—no conscious sadism allowed, no socializing with members outside the group—and reiterated the ideal of plain, straight-up honesty.

Sitting in the circle, I re-enacted the frozen silence of my childhood and school years, held back and down by a familiar chokehold
of dread. I didn't feel like an elective mute; there was no choice
involved. Week by week, I was stirred by the raw emotional courage of
men and women whose unspeakable childhoods of abuse and neglect
made mine look like a teddy bears' picnic. Many of them held down
high-powered jobs and were raising families even as they struggled to
wrest a semblance of meaning and purpose from life.

As people took turns revealing themselves, I strained to respond,
but I was paralyzed by acute self-consciousness. Unlike in school, we
weren't marked or humiliated for making mistakes, yet my past held
my present hostage. If I opened my mouth, the words had to be nothing short of perfect, but I was nothing if not less-than; still, what is
more perfect than a godlike silence? Peter was struck by the split: one-
on-one, face-to-face, held by his sympathetic listening, I was often
passionate, articulate and insightful. But in the group, even with Peter
present, I disappeared.

After months of silence, I was invited to come forward for the
first time, and I spoke haltingly of my terror of speaking. I was handled with a gentle brilliance, but for a long time to come, I still needed
to be "asked out." When I agreed to participate in my first psychodrama, a woman named Susan was cast in the role of my indomitable
narcissistic mother. Standing behind a mattress held up by three
men, she needled, taunted and teased me with the hauteur of a mata-
dor. At first I gave her nothing but silence, but then I cut loose with a
barrage of punching, kicking, bellowing, ranting. While the catharsis
felt pivotal, I sensed I was just starting.

Week by week, year by year, September through June, I trudged
the twenty-five-minute walk from my apartment to group. At first I
felt as if I was marching to my execution, but gradually I forged delicate, tentative links with others. I was, Peter noted in a well-timed
moment, a "classic self-holder"; I still could not trust anyone else to

handle the job. I was learning that as children we are open vessels, immigrants crossing borders, psychologically rooting ourselves deep inside our parents, and they in us, captivated by our captors; much darkness and light comes of it. In time, I would see myself as a diver slipping into a black hole in the arctic ice, descending in slow stages, coming back up for air and attaching to the circle of warm-blooded mammals, the next time plunging a little deeper, as much as I could tolerate, toward the motherless core and the chance of rebirth. But in these early years, I mostly played it safe, clasping my habit of ironic distancing close to my heart.

Pandora's Box was meant to be opened, for hope lay at the bottom. In a black three-ring binder, year by year I captured the fragments of my dreams. Like the bending of a dowser's stick, my unconscious was imparting a radically new sense of direction to my life.

Wave after wave, the dreams came, my own and from the members of the group, sexy-violent head movies of censored and uncensored childhood wish. As actor, writer, set designer and director, I was swept up into dense, intricate narratives, shifting from fantasy to horror, musical to farce, idyll to massacre. "All that one has forgotten," the writer Elias Canetti reminds us, "screams for help in dreams." I experienced the phenomenon of the "day residue": how a seemingly random daytime word or conversation plumbed the bottomless unconscious, rooted around in the archive of imprinted experiences and latched the present experience to a prototype from the past. Dreams, when they were attended to, delivered a state-of-the-art update on your current psychic state. I found that the subtle work of tentative interpretation of a dream in turn generated a problem-solving "correction" dream: the Dream Factory never closed.

And yet, for many of us, the salutary power of dreaming remains a well-kept secret, relegated to the bogs of superstition. We casually dismiss one-third of our lives—decades of sleep and dreaming—as insignificant, even counterproductive. The UCC old boy and work-aholic corporate czar Ted Rogers spoke for more than his own class when he declared, "Sleep is for wimps."

No single theory captures the full mystery of dreams, but any therapy that denies them may as well deny the weather. Do dreams serve an adaptive, evolutionary function, a throwback to our pri-mordial caveman past? Do we dream of fending off the predations of the saber-toothed boss as an undressed rehearsal for when the real thing happens? Freud believed that dreaming is designed to preserve psychic equilibrium, presenting us with sights that we have perceived while awake yet have not fully registered. Unsolved traumas are resubmitted to the dreamer to work through and mas-ter. My own dreams felt like communiqués from the unconscious, frontline bulletins ripped hot off the wire—all the news that's unfit to print. Most dreams melt away entirely, and others are censored or redacted, black bars blocking the eyes of the guilty; still, it's a mistake to neglect the morning mail sitting on your pillow. Just read between the lies.

Step by step I became more consciously aware of my ferocious superego, the sleepless inner critic who flays and lashes with the mania of a slave-driver; no matter what you achieve, it is never good enough. But it is also the source of my conscience: it is good to be good. I started to grasp the dynamics of my resistance to the help I was seeking and my projections and transferences onto people who represented past relationships; I began to understand the rigidity of my defences and why they were vital to my survival. In the stories of my group members, I glimpsed flashes of greatness, victims as slowly self-realizing heroes, struggling to reconcile our gifts and curses. I was intrigued when Peter told me how he was struck by the number of high-powered corporate CEOs who passed through his office with the same complaint: they felt like complete frauds.

The group members were meant to use each other, in the best sense of the word, as emotional surrogates, a flock of black sheep falling in love and hate with one another and everything in between. In a real-life relationship, if you expressed yourself authentically you risked losing that relationship. But here, we did what we couldn't do with a parent or partner and survived each other together. We were not here to make friends, yet what we said to each other could stick for a lifetime: James, you are like a gentle racehorse.

Gradually I felt guilty that people were helping me but I couldn't help them. I never knew true reciprocity or honesty in my own family, so I should not have been surprised. Inch by inch, I felt my unvoiced responses to the struggles of others coming up over the hilltop to meet me. Experiencing moments of seeming telepathic connection, I realized the phenomenon was not supernatural but natural. I dreamed of a woman in the group emerging impossibly defiant and unscathed from a gang rape, but I didn't bring it forward; in an ensuing session, we learned that her mother had survived rape by Russian soldiers, and only then did I reveal my dream. When I guessed from the sight of her empty chair that a young woman of Irish blood, an aspiring writer who physically reminded me of Sally, had attempted to kill herself, my subsequent reaching-out and her reception of it enlivened us both; in the months to come she would credit our relationship in the group as lifesaving.

As Sally had once done, the group slowly oiled the rusted joints of the Tin Man who had stood too long in the rain. Each time I found the courage to speak, I was breaking the silencing guilt of my suicidal childhood household. I was rewarded with irreplaceable, irreducible, face-to-face, voice-to-voice, heart-to-heart human contact.

In the above-ground workaday world, I started to crawl out of my manhole, absorbing the knocks and bumps of everyday interactions with a newfound resilience. I was less quick to bash myself into the ground or let myself off the hook or do the same with my parents. *I relate, therefore I am.* As I stood back and appreciated, for the first time, my parents' strengths and gifts, I realized my own were best invested in anyone but them. Perhaps they believed they loved us, but it was not love if they never gave it.

Working one-on-one with Peter on Mondays and the group on Wednesdays, I experienced a hopeful recurring dream in which I returned to my childhood haunted house on Balmoral, now under a state of renovation by new warm and welcoming owners. But the sunny dreams invariably triggered a backlash: at the foot of my bed, dragons loomed and menaced, and taking them for real, I jerked and thrashed myself awake.

In the years since 1968, Sally kept making unpredictable cameo appearances in my dreams, alive but aloof, pretending she didn't know me, unaware of her fate. Was my desire for the dead still alive, my desire for the living still guilty?

Then, one night, came the rock-bottom mother of all dreams.

I was a newborn baby gripping a long umbilical cord that swung me like a pendulum across a spacious courtyard. My mother, Janet, was standing at the railing of a third-floor balcony, as hypnotically beautiful as a Hollywood star. On my cord, I arced back and forth like a baby Tarzan, reaching for the comfort of her breast. But each time I drew close enough to touch her, her glowing face burst into a grotesque gargoyle of alarm, disgust and revulsion. With each swing, the cycle of beauty and terror repeated. When I awoke, I was convinced that the Janus-faced oscillations would never end.

Was the condition inherited from her own brittle, corseted Victorian mother, and thus ultimately forgivable? No matter; my hesitant, stutter-step adult relationships with women now made sense. How could I woo them when I had failed to court and win my first, primal love? For it was impossible to see the failure as other than my own.

Yet the dream validated what I'd been feeling in my gut as far back as I could remember, and even earlier. The dream persuaded me that even in my wordless infant state, I'd perceived a harsh truth that I could never fundamentally change: my mother's essential unreachable nature. But I did not have to carry on the same as I ever was.

My father and grandfather, scientists both, would likely have dismissed my dreams of Balmoral, of my mother, and of Sally as meaningless brain-flotsam. But they were the blinkered, overreaching racehorses who had both raced off the cliff, and I was not keen to follow. I knew I was not crazy for still dreaming Sally, both a person and a symbol, long after her death. Like all the important figures and pre-figures in my dreams, she was a messenger, and an audience, pushing herself to the centre stage of my nightly shows in an especially insistent way.

I felt that Sally, my first love outside the ring of the family, was telling me that something remained, and would always remain, unfinished, untalked, unlistened, unrealized, unsung, undanced, unswung. At the same time, she stood for everything cosmically possible, like the emotional and spiritual opening of the sixties itself: as if she understood what happened, what was happening and what would happen next; as if agnostic James might yet convert to the faith that the sunlit face of hope, swinging on its pendulum, could hold its own against the dark side of the moon.

In the spring of 2016, while I was revising a sentence in the section above, the uncanny once again paid a surprise visit. I now knew from long experience that *surprising* was the only way it *could* visit.

Originally I had used the word "boomerang" to describe my recurring dreams of a black incubus figure who, despite all my therapeutic work, kept appearing at the foot of my bed, as if to say, Not so fast, I'm not dead yet. Such is the nature of dreaming and healing: two steps forward, one step back.

I decided I did not like the word "boomerang," and in the very moment I tapped the keyboard and substituted the word "backlash," I was startled by a sudden crash and the showering of glass fragments at my feet. I swivelled my chair to find that a framed black-and-white eight-by-ten photograph of my childhood home at 186 Balmoral Avenue, perched on the windowsill behind my back for the past seven years, had fallen on the floor. Had my keyboard turned into a Ouija board?

The photograph of my brother, sister and me standing in front of the house had been taken in the fall of 2009 as my memoir, *What Disturbs Our Blood*, was in the final stages of production; the image, one of dozens, was not published in the book, so I'd decided to frame a single image for myself.

During the shoot, the young photographer, Christine, had been intrigued by the Gothic house built by my grandfather and the suppressed scandal of his mysterious end. She urged me to tell her the secret of his demise, but I insisted she read the book herself; otherwise, it would be like spoiling the narrative of *Citizen Kane* by blurting that Rosebud was a sled.

As Christine packed up her camera, we stood on the sidewalk in front of the house. She had not stopped badgering me to make the Big Reveal, so I relented. I explained how, while under suicide watch in a bed at Toronto General Hospital in 1940, my grandfather, a Canadian medical hero, slipped a knife off his dinner tray and severed his femoral artery, bleeding to death—a scandal that was covered up for decades.

Seconds later, I felt a gust of cold wind brush the left leg of my corduroy pants. I looked down and discovered a surgically precise six-inch rip in the seam, exposing the flesh of my thigh to the October air. The femoral artery is located in the thigh, and my grandfather was left-handed.

I turned to show Christine the uncanny rip in the fabric of my reality: "What do you make of this?"

"Opening old wounds, James?" she replied.

"How about *healing* old wounds?"

I turned to my grandfather's house to salute the crafty spooks. My book cast light on the darkness, yet night forever follows day.

It was Christine's photo of Balmoral, taken that charged October day, that fell to the floor the second I typed "backlash," a phenomenon that Jung would not hesitate to claim as classic synchronicity.

Three hours after the photograph-smashing incident, I appeared at a book club in the city's west end to speak on my memoir to an audience of forty. As I entered the room, my eyes were drawn to a large screen set up to show an introductory video, where instead a photograph of 186 Balmoral Avenue stared back at me. I learned that a member of the book club lived a block south of the house, and only yesterday, after reading my book, she'd walked up to take a photo, then decided to project it on the screen. I didn't tell my hosts of the coincidence; it felt like far too much extra work. What else to do except take yet another mystery in stride?

TWENTY-ONE

The Bell

Across a distance of three thousand miles, Stewart worried that George might succumb to his latest crisis. At the same time, Stewart had never ceased marvelling at his friend's resilience.

In 1984, with a fourth child on the way, Stewart quit his steel-working job and entered teachers' college; like George, he took the long way around to his true calling. Beginning a new career at Valley Heights High School in Port Ryerse in Southwestern Ontario, he taught seventeen subjects, from math to law to art. He'd spent his life refuting the "stupid" label that George's mother and others had so casually flung in his path. He told his students, "I failed Grades 1 and 2. I didn't learn to read till I was eleven and now I'm your teacher. How do you like me so far?" He also loved telling the story of the night he was struggling to read a bedtime story to his exasperated three-year-old daughter (the future Crown attorney), when she exclaimed, "Send in someone who can read!"

In his classroom, Stewart often related how his sudden premonition in Dublin on August 13, 1968—"the single most intense psychic experience of my life"—converted him from an atheist to an agnostic. At the funerals of headstrong teenagers who'd been killed in car crashes, too many to bear counting, he stood firm and open under the twin avalanches of pain and grief. He learned the true value of work and deepened his commitment to the ceaseless asking of questions as the indispensable driver of education. "That's why they forced Socrates to drink hemlock," he said. "It was not what he was saying but the questions he was asking. Our generation no longer asks, Why is this guy lying to us? Mass propaganda is capsizing the facts."

Every crisis conceals an opportunity, and on the basement foundation of a collapsing life George assembled the planks of a new stage. In September 1989, he started teaching at BCIT, the broadcast journalism school from which he'd graduated a decade earlier. In his ten-year run as a reporter, editor and producer, he found the formula for effective broadcast storytelling, and now he was poised to bequeath what he had mastered. Being fired was proving therapeutic.

The split with Ronda deeply affected the kids, and he realized it was time to pay attention to others at work and home; it was not all about him. Nick, the inward contrarian, sided with his father, while Lily, an energized, independent, sassy blonde, allied more with her mother. Religious about seat belts—the simple technology lacking in Sally's bus—George drove the kids to and from school every day and signed them up for soccer, baseball and ballet. He became "The Dad Who Shows Up," chatting up parents on the sidelines on all-weather Saturday mornings. George had no intention of driving his offspring into years of therapy.

At BCIT, he transformed the curriculum into the one he would have liked as a student a decade earlier, synthesizing his hard-won knowledge into a two-year job-ready course in TV news reporting. His students learned how to reduce a news story to a single compelling sentence and how to work up a game plan before heading out the door. He counselled his charges, "If you can't fashion an empathic and imaginative question for a victim of tragedy, you should not be in the business. Never ask a victim, 'How do you feel?' Rather: 'Tell me about your child.'" With a ruthless blue pencil, he exterminated all clichés: "If I find the phrase 'It's only a matter of time' in your copy, I will fail you."

In 1990, George bought a used car from a neighbour named Steve, who told him he was forming a small men's group with his pals Neil and Greg. He asked whether George would like to join? The group afforded a private realm of honest talk unfit for conventional social intercourse, and in he jumped.

One day Greg and Steve returned from a Mastery Workshop, a quasi-therapeutic weekend operating out of Los Angeles that toured North American cities. The men burned with evangelical fire over how the experience—a mix of confrontation, support and primal screaming—could detonate the mid-life psychic roadblocks, the dead-end jobs, the stagnant relationships. George was still George, pushing back hard against anything smacking of a naval command, yet a day later he thought, *My life stands at a crossroad and I need a reboot. I will try anything once.*

On a Friday evening in January 1991, George took a seat among thirty men and women in the Cambrian Hall in downtown Vancouver, nowhere close to realizing how the weekend would rewire his fuse box. When the charismatic American leader invited the group to engage in a screaming exercise to open up their bodies, George shrugged it off as silly. But when a woman started shrieking, he felt pressure welling up inside, and he let 'er rip. He almost loved it.

As the Friday session extended to 4 a.m., the leader assessed George's baggage: too nice, too boring, too cautious, too safe. Too

Canadian. George was given homework: come back tomorrow morning at nine wearing Bermuda shorts, snorkel and flippers, and so he did, clomping through the slush of the parking lot, feeling stupid and small. He was rescued when a tall, striking woman just short of his own height of six feet approached with the irresistible words: "I want to play with you." Her name was Anne.

Into the pool of thirty bodies they plunged, bottom-of-the-lungs waves of howling, bellowing, screaming. Everybody was digging it—or most of them; at day's end, some staggered into the streets, uncorked messes of goo stripped of the basic defences needed to negotiate the world. But for George, it was more than he hoped for: a transformative jolt of theatre.

He learned that Anne was thirty-two, eleven years younger than he was, and unhappily married. She had left her hometown of Calgary for Vancouver in 1975, the same year George quit Ontario, to escape the dead end of her oppressive working-class Catholic family. She was determined to make her own way, taking a criminology degree at Simon Fraser University en route to a career in social work. Because she was set on reshaping herself, George felt an instant identification, but bitter experience told him that this time he should bide his time.

Just as he was drawn to an imagined future with Anne, he felt the tugging fingers of the past—an urge to look back and understand what had happened to his first marriage to Sandy. He invited her out to Vancouver for a visit, and they enjoyed a day out on Mac's boat where everything between them clicked. He visited her in Toronto, but the second encounter proved difficult, and he headed back west, leaving Sandy with the feeling that he was deciding between her and another woman. Six months later, George sat down with Anne's husband, an accountant, and pointed to the writing on the wall: "You and Anne aren't working, but we might."

As he had with Sandy and Ronda, George told Anne about

Sally: "I've been emotionally involved with a dead person for over twenty years." Like his first two wives, Anne was undaunted, but this time George found himself promising that he would not flirt with the ghost.

With her husband, Anne had failed to conceive, even with the aid of in vitro fertilization. Freed of the need for birth control, in June 1992, she joined George on the ferry to Hornby Island to enjoy a weekend getaway in a cabin offered by friends. The obstacles had fallen away, and the uncanny slipped into the bedroom. George and Anne realized that at the precise instant of consummation they both knew she had conceived. The doctor merely confirmed it.

On December 3, 1992, Mac Orr passed his seventieth birthday knowing he was dying of lymphatic cancer. Although the scourge had stripped fifty pounds from his already lean frame, he managed a trip to Toronto for a farewell party with a loyal crew of friends. Back in Vancouver, he was quickly hospitalized. George came to sit at his bedside, father and eldest son grasping at threads of conversation. Anxiously George confessed that Anne was six months pregnant and he had not yet divorced Ronda. "Thank God," came the unexpected reply, for Mac was fond of Anne. "I thought you were going to say my boat sank." In stages, the son heard the father's breathing sink into the shallows, and as the last puff turned to silence, days before Christmas, George felt nothing; or if he did, the emotions escaped his reach.

Three months later, on March 7, 1993, Anne delivered a son whom they named Jordan. When George had suggested filming the great event, Anne balked; some things were best left to memory. As a stepmother, Anne engaged the challenges of a blended family, gradually winning over the recalcitrant preteens Nick and Lily—"We don't do dishes!"—with a mix of affection and discipline. George

insisted on clearing the house of all elephants, inviting the honest
talk absent from his own upbringing. He regarded Anne as a splen-
did person in every respect, possessed of more integrity than himself.
Sally had believed there was order to life, right up to the moment it
ended, and Anne brought the same qualities to their bond—vital,
warm, comfortable in her own skin. This, he now knew, was what he
wanted from life—a steadying influence, a loving home, a partner
capable of spontaneous fun. Through the stability of family, George
admitted his attraction to a state he'd long mistrusted: normal.

Perhaps the timing was no accident, but one day the rejuve-
nated father of three chanced upon a jewellery box he had not
opened in years. Rooting around among the buttons and baby teeth
inside, George pulled out the silver ring that Sally had given him
before heading off on her Odyssey. He tried to slip it on, but the
years had thickened his fingers. Next he picked up the two gifts that
Dr. Wodehouse had found in Sally's suitcase in August 1968 and
passed on to him: a pair of German beer-stein cufflinks and the
Bucherer Swiss watch he'd worn for fifteen years until it stopped
ticking. Pulling out a yellowing newspaper clipping, he realized it
was Sally's death notice. As he scanned the type, something dimly
remembered rose into full consciousness: Sally's birthdate of
May 25, 1950. Then the slap in the head: his daughter, Lily, was
born on May 25, 1984. What was he to make of such a link?

TWENTY-TWO

Kill Your Parents

Holed up in a one-bedroom high-rise apartment, unburdened by wife, children or mortgage, I had stripped my life down to the basics. I delivered my dying Dodge Dart through the gates of the automobile graveyard and took up walking and public transit. I quit smoking but not drinking. To face down the heavy, best travel light.

More intimate with books than women, I found perfect lovers only in the cave of sleep. My social life was sustained by a circle of male friends—Mark, Peter, Craig, Ken, Terry, Frank, Doug—but romantic forays remained few and fraught. I dated the sister of my dead friend Jay, a lively, witty Branksome Hall grad and talented artist, dimly sensing, then denying, a back channel to Sally; what exactly was I trying to resurrect?

One evening at the International Festival of Authors, the novelist John Fowles jammed my flank with a cattle prod when he mouthed the electric words: "If you want to be a writer, you must kill your parents."

I was struggling to carve out a sane distance from my mother, erasing the wheedling-yet-imperious messages left on my answering machine. As my father's physical health deteriorated, unresolved guilts and hatreds were revving my mother and sister up to sixties levels of intensity. If my father was predisposed by family and fate to be driven out of his mind, my mother was the last spike. Unable to acknowledge her unconscious wish for his death even as he tried to take his own life, she'd shifted the burden to my sister, who felt she had no choice but to carry it.

My mother had long since perfected the dark art of gaslighting, delivering steady digs and jabs designed to make her targets doubt their own perceptions of reality. One day Shelagh made the mistake of admiring a piece of jewellery our mother kept in a glass case and expressed a desire to have the maternal heirloom when the time came, not realizing that she was drawing attention to our mother's mortality. Only weeks later, Shelagh happened to see the very same piece displayed in the window of a pawnshop. Of countless provocations, this one was a capper. Then, one day, the levee broke and mother and daughter fell into an all-out, screaming fist fight. In a sense, they had hit a new form of honesty—ugly, but honest—a shift from the covert shivs in the back, death by a thousand cuts.

My own sporadic interactions with my mother seemed to invite a truce, but her words had a way of stopping me cold.

One moment she'd blurt, almost as an accusation: "Why were you so withdrawn as a child?"

Then, in a tone of desperation: "I'd do anything for you!"

Then, accusingly (and truthfully): "We have no relationship!"

When she announced that on her death she wanted her ashes thrown off the ferry to the Toronto Islands, I thought: *Why wait?*

One Christmas, in a tone of accusation mixed with what seemed genuine puzzlement, my mother asked why none of her three children had presented her with grandchildren. When I ever so gently broached the subject of her historical interferences with my romantic choices, she bristled: "You're a nasty piece of work."

When I fished for sympathy in my next session with Peter, he simply responded, "What profiteth it a man if he confronts his mother and ends up feeling crazy?"

Of course.

I'd moved over to run the promotion-publicity department of the Toronto branch of Addison-Wesley, another American-owned publishing house, where I nursed hidden passions for a string of unavailable women. If I marshalled the gumption to ask out one of the available kind, I felt I had only one shot, so I had to make it perfect. Invariably my tremulous intensity leaked through the mask of enforced calm and I recreated the original maternal drama, transforming the smile on the receptive face into an expression of barely disguised alarm. Even so, what would I do if I won? Drop her? Keep her? Then what? One day over lunch, my bright female assistant offered the astute perception that like Plato, I regarded women first as an idea. I responded: "I'll have to think about that."

At a company Christmas party, a tall, thirty-year-old editor with charisma to burn, like Sally a daughter of a doctor, unhappily married to a corporate drone, pulled me by my tie onto the dance floor as "Let's Get Physical" beckoned. Whatever she saw in me, I didn't. Let's Get Metaphysical? Back in my concrete box of an apartment, I thought of the wisdom of Zorba the Greek: "There is one sin God will not forgive: if a woman calls a man to her bed and he will not go."

In the summer of 1988, I hosted the twentieth reunion of the Odyssey. This time, I stood with nine others for the photo shoot— Ross, Dave, Sean, Stu, Rich, Marywinn, Nick and Jane—one fewer than the 1978 reunion. The party proved an inert affair; I was holding on, but why and to what end?

———

After a decade in book publishing, I was fired in the spring of 1989 because I'd confronted a Nurse Ratched–like administrator who routinely bullied the high and the low with impunity. It proved a blessing in disguise. I went to work as an editor on a new trade magazine founded by my friend Mark. Once I was back in journalism, the buttery piano keys of the Mac computer rekindled the writing I had neglected like a bad child, and my life path was reset.

On my thirty-ninth birthday, I hesitantly accepted a honey-toned invitation to travel the six subway stops north to my mother's semi-detached house near Yonge and Eglinton for a dinner with her, my brother and sister. She served Orange Crush, hot dogs and chips in a jokey reference to childhood birthdays, and I was made to feel nine, not thirty-nine. At precise ten-minute intervals, my oldest and closest friends walked through the door, one by one, unfolding a slow, seamlessly orchestrated surprise party. I was a lobster in a pot, boiling by degrees.

Has she de-crypted my address book? I wondered, for she had never met most of my non-UCC friends, as they were hatched outside the Toronto WASP nest. I come close to admiring the disarming, clandestine deception of the stealth attack—in certain parts of the Upper Canadian universe, you don't know you've been fucked until you're nine months pregnant. But mostly I was creeped out by her gambit, playing the gracious chatelaine in an attempt to telegraph to my friends that no matter what I might have told them, she was not the reincarnation of Lady Macbeth.

One night I dreamed of my mother slipping seductively between the sheets of my bed and whispering, "Do you want me to leave?" When I was young, she had never ventured to my bedside and now this? What would have been life to the boy was now death to the man, and within the dream state I was tongue-tied.

Weeks later, when the disturbing incestuous dream recurred, I was able to muster the feeble words, "I'd rather you didn't." When I saw the film *Dead Poets Society,* I was moved by the scene of the English master goading the petrified prep boy to let fly with a Whitmanesque yawp. In the boy I saw a replica of myself. The unconscious mind is relentless, but so was my drive to decipher it in my sessions with Peter. When I dreamed of my mother's bedroom invasion a third time, I was able to scream in her face, blasting her out of the bed and the room. I was decoding the Ultrasecret, my mother the spy, cell by cell.

In a do-or-die moment with her on the telephone, I took a deep breath and stood my ground. Most men are lucky if they reach a semblance of maturity by the age of forty, and I was feeling lucky. I spelled out my terms of disengagement: unless she backed off to a prescribed distance, she risked losing a son permanently, with no chance of reconciliation.

"Are you prepared to live with that?" I asked. "It's your decision."

In her wavering silence I sensed she knew that if she forced my hand, I would, in fact, play it.

The harassing, backbiting phone calls stopped, but my mother never forgave me for shredding the unconscious script and cutting loose from the family emotional plague. In the moment I stopped standing in for her husband, I started becoming myself.

Although eighteen months younger, my brother had always felt like a fraternal twin. For all our family griefs, he had carved out a rewarding career in business, and I appreciated his steady decency and dependability, his dry ironic wit and a subtle psychic radar no doubt born of our early childhood isolation.

As we talked one night over dinner in a downtown restaurant, I sensed the cross-currents of my life coming to a head in the form of a book I thought I wanted to write. I had recently devoured Studs Terkel's oral history *Working,* a collection of tape-recorded and transcribed subjective voices ranging from hookers to hockey players, bus drivers to bank presidents, on the theme of work. Everyone was potentially a walking storybook and all they needed was a competent listener. Terkel's voices delivered a sense of alienation worthy of Karl Marx: most people hated what they did for a living.

What if I applied Terkel's technique to the alumni of the country's most prestigious and exclusive private school and left it up to the reader of the book to interpret the stew of voices? I could slip through the gates of the male, monied, macho, monarchical, military, corporate hierarchy. But I wouldn't treat them like objects, as I had been; I'd treat them like subjects, with unique voices. In fact, together we might even change the subject.

In his apartment bunker, my lithium-dampened, zombie-eyed, TV-addicted father, haunted by the mad end of his own father, was swirling down a slow drain to meet him. On my sporadic visits, I was a paragon of gentle diplomacy, sifting for clues to the paternal generational mysteries, but he gave nothing away except his own pathos; in our silent movie, there were no speaking parts.

During his first mid-life breakdown, I had seen my father fall into a state of abject vulnerability, reaching out for help like a wounded child. There was something hopeful about it, something very sixties: he was fed up with the false life thrust upon him and wanted to change. At this critical, revolutionary moment, he was reachable, and as a teenager I sensed it. Breakdown can be breakthrough.

But he became a victim of shocking psychiatric malpractice and learned a final lesson: to never again permit himself an iota of vulnerability. Naively I kept returning to the well, hoping to revive the gentle, sensitive, witty man I'd glimpsed under the armour, but we had no historical ground on which to stand. My tactful attempts to stir memories of his own father, the eminent man who had killed himself, shaming the family, only raised the drawbridge; in fact, my very presence posed a threat, as it had from my birth, because it triggered the loathed emotional vulnerability. In the reflection of his wily, wary eyes I saw myself, the subversive son failing to spark the conversation that might set us free.

During his declining months, I reached a point when I realized, as with my mother, that I had nothing to lose. When I confronted him for his maltreatment of my too-eager-to-please sister, I broke a long-standing taboo by going to bat for a sibling. Mortified, he rocketed out his chair and dragged me up and down the corridor of his apartment building to work off his agitation; like my mother, he neither tolerated nor forgave direct talk.

In our last tense, terse exchanges, he muttered jibes and sarcasms; under the genteel veneer of the doctor, the sneer was revealed. I had quit my magazine job to work on the UCC book full-time, but he had no reaction when I revealed that I was about to become a published author—giving me the very nothing that had galvanized my book to life, a subject that had, at bottom, everything to do with him. To the end, he remained the slippery politician behind the press conference podium, evading the questions, hard or soft.

Yet in the world outside the apartment of the dying father, the son kept shouldering the wheel. Many of the men formed under the shadow of the great clock tower on the hill were pouring words into my tape recorder, talking, confessing, thinking, feeling, loving, hating, searching, opening up— everything my father could not do. I was cutting open white male privilege to see what spilled out, and sometimes it turned out to be real guts. A different brand of courage. Month by month, Peter listened to me and I listened to the men. My incorrigible father was left to his deserted island and the terror of his own end. When he died on a May dawn in 1992, two days after his seventy-fifth birthday, he was alone.

I found my father's naval uniform and medals hanging in his closet, artifacts of the trembling hunter of Nazi U-boats, pressed by the social conformity of a peacetime world to sire children he never wanted. Jack FitzGerald, father-dead from the first, was dead at last, and the son was free to step into his own life.

TWENTY-THREE

Therajournalism

A smoker since age sixteen, Dorothy Orr had led a sedentary life, constrained by a husband lashed to his own misery, and now unforgiving cancers riddled her body. For a year, George devoted himself to her daily needs, suspending his teaching job and, while Anne worked, looked after their toddler, Jordan. He anticipated the wasp stings of a chronically difficult mother, but month by month, as he sat at her bedside in the Lions Gate Hospital, the doors of reconciliation unexpectedly opened.

Seemingly undisturbed by her impending end, Dorothy reminisced freely. Unable to quit cigarettes, she was often found sitting alone outside, smoking and coughing up spots of blood. As a son's compassion eased old animosities, she was relieved to discover that George had evolved into a mature, accomplished man with a strong, sweet partner and a trio of wonderful children. As a child, he had loved listening to his mother's mother, Grace, and now he was achieving something of a state of grace he never knew with the woman who gave him life.

On a day when George visited the hospice with two-year-old Jordan, the irony deepened: running down the hall, the boy bounded into her room and yelled, "Grandma!"

It was the only time in George's life he saw his mother hug another human being.

When she revealed to him that the death of Sally had broken her heart, the simple purity of the words, disastrously absent in August 1968, landed better late than never.

On an April day in 1995, George, his brother, Mike, and their aunt Nancy gathered for the dying. When George stepped out for a coffee, his mother stopped breathing. "She was sparing your feelings," Nancy offered.

Following her husband, Dorothy's body was cremated and transported back east. She was buried on the eastern divide of Mount Pleasant Cemetery, opposite Sally on the west.

In 1996, George fulfilled an ambition from years earlier when he'd built a desk for Peter Gzowski in the basement of the CBC building: he became the host of his own television talk show. *Studio B.C.* was a weekly one-hour public affairs show on the Knowledge Network, a provincial educational station that pulled in forty thousand viewers. Loving the knife edge of live TV, he interviewed guests, along with a female co-host, and covered current affairs from First Nations fish farming to pot legalization to teenage violence.

In an interview with the American poet Robert Bly, author of *Iron John*, George was amazed he could hold up his end of a conversation that struck close to home: the dearth of strong fathers common to the boomer generation. To become truly free and wild, Bly counselled, "boys need to steal the key from under the pillow of the sleeping mother." Had his own mother's dreams for him come true, George knew he would never have landed here, trading words with a poet, under the spotlight. "Where a man's wound is," Bly insisted, "there his genius will be."

In 1999, while caught up in a free-flowing interview with a guest,

George heard in his earpiece the chiding voice of the female producer: "Do not deviate from the script." Irritated by echoes of Maternal Control, he deviated and was fired. The timing worked, for together with Ross Howard, his old boss at the York student newspaper, *Excalibur*, he had been making a documentary on sockeye salmon, a two-year project that demanded his full energy, trekking out every weekend to a Vancouver Island hatchery to interview Indigenous people. When their film *Against the Current* aired on the CBC program *Rough Cuts*, the documentary won a Jack Webster Award for outstanding British Columbia journalism.

Over the course of nearly three years, I tape-recorded, transcribed and edited oral history interviews with three generations of Upper Canada College old boys. To cover my working and living expenses, I burned through a $22,000 publisher's advance and a $40,000 inheritance from my father, fitting given that the book was ultimately about the eternal drama of fathers and sons.

I was on a deeply personal quest to find out what drives the privileged male of the species. How aware were the so-called best and brightest, the leaders of tomorrow, of the forces of family and school that had shaped their choices and actions? Did they notice? Did they care?

Over the course of three hundred interviews, a chain of coincidental links set the organizing principle of the book: the juxtaposition of disparate yet overlapping voices arrayed across a three-generational spectrum. I chose not to interview George Orr, class of 1965; I sensed a book in his story alone, and I was content, for the moment, to let a large sleeping dog lie.

But I did encounter a jostling gamut of characters: famous and obscure, carpenters and cabinet ministers, bullies and victims, naïfs and Machiavellians, con men and true believers, cynics and idealists, dullards and charismatics, braggarts and milquetoasts, hotshots and lowlifes, Canadian-born WASPs and immigrants, the decent and the thoughtful, the shallow and vain, the corrupt and the pure of heart, and the occasional born leader. I rattled their cages, and they rattled mine. Vulnerability was the great equalizer.

Some were clearly in the grip of Stockholm Syndrome, fallen compliantly in love with their captors; others had become creative rebels. In every face, I recognized pieces of myself. The stubborn absence of the female-as-equal was the elephant in this room; when a former chairman of the school's board of governors proclaimed with a straight face the school was "the best in the country," "turning out a quality product," not pausing to consider that admitting the brightest girls would raise the overall academic standard—not to mention deliver multiple tangible and intangible qualities beyond capitalist units of production—I waited, in vain, for him to catch on to his own absurdity.

I was amazed when David Thomson the multi-billionaire scion of one of Canada's the wealthiest families, agreed to an interview. Of all the voices, he showed himself one of the most intuitive, understanding that I was "trolling the collective unconscious" of a mythologized institution. He knew a Trojan horse when he saw one, but he seemed unconcerned.

He struck me as a frustrated artist mandated to inherit the role of ruthless, bottom-line businessman in a world where legal tender ruled, where tenderness was illegal. In one telling moment among many, he confessed, "Your best friend is your dog, if you are lucky." People wanted to know him not for who he was but for his wealth and connections, and thus he trusted no one. Within the confines of the plutocracy, only when money talked did people listen. As I left, I wanted to exclaim, For your integrity, your true self, your soul, walk away from it all. You've got the brains and drive—start from scratch. But I didn't, and neither did he.

I thought of the air-brushed "success stories" in the glossy pages of *Old Times*, UCC's alumni magazine. But if we dared to conjure the figures lingering outside of the frame, we found a different breed of archetype: the middle-aged multi-millionaire bloated with Scotch and self-betrayal, shuttling between the luxury car, the mansion and the belief in his heart that he was too far gone to change course; the alpha male CEO, justified by an impregnable sense of entitlement, tossing his wife of thirty years over the side and hauling up the shapely, gold-digging secretary; bodies hurled on subway tracks, cars careering off cliffs, heads of head boys hanging in nooses in Muskoka boathouses. I lost count of the number of brothers locked in states of uncivil war. Generation after generation, the school administrators reflexively swept under the Persian rug the toxic cycles: bullying, drugs, cheating, misogyny, racism, depression, hubris, affluenza, child abuse and neglect.

When the book was published in October 1994, one old boy aptly dubbed it "an encyclopedia of arrogance and pain." While it attracted some radio and newspaper coverage, no one risked unpacking the sex-and-death content, and a lesson emerged: asking questions remained out of the question. I had committed the unpardonable sin of pulling back the curtain of male vulnerability.

That same year of 1994, Nick Duffell, an English boarding-school survivor, made a BBC documentary and published a book, *The Making of Them: The British Attitude to Children and the Boarding School System*. In his succinct description of the inner life of young boys exiled to boarding schools, he captured the classic double bind that shut down my own father as a boy in the 1920s:

"Mummy and Daddy sent me away. If they loved me, why did they send me away? But I know it's important to them and it costs a lot of money. If I show I hate it, they will be disappointed, and if they are disappointed, they won't love me. So I won't show them that I hate it. If I hate it, there must be something wrong with me. Maybe that's why they sent me away." The boy can survive only by repressing his feelings and thus betray himself.

"The British are mad," commented the author John le Carré. "But in the maiming of their privileged youth, they are criminally insane."

With the publication of *Old Boys*, I met the face of my father and the school, which were fused as one; I was forced to accept the impossibility of either one experiencing honest confrontation as an act of love. But if you don't struggle to tell the truth, most of all to yourself, you grow sick; if you fail to acknowledge and experience your own fallibility and mortality—to sink down, experience it, and come back up stronger—you will skim the surfaces of life, never knowing what it means to let in and love others. I had had no clue how to love Sally or anyone else. And I was still nowhere close to prepared.

The brave self-exposures of people in the privacy of my weekly group continued to move and inspire me, together with the many old boys who had opened themselves up to me and risked the sting of public backlash. At the same time, when Fred, a book editor friend whom I had steered into therapy, walked out of his session one evening and jumped into the path of a subway train, I learned the limits of even the best of human help.

Over weekends and evenings, I bore down on my family history, untangling the convoluted fate of my mysterious grandfather, leading darkly down through my father to me. I was slowly learning how to live with myself—and maybe even, down the road, with someone else. But first that meant finding, or refinding, my own voice.

Two months after the publication of *Old Boys*, I discovered in an archive a cache of dozens of heart-rending, painfully confessional letters written by my grandfather in a New England asylum from 1939 to 1940, the last year of his life. Parked on a dusty shelf, untouched for forty-five years, the letters had only been deposited in the archive the very week I walked in.

A second serendipity led me to an aging doctor in a Vancouver nursing home who turned out to be the last person alive who knew the suppressed details of my grandfather's suicide. The old man's harrowing revelation confirmed my own decades-old intuitions. Over the years, a series of epiphanies had popped like flashbulbs, melting the generational sheets of body ice, leading me inexorably to our buried family secret. At last I understood—and could begin to forgive— my father's silence. From terror was born liberation, and although fifteen years of work lay ahead, I had conceived a second book.

My weekly group work continued to bring my body and soul back from the dead. On a weekend marathon, I brought up the silent-scream nightmare from my third session with Peter back in 1983; surviving shards had disturbed my sleep ever since. I could not shake the conviction, without external corroboration, that as a child of five I had actually witnessed my brother suffer the sexual predations of the live-in "help" on the third floor of our childhood Balmoral home.

In a psychodrama reconstructing the dream, a man lay on a mat on the floor, conjuring up a memory image of my three-year-old brother. I was thrown into a state of stark terror that pitched me out of my chair; this time I uttered the scream that my throat could not claim in the dream.

If the psychodrama had stopped there, it would have only re-traumatized me. But as my nervous system calmed down, I was able to take in the group's sensitive, attuned responses. More than one person felt that the drama had a "devouring energy," which resonated with my own experience. In my five-year-old mind, I was watching an act of cannibalism, and in my identification with my innocent and unprotected brother, I might as well have melded my body with his. It now all made a kind of sense.

Over a restaurant dinner with Mike a few weeks later, I did not mention the psychodrama. But it was if he was reading my mind: for the first time, he broached the taboo of the open family secret that lived inside us like a forgotten movie. The understated sexual content of the recently published *Old Boys*, woven through the oral histories, had given him tacit permission to talk.

Mike described how, night after night, a large figure softly approached his bedside. Mike had split from the experience of the molestation, ascending to the ceiling, watching himself from above like a camera. As he spoke, I felt a violent roiling, as if feeling his feelings for him, as if I was responsible for saving him but powerless, helpless, desperate beyond words. Or had I betrayed him? Did I somehow manage to kick the predator away from me, as my dreams suggested, only to deflect the abuse upon Mike?

Together we told our mother of our conversation. She confirmed that in 1960, three years after we had moved out of the Balmoral house, she had received a phone call from the wife of the abuser; she wanted my mother to know that her husband, Hank Besselar, had been jailed for molesting small boys and that Michael had been one of his victims. Although my first impulse was to berate my mother for her failure to protect us, I decided to simply thank her for the information she had withheld all these years. The abuse was now established as historical fact, something that actually happened and was acknowledged as such. My dream was not a delusion, and even better, healing was now possible, layer upon subtle layer.

Still, at forty-five, I remained a commitment-phobic master of hit-and-run relationships, ill-fated triangles piling up like a kindergarten orchestra, mixed with long stretches of sexless solitude. The certainty of isolation was preferable to the risk of hope.

Old Boys sold five thousand copies, Canadian bestseller territory but not enough to pay back my advance. After the honeymoon rush of publication, I felt a mild postpartum depression. I ground out hack freelance articles at 50 cents a word, and supplemented them with a courier job, living hand-to-mouth on a negative net worth, drawing off a line of credit, barely covering the rent.

In April 1996, my eye caught an obituary for George Wodehouse, who had died just short of his eightieth year. I chose not to attend the funeral. That fall, my parents' closest childhood friends of nearly seventy years, Jack and Marjorie, died within weeks of each other. As we flanked Marjorie on her deathbed, I was appalled by my mother's rigid posture. On the drive home, she confessed, "I didn't know what to say."

Marjorie's daughter Janet was, like Sally, one of the few girls I knew growing up. Seeing her at her parents' funerals, after so many years, evoked a familiar fusion of grief and the erotic. I realized I had never lost a sweet spot for her. At age six, we were abandoned to the same month-long summer camp in the Ontario wild, and I recalled her piercing, unanswered wails. I unearthed and presented a 1956 photograph of her, a blue-eyed, curly-haired cutie, perched on the steps of our rented De Grassi cottage, and she was charmed. Even though she lived three thousand miles away in British Columbia, or because she did, I stoked romantic fantasies and churned out feverish letters. Even as I knew it was no coincidence that I was spellbound by an unavailable woman named Janet, I persisted all the same. Events unfolded, yet another thwarting triangle emerged, the spell snapped and we evolved into the passionate friends we were destined to be.

For the 1998 Odyssey reunion, our thirtieth, once again I was driving the bus. Together with Nan, living in Victoria, B.C., we started tracking down people over the months of July and August via the internet, a magical new tool that seemed expressly made for our purpose. When

Nick offered his house as a venue, he cracked, "Should I build an amphitheatre in my backyard?"

Nan and I solicited written memories of the trip and compiled a scrapbook of photos: "1968–1998: A Space-Time Odyssey." I wrote a letter to Sally's mother, and she responded with a hand-written note: "George and I thought Sally was a wonderful gal and we were extremely proud of her. We felt fortunate to have had her for 18 years."

When I located Will, I learned that he was a doctor working in a London, Ontario, hospital; when I located Liz, I discovered that she was a nurse at the same hospital. Neither was aware of the other's presence under the same roof. When I phoned Peter in B.C., his voice unheard in three decades, I tested his memory by simply saying, "It's Fitz." I expected him to say, "Who?" but instead he gasped. Preparing to step out with his wife to celebrate their twenty-fifth wedding anniversary, he reported that at the very moment the phone rang, he was gazing at the Rüdesheim group picture taken on August 12, 1968, wondering what we were all doing.

From Nick I retrieved the reel of the Odyssey promotional film that Bernie had made in 1968; I transferred it to video and made twenty-seven copies to distribute to everyone. I blew up the totemic Rüdesheim photo to poster size to bring to the reunion, wondering what force was compelling me to do such a thing. Was I expecting some mystical revelation to burst out of the concentrated dots composing the image of Sally's head, tilting next to mine?

In my spare hours I was researching the life of my elusive grand-father, building a pitch that I hoped would translate into a book. One day I visited the City of Toronto Archives seeking information on his brother's suicide. As the archivist directed me to the police reports, I smiled when she revealed that her name was Sally; then she intro-duced her colleague whose name, of course, was George.

Cycling home a few nights later, I failed to see a speed bump in a darkened laneway, and I pitched over the handlebars. I snapped my collarbone, but my helmet buffered my skull from cracking like an egg on the pavement. Destiny had ensured that our thirtieth reunion would not be killed by my own funeral.

On August 12, the thirtieth anniversary of Sally's last night on earth, I dream we are all back on the trip, a year later, travelling in the same VW mini-buses. I am sitting beside Sally, vivid in her floral dress; I know she was killed on August 13 the previous summer, but she has returned to luminous life. As we move along the same German highway to Luxembourg, my dread mounts—I'm terrified she will die a second time. I want to warn her, but as the words stall in my throat, I surface from the underworld.

The reunion was set for October 2. The night before, as I had done for the two previous reunions in 1978 and 1988, I called George in Vancouver to catch up on our lives. In a subdued voice, he told me that on Christmas night 1967 he dreamed that Sally would die in Europe, and that the premonition fulfilled itself hours after he sent his telegram proposing marriage. At first I didn't let the story sink in. Why was he telling me this now?

Then I experienced an obscure feeling that he had told me about the dream in 1968 at De Grassi Point, that I had always known it, but I had forgotten, and now here we were again, held in a dream state together. I felt a link to my brother's recent confession, a sense of cracking a silence, that finding out things I was not supposed to know drove the wheel of my existence.

The morning after speaking with George, the day of the reunion, he sent me an email that relieved my sense of transgression: "The conversation we had last night took me back to some very dark places in my life—and I do appreciate that."

The night of the party, I was as keyed up as if I were getting married. One by one, twenty of the surviving twenty-seven Odysseyites flowed through the door. Now divorced, Nick and Tammy had each remarried and lived a block apart on the same street. We took turns talking on the phone to the other seven in Vancouver and Halifax, passing the receiver around the room. Nick said, "You guys will always be eighteen to me."

In Nick's basement, we jammed together on the floor and sofas to watch the 1968 promotional video we had never seen. The soundtrack played the pop song "Love Is Blue" and the theme of *The Dating Game* driven by cheesy Herb Alpert horns. As Bernie's sonorous, senatorial voice-over narration was drowned out by our explosive bursts of hilarity, I was pitched into 1968: the Sorrento bikinis, Vesuvius looming across the Bay of Naples, Nick in his black Peter Sellers glasses leading us up the steps of Giotto's bell tower in Florence, the bronze baptistery doors depicting biblical scenes, "the Gates of Paradise" said to have started the Renaissance. "Such scenes," intones Bernie, "require interpretation." In the grainy film transfer, I strained to catch a glimpse of Sally amid our bodies shuffling through the Uffizi Gallery—she was alive in Italy; is she alive now?—but her image never appeared, as if cut by a censor. In the final scenes in London, I saw myself boarding the bus to Heathrow, a dream within a dream, my dissociative grin translating her absence into a detail of no importance.

Herding everyone upstairs, I orchestrated a re-enactment of the Rüdesheim group photo taken on August 12, 1968, hours before the catastrophe, everyone posing in the original configuration. As I stood in the back row beside where Sally should have been, I was engulfed in a cascade of joshing and kibitzing, as it was back then. In the front row, Nick and Tammy held the blow-up of the 1968 photo I had made: a photo within a photo. I couldn't bring myself to tell anybody about George's dream; I'd have felt like a killjoy, and

I wanted the party to rage into the dawn. I couldn't bear it when the bodies slipped one by one into the night. I was the last dog hung.

In the months to follow, I pondered writing a magazine article about George's dream, but I was consumed by my family memoir. Still, I allowed myself to imagine a book, my third, down the road, knitting scenes of a half-lived life, cinched by threads of inarticulate strangeness.

TWENTY-FOUR

"I'm Not Dying"

I n June 2001, I was delivering a lecture on my work-in-progress at the Centre for Training in Psychotherapy on Dupont Street to an audience of forty psychotherapists. I stood in the room where I had spent countless hours over the past seventeen years. Wearing hard-won emotional stripes, I had recently "graduated" from the group at age fifty.

An unknown, unattached woman my own age tagged along to a post-talk lunch with friends. Although Katy was a full foot shorter than me, her live-wire energy was large, and I was drawn to her easy smile, pale white skin and curious, kind brown eyes. When I learned she had graduated from the training school only days earlier, I thought about asking her out but hesitated, still touchy about letting the right one in.

Weeks later, on August 1, a scandal rocked UCC when Doug Brown, a former master, was charged with multiple counts of sexual assault of pubescent boys in the prep boarding house during the 1970s and '80s—enacted in the same curtained cubicles where my belea-guered young father once slept. Four years earlier, another former UCC master, Clark "Nobby" Noble, scion of a prominent medical family, had been charged with the sexual assault of two students from

UCC and Appleby College; the testimony of his UCC victim, a schizophrenic, was deemed unreliable and Noble was given a one-year suspended sentence and eventually pardoned. At the time, I was disappointed by the minimal media coverage, but the Brown charges were once again exposing the dark, ignoble side of the institution.

Only now did I allow myself the thought that my deepest unconscious motivation for publishing *Old Boys* traced back to the shadows of the Balmoral nursery and the trauma of the powerless boy (father-brother-self) long forsworn. Eventually, Brown was sentenced to three years in jail and a multi-million-dollar class-action suit forced the school to compensate the multiple victims. In yet another eerie coincidence, I learned that the UCC prep headmaster Richard Howard was instrumental in covering up the abuse when it was first reported, and the offender was allowed to run amok for years. As a child in the 1930s, that same Richard Howard lived with his family as a tenant in the third-floor apartment of my grandfather's house on Balmoral Avenue, the same third floor where my brother was abused.

When a mutual acquaintance separately invited Katy and me to a camping weekend with a circle of friends, I sensed a set-up, but I decided not to resist. As I was carless, Katy offered me a ride; over the two-hour trip into the eastern Ontario woods, I babbled with abandon as she listened, my captive audience behind the wheel. As we dipped our bodies in a rushing river, I fell for her. The weekend was August 17–18, 2001, three weeks before 9/11; as Western triumphalism was to begin its slow unravelling, the puzzle pieces of my personal life started to come together.

At first blush, our different backgrounds suggested we were not a match. Traumatized as teenagers, Katy's German Catholic parents barely survived death by starvation in a Serbian slave-labour camp at the end of World War II. In 1954, Katy's mother, stripped of her family home and possessions when the Red Army invaded her village, landed in Toronto's Union Station not speaking a word of English; besides five-year-old Katy and her sister, Heidi, nestled in a baby carriage, she carried a single cooking pot. So began the classic 1950s narrative of working-class immigrants, a bricklayer and a cleaning lady with Grade 8 educations, hacking out a new life in the New World.

Parental uber-pragmatism ruled Katy's childhood, and she learned to hide her true self. Hungry to break free, she discovered, hand in hand with sixties liberation, her innate talents and sturdy self-reliance: aesthete, fashion plate, gourmet, gardener, award-winning flower arranger, steady reader, photographer, film buff, world traveller, counsellor of disturbed kids.

In time, I realized that with Katy I was not swinging on a pendulum but settling into the creative tension of yin and yang. Growing up, she lived in a humble home but felt internally rich; I lived in affluence but felt internally poor; somehow we met in the middle. While my mother never touched me, her mother over-hugged. We discovered we were both veteran serial monogamists serially disappointed and found common ground; her earthbound constancy and the giving of the simple gesture grounded my floating Kubrickian intronaut. In the magpie hunt of the Saturday morning garage sale, she took pleasure in spontaneous interactions with strangers and the spearing of the desirable tchotchke; because money was not an obsession, she was rich. In 1984, in a savvy move, she'd bought on a teacher's salary a grand but rundown three-storey 1910 red-brick house in High Park, complete with wraparound veranda and garden butterflies. Renting out apartments to cover the mortgage, she'd carried out gradual renovations. When I first visited the place, it felt like a fusion of my grandparents' homes on Balmoral and Delisle but blessedly cleansed of the bleak, *unheimlich* vibe.

Crucially and invaluably, we spoke the same language of the dream: hers sweeping Flight-of-the-Valkyrie epics, mine compressed

WASP puzzles. When we fought, we learned to fight fair, each hearing the other out. She did not flinch from self-reflection, or if she did she came back for more. If we hit the black holes of our respective mothers, we rode out the storm. What could come of this except appreciation and gratitude?

Given my mother's history of divide and conquer in my romantic life, I delayed introducing her to Katy. But I need not have worried. On the appointed day, Janet set the first in what would become a series of leg traps by placing a bolt of cloth by the door of her condo with the intention of throwing it away; when Katy admired its texture, my mother offered to let her have it. Minutes later, she recanted, and into my ear Katy whispered, "I think I am getting negatively attached to your mother." She had spotted the quicksand, which drew her even more closely to me. Later I posed the inevitable question, "What was it about my family history that attracted you to me? The bitch goddess mother? The suicidal fathers? The addictions? The pedophilia? The madness?" It was, she said, my endearing blend of nervousness and enthusiasm.

On August 13, 2004, I flew with Katy to Europe on a holiday-cum-book-research trip to explore my paternal roots in medieval Ireland and track my grandfather's career path through the pathology labs of pre–World War I Germany. Visiting Katy's relatives near Cologne, I did not plan on retracing my last days of the Odyssey, but we found ourselves on the open deck of a Rhine cruiser, heading south in the opposite direction from 1968, from Oberwesel to Boppard, stopping short of Rüdesheim, the wine village of Sally's last revel.

Boarding an open chairlift up a thousand-metre mountain that overlooked the forested vista of the Rhine Valley, I was overcome by agoraphobia and I clutched Katy's arm. Matrix of good and evil,

Freud and Hitler and quantum mechanics, Europe remained, more deeply than I realized, my haunted yet precious memory palace of beauty and loss. Maybe with Katy, a European in her soul, I could step into the same river twice. Or maybe for the first time.

Tortured by fibromyalgia and assorted psychogenic ailments, my mother had built up a superwoman tolerance for physical pain, a self-punishment, I was guessing, to gratify the backed-up unconscious guilt she had never faced. In the fall of 2005, she hosted a launch for her self-published book on John Ewart, her maternal great-great-grandfather and a pioneering Toronto architect; when she strangely declined to address her invited guests, I took it as an act of emotional cowardice. Though I had helped her find a freelance editor, she was peeved when I chose to focus on my own book and not hers. In her acknowledgements, she thanked my brother and sister but conspicuously left me out.

Only months later, as she lay dying of pneumonia in her eighty-eighth year, I asked if she believed in an afterlife. "I'm *not* dying!" came her brusque retort. For a single open-ended heartfelt conversation I might have forgiven everything. Maybe that's what I should have told her.

In February 2006, during the last week of my mother's life, I submitted a massively overwritten first draft of my family memoir to my publisher. I still had trouble believing anyone was listening, even when they were; was it any coincidence that the death of each of my parents coincided with the birth of a book? In the intensive care ward, I stood over my mother and enthused: "The book is very exciting, it's going to be big," as if speaking of a flight to the moon. Instead of the maternal pride I vainly hoped to raise—why had I not learned my lesson?—she rolled her brown eyes and snorted under her oxygen mask.

Days later, my brother telephoned to tell me that the pneumonia was reaching its endgame, but I arrived at the hospital half an hour late. Mike left the room so I might sit with her alone. I perched at the foot of the bed, moving no closer, my gaze deflecting off the mask of her face. Then I became aware I was assuming the position of my first day on earth, when I was squeezed from her labouring body, then placed at a safe distance as she sank into her postpartum depression. My fingers skimmed over her upright white-sheeted feet, breaking the royal protocol: Never touch the queen. No tears of rage, no tears of grief. How was it humanly possible that on the death of a mother a son would feel next to nothing?

Passing on a church funeral, my sister, brother and I showed a video collage of her life at a memorial service at the University of Toronto. I would have felt like a whitewashing hypocrite had I mouthed the conventional homilies, so I let the glamorous surfaces speak for themselves.

As we cleared out her condominium, we agreed that I should take her vintage wooden bookcase with glass doors and the pick of her hardcover tomes. She habitually wrote fan letters to her favourite authors such as Farley Mowat, Mordecai Richler and Muriel Spark and stuffed their responses between the pages of their works. I recognized several of the books as my inscribed gifts of Christmases and birthdays past. For her last birthday I had presented her with Gore Vidal's *The Golden Age*, alive with detail of 1940s New York City, where she had worked during and after the war. I suspected that happiness might have been hers in Manhattan had she stayed and never had me; yet she never told me whether she liked the book or even read it. Perhaps she saw the gift as a dig at her unlived life, and perhaps she was right.

Among her possessions, we found several charcoal sketches of nude figures that had never seen the light, love letters from blindly passionate suitors and folders filled with scribbled fragments—dates, musings, regrets, guilt. On a page headed "My Mistakes," she brooded over the fact that all three of her middle-aged children were single and childless. She berated herself for "not facing the truth that Jack did not like children and should never have had any. He was not the faintest bit interested in them." During my father's descent into madness, she wrote, "I can't help but feel dreadful guilt feelings but I must keep them down for my own salvation; if I keep my cool, I should be able to control things." She decided that her own diarist mother "very wisely wrote for posterity, not baring her soul; daily events are more interesting than introspective rambles." Another note read, "I keep hoping that you will understand me and my inner sadness, that our life has not been fulfilled in the way I had hoped." In yet another, she wrote that she felt awful that she "never found the nerve to tell my three children that I loved them to their handsome faces."

Of course, from the start, my childhood intuition understood her better than she understood herself. Early on, I read her like a book, but I didn't yet know what I knew. But now, as I read her words, I knew she intended me to find her diary, a perfect last testament to a perfect last thwarting, where she dangled high promise from the far swing of the pendulum, then died before I could reach her. Some things you will never know.

Then came the motherlode. Stashed in a gold-yellow folder, I discovered my childish scribblings that survived her impulsive, censorious purgings of family artifacts. Pulling out an ancient, elementary school story titled "The New Rokeit," printed in my wobbly six-year-old hand, I felt the thrill of the archaeologist discovering Pompeii. This was the story my mother had promised to show me when I turned thirty—"maybe one day you will be a writer"—but then forgot. Perhaps it was no coincidence that when I turned thirty, I passed a decade of *not* writing.

Onece upon a time there was a man who made the first Rokeit.
He was very proud of his Rokeit but he could not find a man
who would go to the moon in it. So he decided that he would go
himself. Lots of men storded in food for him so he would not
starve. He was going to start at seven o'clock in the night. So
when he was all redy he said to turn on the Rokeit. Soon as he
was going to say good-bye he was one hundred miles away. He
saw all the stars. Then he landed on the moon. He got out and
put his helmet on. He walked and walked till he was out of
breth. He sat down and went to sleep. When he woke up he
went back to the Rokeit but the Rokeit was not there. He
would die if he did not have food. But he lived very long. One
day he was walking and he saw a very nice Rokeit. He looked
for the pursun who owned the Rokeit but there was no one. So
he got in and went right back home agen and he never found
who owned the Rokeit.

A close reading revealed an unconsciously attuned fable from
the front lines of a boy's hope and desolation. My first "exposé"
revealed the secret of the genteel nursery: an airless coffin of emotional starvation where only lunar flights of imagination saved my
psyche from crashing and burning. How stunning that my stun-
ningly beautiful mother, Planet Janet, was not the earth mother falsely
advertised by the glossy surface but a breed of female impersonator;
all the more stunning that some children are able to find alternate
landing strips, and ways to keep breathing. Though she chose to save
my story, she never got the message. The day had come when, finally,
I did: from the start, my outwardly vital mother was inwardly as
petrified as wood, beyond softening, beyond saving, my childhood
of endless effort all for naught.

As the lawyer read us her will, I was amazed by my one-third
inheritance—money that she herself had largely inherited. She had

often threatened to disinherit me, and I had called her bluff, but here it was. While I did not join the millionaire class of many of my UCC peers, I was able to clear my debts, stabilize my life and, ironically, finish the family memoir that, had my mother lived long enough to read, would have finished her.

As a pre-verbal child, I could have my mother, my first love and first death, only by sitting stone-silent at her feet, pretending to read a book upside-down, my head turning backward to check, like Orpheus, if she was still there—finding her forever there-but-not-there. I waited her out, a misguided act of faith and hope, as if we had nothing but time for her to wake up and love me, so that I might love others. Mortally fearful of spontaneous play, my mother once branded me "a nasty piece of work." Even as I type out those words, I wonder, yet again, if it is true that most or all working writers write for their mothers. Is giving up the nasty work of writing the only, or best, way to let her die for good?

Odyssey 30th Reunion, Toronto, 1998,
restaging 1968 Rüdesheim photo

PART V

In a vacuum, any object hanging from a weightless and unstretchable wire free of air resistance and friction will oscillate for eternity.

—UMBERTO ECO, *Foucault's Pendulum*

TWENTY-FIVE

Reunion

On August 12, 2008, exactly four decades since I had crossed the threshold of the Rüdesheim hotel room to find Sally clutching George's telegram, Katy and I boarded a plane for Vancouver Island where we planned a two-week car trip. The holiday was designed to culminate with a weekend-long Odyssey reunion, our fortieth, hosted by Nan in late August at her summer cottage on Salt Spring Island.

I had not spoken with George since our last reunion in 1998 when over the phone he revealed his prescient dream of Sally's death. I had kept the dream on ice for a decade now, telling only a select few, and then in muted tones, as if testing the listener's—and my own—credulity.

Only ten of the twenty-seven members were making the trek—Nan, Robin, Rich, Walter, Steve, Peter, Stan, Kathy, Kat, me—but several were bringing spouses, curious to meet a group bound together by the strangely far-fetched story of a doomed girl from the doomed sixties. Our three previous reunions were held in Toronto, so I had not seen the "West Coast girls" in forty years; maybe this would be the one when I finally cracked open whatever it was I felt I must feel. As I stood in Nan's living room, a sweet vermouth in hand, I felt as if I had set up a camera on a tripod to shoot a lucid dream, my anticipation of the evening pulling from my gut a queasy thrill.

In strode Kat Joy, the unforgotten, feline seventeen-year-old matured by the decades, hair now streaked with vibrant grey, and it was a joy to see her. Within no time we were swept back to the West German highway, for she was one of the six eyewitnesses. As we reconnected, I realized that all this time I had been tending a safe, sanitized, stuck-in-neutral picture of what had happened on the afternoon of Tuesday, August 13, 1968.

As Kat's passionate, detailed account of the accident poured out—"I was traumatized"—my body rippled with adrenalin. All this time, the obvious had escaped me: no one had ever had ever used the word "trauma" when speaking of the impact of Sally's death. For three days afterwards, Kat revealed, her body had shaken, robbed of sleep despite the sedatives Tammy gave her, for she could not stem the hammering thought, *it could have been me*. As she spoke, I was pitched back to the courtyard of the Paris hotel. What had stopped me from reaching out to Kat in the nights of her terrible distress? Or John? I denied her, denied him, and Sally, and all the others, most of all myself. For the trance broken with a rush of words, for the image of the head wound I was finally admitting through the temples of my own head, I gave quiet thanks.

That first evening, dining at a local restaurant, we took turns voicing sweet soliloquies on the summer of '68, our personal, state-of-the-reunion addresses. The next day, Nan organized a scavenger hunt, twelve of us stuffed into three cars, zipping around leafy backroads like rowdy teenagers. Conference calling with missing bodies in Toronto and Vancouver, I tapped into the vein of indefinable Odyssey euphoria; I knew it when I felt it, and I knew it would pass.

Before we headed to the ferry back to the mainland, Nan suggested what I sensed was coming. She knew I was currently struggling to pull together the final scenes of my emotionally exhausting family memoir in which I had assembled the deeply repressed secrets of my eminent yet self-destructive grandfather. I was drawn to the tragic, so why not write Sally's story? I protested, "I wouldn't dream of approaching George. Her death has haunted him for years."

Failing to add, *as if it has not haunted me.*

But Nan's words endured as a kind of permission. Whether confronting unloving parents, or shame-driven prep schools, or heartless psych wards, I felt a familiar prod to serve as the detective on the case—to chalk outlines on the asphalt, to circle the obscenities no one wanted to see or hear or remember or speak or feel—torn between needing to know, and not know, more. The French writer Georges Bataille once said there were three things on which humans cannot bear to steadily fix their gaze—the sun, the genitals and death. But were not artists compelled to challenge the gods? Why did I keep fixing my gaze on the rearview mirror? What was it I was trying to retrieve, fix, restore? My horror of the random?

With *What Disturbs Our Blood* in the final stage of production, I was reaching another crossroad in my life. I had come a long way since the day twenty-six years earlier when I'd retreated into the eighth floor of a concrete apartment block in downtown Toronto, suspended in a holding pattern, waiting for exactly I knew not what.

In the crucible of two difficult books, I had slowly expanded my range (and rage), struggling to balance my inner and outer lives. By August 2009, I felt ready to make a not-so-sudden move—moving in with Katy. In the unconscious script of my life, my mother had written in invisible ink that I would never know intimacy with a woman other than her; living common law with an uncommon woman felt like smashing the ultimate taboo.

I rented the first-floor apartment of Katy's house while she occupied the upper two floors, and we split our time evenly, alone and together. Three years had passed since my mother's death, and in sudden, unguarded moments I experienced her absence as a powerful presence. In our disconnected, over-controlling mothers, Katy and I intuitively shared something profound, and each day, each night, I let the emptiness fill, like hot water running into a tub.

By making a wide berth for my mother-made pendulum swings, we moved closer to each other. For the first time I allowed tears to coincide with sex. But in unpredictable moments, the monster-nightmares of the third floor of Balmoral slipped through the newly formed opening. I curled up and played possum, eyes wide shut, emitting the low growl of the terrified prey. Session by session with Peter, I learned to drop my childhood defences, open my eyes to the darkness, and stare down the body-snatching beast; each time, Katy remained a calm ally. Gradually the nocturnal break-and-enters tapered off to next to nothing. The power of love was forcing my own silent complicity into retreat.

As I put *What Disturbs Our Blood* to bed, I was aware that I was laying my father-ghosts to rest; on its heels came the half-realization that if I invoked the ghost of Sally through the rite of writing, I was now invoking the motherlode. After an epic run of twenty-six years, I left Peter, and via the timely recommendation of a friend, I started working with a woman psychotherapist, Eva, aptly of German blood, trained in art therapy and relational psychoanalysis. I was much taken, then stirred up, by the coincidence that she worked out of a three-storey stone house in the epicentre of my primal dreamscape at Dunvegan Road and St. Clair Avenue, precisely equidistant between my two childhood homes. As with Peter, I felt lucky to find a workable rapport with a strong, gifted and compassionate human being; as with Peter, I used the sessions to keep open the channels of my unconscious and construct the narrative of the three generations of my family history. I knew that killing your parents and grandparents took time; but now it was more about letting them die.

With Eva, I defied the biblical-parental injunction against curiosity and deepened my pursuit of the forbidden fruit of unconscious knowledge. I read her the "Rokeit Man" story, and unlike my mother, she instantly got it. Gradually, new patterns and meanings emerged; I realized I was enacting a transference, the glib song-and-dance man reviving the dead mother with the spinning plates of jokes and stories, planting a fixed image of the past on the face of the real, responsive, in-the-moment person sitting directly in front of me. "Let me help paddle the canoe," Eva interjected one day, and I felt a subtle loosening of my rigorous Upper Canadian literacy sinking into something freer, looser, unscripted. This time, could I safely throw off the harness of my Grade 8 thesaurus?

Jane Wodehouse was now living in a retirement home, the Balmoral Club, a five-minute stroll from Eva's office. Over the phone, I explained my recent contact with George and the fact that I wished to write a book on her long-dead daughter. I tried to explain my motives, even as I didn't fully understand them myself. She invited me for lunch. Coincidentally, Sally's sister, Diana, was visiting from her home in Nova Scotia, so it was the three of us.

A year short of her ninetieth birthday, Jane appeared at her door impeccably attired, impossibly youthful. When she extended her hand—she called me by my De Grassi name of Jamie—I insisted on a hug. After lunch, we moved upstairs to her apartment. For an hour Jane reminisced poignantly about her lost daughter. Mostly I felt awkward and intrusive; I couldn't bring myself to ask, Why was Sally's funeral rushed? Why didn't you wait for us? As I rose to leave, she pulled from memory an image of my newlywed parents visiting De Grassi in the summer of 1947, myself unborn, smooching in their parked car as Jane drove past.

Next came a chain of one-on-one talks with each member of the Odyssey, as if I was emulating the film *56 Up*. Our group now formed a generally healthy, standard-bearing cross-section of decent, responsible, middle-class, liberal-minded Canadian civilization: teaching, law, medicine, nursing, accounting, engineering, business, journalism, philanthropy. Rich was a co-recipient, with eight hundred other scientists, of a 2007 Nobel Prize recognizing the work of the Intergovernmental Panel on Climate Change headed by Al Gore—the same Rich who, after an all-night Odyssey bacchanal, laid himself open to the weather conditions of the late sixties as we stepped over his unconscious body sprawled across a morning-dewed lawn.

Only five of us were unmarried and childless; some were reclusive, alcoholic, divorced, dogged by chronic illness, the inevitable shocks of life that no class privilege could stave off. But there was a high rate of long-lived marriages, thriving lines of children and grandchildren, niches of bourgeois solidity I once disdained and now often envied. One night during the round of interviewing, I dreamed that I was toking up with Eric, Jack and Ginger, the feuding power trio of Cream, urging them to stay together. What was it about 1968?

I gathered up the memory fragments of the six other occupants of Sally's bus, piecing together a mosaic of the accident. Like my experience with the making of *Old Boys*, I encountered the Rashomon effect—the inevitable variability in the accounts of witnesses to a single scene, the proverbial blind men groping for the elephant of memory. But as each witness stepped into the box of my digital recorder, as their voices raised Sally's ghost, I did sense something close to certainty—spokes of guilt radiating from the hub of a turning wheel—and I flattered myself to think that in the act of listening, and writing, I might deliver a quantum of absolution. For myself as much as anyone.

———

How quickly, one by one, the sound of each familiar voice spirits me back there, back to the dock in Koblenz where I am lingering on the deck of the Rhine steamer, catching from above the sight of Sally below, vivid and laughing in her floral dress, the best thing I never had, sprinting ahead to the waiting buses. In the flush of George's telegrammed proposal, she's belting out "See You in September."

Under a drizzling sky, our convoy is heading westward through the Mosel Valley on a short 120-kilometre jaunt to Luxembourg, with Steve's bus in the lead. Over the first hour, John badgers Steve to let him take the wheel; Steve does not realize that Nick has forbidden John to drive, but his head is throbbing with a hangover, so he is tempted. As he pulls into a village gas station to refuel, Steve thinks, *It's just a short run to Luxembourg, so what's the harm?* Simultaneously, Sally asks Kat, who has been serving as navigator, if they can change places; over the six weeks of the trip so far, she has yet to ride up front. For both John and Sally, it feels like a last chance because after Paris we are surrendering the buses for trains.

I am the map reader in the front seat of Nick's bus, the second in the convoy, and cruising toward the gas station we notice Steve's bus refuelling. Our heads swing to look long enough to see John climbing into the driver's seat, taking over from Steve; long enough to see Sally climb in next to him, taking over from Kat; long enough for the ever-vigilant Nick, at my side, to speak the words I will never forget: "That's a mistake."

As Sally settles into the front seat, she hears a joshing voice from the back: "You're in the suicide seat now." John pulls the bus to the lip of the highway; a construction barrier partly obscures his westward view. Map spread on her lap, leaning her back against the door and facing John, Nurse Sally, ever the caretaker, tries to help the driver untested in Europe negotiate the move. In his nervous excitement, he releases the clutch and presses the gas pedal a touch out of sync, and the bus lurches into the middle of the road and stalls. He turns the key to restart, and as he grinds the gear into reverse, trying to pull back, a black Mercedes sweeps up from the right side; John sees it coming, everyone in the back seats sees it coming, everyone but Sally, and time slows to a crawl.

The Mercedes is moving at roughly 30 mph when the driver sees the bus nosing the middle white line. He hits the brakes, horn blaring, swerving to the right to avoid a collision, which he does, except something known as fate determines that his bumper clips the hinged edge of the passenger door ever so slightly, yet with enough force to swing the rear of the bus roughly two feet in a semi-circle and pitch open Sally's door. In a slow, arching, dream-like motion, she falls— *zufall* is German for "coincidence"—blindsided, backwards and downward, heels over head, onto the middle of the road.

Steve is the first to her side. "I've hurt my head," she rasps. He asks for something to place under her neck, and Liz throws her raincoat from the back seat. Lying in the westbound lane, Sally is conscious, talking, and as people gather in a circle, traffic backs up both ways. The girls are hysterical, the boys stoic. Even as American GIs arrive, like the 7th Cavalry, lugging a stretcher from a nearby army base, even as Steve does not consider her injury serious, the seven minds of the bus have split in seven directions.

In Kat's mind, she hears Sally unleashing a torrent of profanity— "motherfucker, cocksucker, fuck shit fuck shit fuck fuck fuck"—yet the others hear nothing of the kind. John and Liz and Kat and Ross and Walter blank out, each in their own ways, retaining nothing of the hours to come. Ross saw the car coming, but what stopped him from warning Sally? For years into the future, whenever Walter hears the everyday sound of gears grinding in traffic, his mind will flood with the image of Sally in the middle of the road. The source of Liz's blanking out traces back four years to the time when, as a fourteen-year-old, she lost three family members within a year—her uncle to suicide, her father to a car crash and a grandfather to a fire—and the past petrifies the present and the future.

Our third and fourth buses are backed up in the traffic jam a hundred yards down the road. Although she can't see anything from the window, Marywinn thinks, *Sally has been in an accident*, a conviction reinforced as she sees Ross sprinting down the road toward them. Tammy pulls over and walks up with Ross to the accident scene. When she returns, she tells Marywinn: "Sally is hurt. Do you want to go with her in the ambulance?"

Marywinn finds Sally lying on her back in the middle of the road. She has lost consciousness and blood is trickling from her left ear. From the shoulder of the road Tammy's bus pulls in, but people are not allowed to crowd around. Nan's first thought: *Sally's father is a doctor and he will save her.* An ambulance pulls up, operated by a farmer and his wife. After a policeman draws a chalk outline around the limp body on the black asphalt, Sally is lifted into the back on a stretcher, Marywinn climbing in beside her.

Promising to meet her at the hospital, Tammy presses ahead to Luxembourg to fetch Nick. As the ambulance races back toward Koblenz, Sally rolls over and throws up, but she does not wake up. Trembling at the sight and plight of her friend and classmate, Marywinn holds back a wail that yearns to fuse with the siren, and the woman up front who speaks no English reaches for her hand.

Within half an hour, the ambulance pulls into a small Catholic hospital. In the rush, Marywinn had forgotten her purse and passport; she is alone and she can't speak a word of German. A nurse needs to know the identity of the unconscious girl, but Marywinn can't remember her surname, repeating "Sally, Sally, Sally" over and over and over. In the waiting room she sits, one hour becoming two, nodding senselessly as a passing nun, shrouded in black, babbles in the unrecognizable tongue of a childhood nightmare. At last Nick and Tammy arrive, and the trio climb the stairs. The image of the second-floor hospital room—stark, white, plain—burns into their memories a permanent frame: Sally lying in the bed, an IV tube infusing her arm, her head heavily bandaged on the left side, covering the ear, a spot of red seeping through the layers of white gauze. To calm herself, Marywinn murmurs, "She's only sleeping."

Marywinn finds herself sitting in Sally's seat in the damaged bus with Steve at the wheel, or so the frame of retrospective memory will tell her. Steve has used his belt to cinch tight the semi-unhinged door, and they putter at 20 mph back down the highway, passing the scene of the accident, driving over the spot where the chalk outline of Sally's body had been marked, though it has now been erased by the tearful rain. In the back seat John sprawls white-faced, near-catatonic, held together by the murmuring words of Steve. In his head John carries a hyper-vivid replay of the collision, but all details of what happened before and after will be erased into nothingness. By the time they cross the border into Luxembourg, darkness has fallen.

Circling the unconscious Canadian girl, the German doctors corner the hard clinical truth: with the initial blow to the back of her head, and the contrecoup of the brain against the forehead, bone fragments have torn the blood vessels that radiate over the cranium like the tributaries of a river. The withdrawal state of the coma is easing demand on her system, but as her blood pressure rises, the force of the trauma is cascading like the breached watertight compartments of an ocean liner. The more the blood vessels leak, the more oxygen the brain needs, the more it swells, encased in the skull; expansion and pressure destroy more brain tissue, jamming the brain stem, in turn ramming down into the canal of the spinal column. Lacking the expertise needed to trepan the swelling of her brain, the doctors know they must transfer Sally to the city of Mainz, over a hundred kilometres back down the Rhine.

Past the romantic doom-rock of the Lorelei, past the ancient village of Rüdesheim, the wheels spin southward, backtracking along the path of her summer fling. Down and up, up and down surge the unfathomable, pulsating forces of love and death, churning in the wake of a single human life, gliding back down the throat of the darkly dreaming Rhine one last time, bearing her toward her destination. Sinking down into the gentle fingers of light, Sally reunites with the source, seeing and hearing and feeling and touching and understanding everything now, all within all, all at once, her eighteen years and eighty days melting into the timeless flow, without beginning, without end, remembering, forgetting and remembering anew. Everything changes, nothing is lost.

TWENTY-SIX

Funeral in White

I n 2010, George quit teaching after a twenty-year run. Inhabiting an empty nest, he and Anne prepared to sell their North Vancouver home and move to a smaller townhouse. Painfully he culled a lifetime of omnivorous archiving and hoarding, the filing-cabinet memory palaces stuffed with letters, videotapes, cassette tapes, vinyl albums, CDs, DVDs, books, magazines, manuscripts, photographs, film canisters, posters, artifacts, story ideas and research, family correspondence dating from the mid-nineteenth century, future projects that will never see the future. He could not yet bear to dispose of the physical traces of Sally, the expired Swiss wristwatch, the cufflinks, the photos, the letters, the fatal telegram. *I'll read it all over one day*, he told himself. *One last time. But then what? Burn it? Bury it? Give it away? But to whom?*

When my memoir *What Disturbs Our Blood* was published in that same year of 2010, my life path swerved in an unanticipated direction. The title, drawn from a line from Yeats, referred to the death wish, yet here I was, enlivened and revitalized as I embraced my sixties. My dreams of my haunted father and grandfather evaporated together with my fear of public speaking; holding forth on the book in dozens of venues, I experienced validation in the sound of my own voice, legs and spine planted on equal parts fact and feeling.

Writers are wise not to care how others judge their work, and when praise came my way, I felt a subtle, reflexive resistance; such was the tragic legacy of father and grandfather, neither of whom were able to savour the fruits of their labours, and starved amid plenty. Trace elements of the dead pathologists still lived inside me, and still deeper down the well dwelt the primal mother: She Who Is Never Satisfied.

As I emerged from my dreams each morning, my body vibrated with intense but just-bearable psychic pressure. I was still working for my dead mother, and working *on* her, dropping opposite Eva week by week into tender and savage places. At her suggestion, I drew sketches of Sally and the labyrinths of images driving my dreams. Often I longed to retire from the battlefront, yet quiescence still felt too close to premature death. I started to feel a third wave, a culminating vow to finish my impossible homework.

In the spring of 2012, a friend of Katy's offered us a free apartment for a week in Place de la République in Paris. At first I hesitated, nagged by an ancient ambivalence; for me, Paris was never a movable feast but a courtyard of death. But how could we refuse such a gift, for surely I was over August 1968 by now?

Wandering the streets, I discovered that our Odyssey hotel, in the haute-chic first arrondisement, had been upgraded to five stars and renamed Hôtel Costes. Walking down Rue St-Honoré toward number 239, we passed through a Cartier-Gucci-Fauchon boutique land of gold-rimmed windows radiant with cashmere sweaters, lace negligees and silk undergarments. Expecting a snooty hotel doorman would peer down his nose at two mundane Canadian tourists, I could feel my guts sink into a churning bag of liquid.

I couldn't bear seeing the place; I couldn't bear not seeing it. But as I approached the young restaurant manager, her face lit up with kindness, and the second she smiled and spoke in charming broken English, the moment I caught the sweet name on her lapel badge— Chloe Tatin—my stomach relaxed. When I showed her my 1968 photos of the hotel, she led us on a tour of the candlelit, bed-lined sauna in the basement, then a plush, multi-mirrored upstairs suite, wallpapered as red as a Belle Époque bordello.

"May I take a picture of the courtyard?

"Mais oui," she responded. "You know, I was not even alive in 1968!"

Katy at my side, I stood in the corner of the courtyard where Bernie, gripping my hand, spoke the incomprehensible letters "DOA." I conjured the seventeen-year-old prep boy, aflame with shame, fleeing upstairs, ahead of his tears.

The next day we visited the Panthéon, unseen in 1968, where I was stunned to find Foucault's Pendulum. Assembled a century before my birth, a twenty-eight-kilogram brass-coated lead bob was attached to a sixty-seven-metre-long wire suspended from the crown of the dome; the plane of the swing rotated relative to the spin of the earth, taking a full day to complete a rotation. Transfixed, I recalled my pendulum dream, born in the early weeks of my psychotherapy: the image of my swaying infant body clutching the umbilical cord, suspended from the ceiling of a courtyard, my mother's face shifting from radiance to repulsion in eternal sync with my approaches and retreats, a first and final statement of my failure to court her. First love, sudden death. I felt as if I was back on the chairlift in the Rhine Valley; without the loving, earthbound presence of Katy, I'd have been lost in space.

On our last day in Paris, trolling through the Pompidou Centre, I experienced with a surprising sangfroid yet another uncanny moment when I happened upon a video installation, *Kulik Is a Bird in Fact*. In a courtyard, naked as a newborn, Oleg Kulik, a wild-eyed Russian artist, was swinging back and forth in a suspended harness, echoing the courtyard of the Paris hotel, echoing Foucault's Pendulum in the Panthéon, echoing my primal mother dream. Of course, of course, of course: such things come in threes.

Over the past three years, George and I had been cultivating a friendship, as much as the distance could allow, talking regularly on the phone. I was delaying pitching *Dreaming Sally* to my editor as I was worried I had no ending to the story.

On Sunday, July 14, 2013, George flew to Toronto for a week to visit his brother and conduct what he called a "roots tour." I was surprised, given his unvarnished revulsion for the city, but he was riding his own pendulum. Before he came, he'd asked me whether he should visit Sally's ninety-three-year-old mother, Jane, in her retirement home. Over the years, a sense of duty, or good manners, or lingering guilt, had compelled him to drop in on Jane when he was in town. But he knew that each time, Sally crossed the threshold at his side. Why remind a mother of the pain of a long-lost daughter?

On Monday, George and I squeezed into a booth at the Ace, a retro restaurant on Roncesvalles Avenue; all that was missing was a jukebox of sixties pop. He told me that the day before, an old friend had confided that her outside perception of George's childhood was that his parents perpetually tried to tamp down his precocity: *Do Not Ever Outshine Us*. I nodded; like George, I'd negotiated a long and twisted road before I could grasp that thwarted parents can actually envy and hate their own children. Or worse: I told him about the times my mother had tried to deep-six my romantic relationships. As I heard my own words, I experienced a flash of shame that I hadn't stood up to her sooner.

After dinner, as George and I strolled through the July night, the sounding cicadas evoked reveries of child-play in the ravines of the summering city. George said he had left a message with Jane, and from her voicemail she sounded as lively as ever. She hadn't responded yet, but he expected to see her.

I couldn't resist the impossible question: "What if your dream had not come true and you'd married Sally—parent-pleasing career, three-storey house, kids, dog, everything she said she wanted, the 'full catastrophe,' as Zorba called it? Or might she have been diverted by the late sixties?"

"I think we would have likely imploded by our forties," he responded more quickly than I'd anticipated. "I'm guessing I would have become a rigid, humourless boozer."

I wanted to protest, but I realized he might be right. God knows, he had been all too right before. I thought of my young self-betraying father: the radical consumed by the reactionary.

When I found myself telling him stories of my ecstatic rambles across Europe with Sally, unsure of exactly what I was trying to confess, George said what I could not: "You must have hated me!"

For a second I held my breath, then laughed nervously. From birth I had been schooled to bury my hatreds so fast and deep that I never knew I felt them.

"If I did hate you, George, the feeling must have been mutual."

We mused on about the sixties, that inscrutable confluence of historical forces that coincided with our own coming of age and held us still, now in our aging sixties. I quoted the line from "Sympathy for the Devil," and I wondered who, or what, killed Sally, as if an answer were possible. Fate? Hate? Fear? Envy? Rage? Lust? Love? Luck? Hope? The lineup of four-letter suspects.

"I hate to say it, but maybe Sally's death was a blessing in disguise," George offered. "My life path was reset and I ended up where I should be. Sometimes bad luck is protection against worse luck."

Then he paused. "But she had that spark; if she'd gone radical, I'd have gone with her."

I thought of the countless films we had watched, the constellated archetypal characters we had identified with and become. I recalled *Coming Home*, with Jane Fonda playing the character of Sally, a naive, culturally programmed, selfless nurse married to a nasty gung-ho marine. When Sally was emotionally transformed by a paraplegic Vietnam vet, blossoming into her loving, authentic true self, her incorrigible husband ran naked into the surf to his death.

"That was us, George, life imitating art. Aspects of those characters, our various possibilities, lived in all three of us."

"Sally was spared the nightmare of getting what she wanted," George said.

Then we totted up the numerous, and numinous, life coincidences that connected us, which included and extended beyond Sally. What to make of our near clone-like family constellations; our idiosyncratic penchants for writing friends and family long, entertaining letters that extended into newsgathering proper; our back-door drifts into, and evolutions out of, journalism; our synchronistic resettings of career paths in the spring of 1989, another hinge year when we were both usefully fired from our stuck, mid-life jobs; our "lucky" dodgings of death, near-death or life-in-death?

I segued into a story about my recent trip to Ireland, land of the uncanny, where I'd showed my brother the medieval crypts where the ancestral FitzGerald bodies lay buried. We'd visited the Lake Isle of Innisfree, the inspiration for the famous Yeats poem; the name "Innisfree" resonated for me, as the founders of De Grassi Point gave it that name. De Grassi and the Odyssey were the only two chapters in my life when I felt weightless, blissful moments of self-forgetting; only now in my anchored life with Katy was I dreaming my way into a third.

When Mike and I boarded a boat to tour the lake, we were told that the captain liked to recite the poetry of Yeats over the loudspeaker.

As we shoved off, he introduced himself as George. *Naturally*. I smiled to myself.

Then I turned to my brother: "I bet you all the spuds in Ireland that he is now going to recite 'Down by the Salley Gardens.'"

On cue, George's melodious Donegal accent fused with the sheen of the green water:

Down by the salley gardens my love and I did meet;
She passed the salley gardens with little snow-white feet.
She bid me take love easy, as the leaves grow on the tree;
But I, being young and foolish, with her would not agree.

In a field by the river my love and I did stand,
And on my leaning shoulder she laid her snow-white hand.
She bid me take life easy, as the grass grows on the weirs;
But I was young and foolish, and now am full of tears.

In the days after our dinner at the Ace, George explored the landmarks of his youth for the last time. Most were altered or rebuilt— 189 Gordon Road, 30 Chestnut Park Road, 7 Inkerman Street, the Wodehouses' De Grassi Point cottage, the Nice Furniture factory in Barrie, Yorkville Village, Rochdale College. Only Branksome Hall, last seen on June 11, 1968, on Sally's graduation day, held something of the way it was.

Four days passed. On Friday morning, a flurry of emails pinged my inbox. Did I see the obituary in the *Globe and Mail*? Jane Wodehouse had died on Sunday—the very day George chose to fly to Toronto. Over our Monday dinner, we were talking about her as if she were still alive.

I punched in George's cellphone number, needing to know how he was handling this latest wild stroke of synchronicity. The cell signal was weak, but I could make out his crackling voice: he was staying at a friend's cottage near Gravenhurst and right now he was huddled under the stairs; only minutes earlier, an Oz-like tornado had toppled two massive trees, which had crashed neatly on either side of the cottage. They could have all been killed. If this were a dream, did the two trees, like twin towers, symbolize Sally and her mother? And why was George handling the news with far more equanimity than I was?

Then I recalled a scene from De Grassi Point in August 1956, when I first met six-year-old Sally in Sunday school. A hurricane had swept the point that summer, driving our family to huddle under the stairwell. A massive oak tree flattened a station wagon twenty feet from our rented cottage. We could have all been killed. On the Odyssey, Sally and I used to talk about how that storm had scared us half to death.

To attend the Sunday funeral of Sally's mother, George delayed his return to Vancouver by a day. Meeting at the Miles Funeral Home on Bayview Avenue, we occupied the last pew. As the presiding minister quoted William Blake—"Joy and woe are woven silken fine"—I felt the surge of a wish that the entire Odyssey were here, now, all four buses full, filling the rows, Nick, Tammy, Sean, Jane, Robin, everyone—all party to the communal mourning denied us in 1968.

Family and friends stepped forward to eulogize Jane. Sally's nephew, Scott, decked out in a white uniform as lieutenant-commander of the frigate HMCS *York*, spoke fondly of his grandmother, revealing that she carried a four-leaf clover in her purse for years. Scott's mother, Diana, had died of cancer three years less a day earlier, at sixty-four; at the premature loss of her second child, Jane Wodehouse wept for two days.

Tales were told of Jane's marriage to George in August 1941 at age twenty-one; how they were quickly separated by years of war; her caring for the returned, decorated stranger and his invisible wounds;

her fondness for bridge and gin, ungladly suffering fools, a "great tiny lady," tough, resilient and smart. In St. Michael's Hospital, sensing the end, she roused herself from bed and slipped into her high heels, determined to enjoy a last supper with family at her retirement home on Balmoral Avenue. Hours later, on Sunday morning, she died, even as George's plane winged eastward. She'd outlived Sally by forty-five years.

As the funeral party departed down the aisle, Scott's wife, Nancy, a lieutenant-commander of the Halifax-based frigate HMCS *Montreal*, glided past our pew in her own blazing white uniform. In the brief seconds of her passing by, mere feet away, I felt yet another shiver of the uncanny: her face, her expression, her bearing, the composed way she carried herself, everything about her fused to form a dead ringer for Sally. Then, ghost-like, she was gone from the chapel.

I turned to George—"Did you see what I saw?"—and he nodded gravely.

At the reception in the aptly named Rosedale Room, framed photographs of Sally and her father stood side by side on a mahogany table, gazing at me over the plates of crustless tuna sandwiches and cups of tea. That secret, knowing Sphinx-like smile. I was so rattled that I couldn't bring myself to speak to Nancy, the seeming reincarnation, and neither could George. But I managed to introduce myself to her husband, Scott, and gripping his hand as Bernie had once gripped mine, I cut to the chase: "I was with Sally in Europe in 1968."

His eyes widened. Naturally he was curious about his mythic aunt whom he had never known, even in stories, for his mother rarely talked about the past.

"Was she like my mother?"

"No, very different, in fact," I responded, but I did not elaborate. *Don't get me started.*

Then we introduced ourselves to Diana's husband, Mark. He did not know the full story of Sally's death, so I reported a short version, aware of George at my side and that an animated retelling would have seemed close to obscene at this time, in this space.

Then Mark slipped yet another piece of synchronistic data into my bursting portfolio: in mid-August 1968, he and Diana had been set up on a blind date. That very day, Sally's ashes arrived from West Germany, so the date was cancelled. A year later, Mark and Diana met by accident; love at first sight sparked their marriage.

Absorbing the strangeness of it all, I struggled to manage my public face. I couldn't decide if I was excited, or sad, or dreaming, a reporter scoring a lucky scoop but with nowhere to file. Then George whispered, "I'm sorry, I can't stand it any more. It's just visceral."

I suggested lunch at the Jolly Miller, one of his adolescent haunts in Hogg's Hollow. As we took our seats in the sunlit patio, he ripped off his borrowed tie. The restaurant was aptly named; an offbeat lightness and jocularity sometimes seized me at post-funeral receptions, either a manic defence, or a culturally inherited Irish Wake-fulness, or both.

Ever the storyteller, George pointed to a nearby gully where he'd played as a boy.

"During Hurricane Hazel in 1954, when I was seven, five workers were killed right here. A sewer tunnel under the stream at York Mills and Yonge collapsed. Their bodies are still there."

"There's a metaphor in there somewhere," I quipped, and we laughed. "Let's face it, we're both stand-up tragedians—blended bits of Odysseus, Oedipus and Orpheus."

"How can you stand Toronto?" he suddenly interjected.

"I guess I have *with*stood it," I answered. "And done my Irish best to mirror it all back to them."

When George confessed that he had always felt like an outsider, I was quick to rejoin: "But so have I, and I was born into the dead centre of upper-middle-class Toronto. The inner circle that expels all inner life. If you're lucky, or predestined, you learn that lingering on the periphery can be an advantage—there's a better chance of spotting the herds of elephants filling the room. Then again, elephants aren't all bad."

We had graduated from handshakes to hugs, and as we parted, he left me with words that seemed to say it all: "You know, the poor have one thing over the rich—at least they know when they have been loved for themselves."

On my drive home, the radio news swooned with a fresh piece of synchronicity: the birth of a British prince and future king, future Canadian head of state. His name, of course, was George. I thought, *The little prince will be lucky if he is loved for himself.*

That night, Sally once again appeared in my dreams. It's 1968, she's still eighteen, but I'm aging apace. I'm both thrilled and unnerved to see her again, exactly as she was, in every numinous detail, except she seems aloof, like that mythic day at De Grassi when I saw her lying on the dock in her dark blue bathing suit. I want to say, Don't you know me? It's Fitz. Don't you know that you were killed on the trip in the 1960s? But I hold my tongue in case words could kill her once again. Or maybe bring her back to life.

But this new dream is subtly different. Here she is, forever eighteen, and now I'm old enough to be her grandfather. She's standing behind a half-opened door, smiling, eating a chocolate doughnut, savouring it, like Eve. Or is it the Mona Lisa? She remains the invisible hand; the book is writing me; the story never ends. Since 1968, several members of the Odyssey have suffered cancer, a heart attack, a liver transplant, yet no one has died. I imagine more tiny miracles to come, more deaths, more births.

Two days later, I received an email from George, who was back in Vancouver. After our lunch, he reported, he spent three hours wandering alone in the renovated Royal Ontario Museum, a far cry from the musty dinosaur rooms of his childhood. At first he couldn't bring himself to visit the Wodehouse family headstone in Mount Pleasant Cemetery, Sally's name and dates carved on the smooth granite face next to the father and sister, soon to be joined by the mother. Then he changed his mind and went. His email ended with the words "My visit felt like a door closing."

I was struck by the image, echoing my recent dream of Sally smiling her secret smile behind a half-closed door. I was glad he didn't say "a door closed," past tense. There's no closure, except the mystery of death, but even then, who knows? Maybe it was an opening. You don't get over life, you travel through it.

But with his parting words, I did feel a rush of relief, and not just for him. Forty-five summers on, something was shifting. Maybe, just maybe, we were all off the hook. And maybe it was true: "Nothing is written."

TWENTY-SEVEN

Unheimlich

Over the Christmas holidays of 2013, I visited the Museum of Contemporary Canadian Art on Queen Street West to view a collection of installations—videos, sculptures, paintings—inspired by the films of David Cronenberg. Two years earlier, I had sent the director a copy of my family memoir in the hope he would adapt it into a film; he was, after all, an explorer of the demented side of science.

In the gallery, I was drawn to a video booth showing a looped five-minute clip of *The Brood*, a 1979 horror film that Cronenberg made during the breakup of his marriage. For the director, the film was a form of art therapy, a catharsis of the primal feelings aroused by the rupturing of his young daughter's life.

The scene depicted a wild psychiatrist played by Oliver Reed working in a session with a borderline patient played by Samantha Eggar. Fascinated, I rented the full film and watched it with Katy on New Year's Day. The cover art of the DVD showed a five-year-old girl with a traumatized expression, and I linked it to the image of my three-year-old self on the cover of my book, standing in front of my grandfather's (and father's) haunted house at 186 Balmoral Avenue, squinting into my mother's box camera, curious yet fearful. Chanelling something, as children and animals do.

My attention was riveted when Cronenberg's camera swooped over my childhood dreamscape of St. Clair and Avenue Road—the Imperial Oil Building, Peter Pan Park, Brown School. My parents first met as five-year-olds in the kindergarten classroom of Brown School in 1922 but did not discover that fact till they met again over thirty years later; I, too, had occupied the same kindergarten class-room in 1955.

Playing the husband of Samantha Eggar's character, Art Hindle stepped out into the Brown School playground after discovering the body of his daughter's kindergarten teacher, murdered by the brood of feral children. I turned to Katy: "I *loved* my kindergarten teacher! I would have never killed *my* kindergarten teacher!"

Pointing his camera westward to Poplar Plains Road, the direc-tor panned south along the playground fence and the houses lining Balmoral Avenue. Then, for two seconds, the camera stopped to fix its gaze precisely on the rear of my grandfather's house at number 186. Scarcely believing my eyes, I grabbed the remote to reverse and freeze-frame the image. Of all the houses, why did Cronenberg need the viewer to look at this particular one?

Strange enough; something stranger still.

Gazing at the image, I was rushed back to the day in 1995 when my brother had revealed his sexual abuse on the third floor of the house—in fact, in the back bedroom shown clearly by the camera.

Then a second realization landed. When I first entered therapy in 1983, four years after the release of *The Brood*, I'd brought a powerful dream in to my third session with Peter. In it, I was standing in the playground of Brown School, a five-year-old kindergartener, looking at the rear of the Balmoral house. Eerily, I'd been in precisely the same spot as Cronenberg's camera.

I checked my dream diary and there it all was, written down just as I recalled it. In the dream, the image of a small boy being impaled on a stake heaved into view, and my mouth opened a voiceless scream of terror.

I emailed Cronenberg to report the strange chain of coincidences. Responding within half an hour, he tossed another bone into the stew: the young actress, five-year-old Cindy Hinds, who played Candice Carveth in the film, had contacted him *that very day*. Now forty, she forwarded a tribute to the director she'd contributed to a film magazine, waxing rhapsodic that working on the set was the highlight of her childhood.

The mysterious witnessing of *The Brood* felt like a personally customized bout of art therapy, the unconscious made conscious; I was left in a state of grateful wonderment.

From my readings of Freud, I knew the German word for "uncanny" is *unheimlich*, the flip side of *heimlich*, the word for "secret," while *heim* means "home." With this cascade of recent experiences, I felt the truth, more deeply than ever, that over the years of our Balmoral childhood we were routinely left alone, estranged and unprotected— "homeless"—within our childhood cage, awash in the uncanny. The *unheimlich*, according to Freud, is a home truth that ought to have remained secret and repressed but has suddenly come to light, awakening an uncertainty about whether an object was alive or dead, animate or inanimate, like a ventriloquist's puppet. The uncanny tricks the unknowability of death by seeming to make contact with the dead.

"When life events seem to conform to old, discarded beliefs, we feel uncanny," observed Freud. In a molten tantrum with his beloved yet frustrating mother, the boy-child wished her dead, then forgot he had. Years later, his teenage girlfriend, a second love-and-hate as passionate as his first, died suddenly, unhinging the door to the uncanny, and in the boy rose a conviction: "So, it *is* true we can kill people with our thoughts."

———

Six months after watching *The Brood*, I was contacted by Don Carveth, the director of the Toronto Psychoanalytic Institute, based in the same building as the Deer Park Library where as a child I'd first encountered storybooks. An admirer of my memoir, Don invited me to dine at a restaurant at Yonge and Eglinton, my father's last neighbourhood, and a fresh round of synchronicities unfolded.

I experienced Don as a charming, loquacious freethinker, the opposite of my buried father. A challenger of convention, Don was known for his confrontation of the rigid, paint-by-numbers orthodoxy that can afflict psychoanalytic societies the world over. The son of a doctor, he'd attended UCC five years ahead of me and hated it; as a boy he was treated for asthma by my allergist father; he currently lived on Orchard View Boulevard, the very street where my flat-lined father ground out the last eighteen years of his life in a one-bedroom high-rise apartment.

When I started to relate my recent experience with David Cronenberg and Balmoral Avenue, he interrupted the moment I spoke the words *The Brood*. During the shooting of the film in 1978, he'd lived at 184 Cottingham Street, four blocks south of 186 Balmoral Avenue, and directly opposite Cronenberg's home. The two men would often talk over coffee, as the director's marriage was breaking up. In his honour, Cronenberg gave the family characters of *The Brood*—the couple played by Art Hindle and Samantha Eggar and their five-year-old daughter, played by Cindy Hinds—Don's last name of Carveth.

During this period, Don sold his house, 184 Cottingam Street, to Cronenberg. As if such a string of revelations were not enough to found a religion based on synchronicity, I recalled that Gary Ross, my editor and the publisher of *Old Boys* twenty years earlier, had grown up in that very house in the sixties.

Curiouser and curiouser. Uncanny, yes, but strangely reassuring, as if meaning were attached to my life, after all.

In the winter of 2014, after talking to George on the phone for two hours, I fall into a dream.

I'm back with Sally on the Odyssey on the sunny Mediterranean. I'm not sure whether it's 1968 or 1969. She's still a bit aloof, but gradually I get to know her again. She asks me to fetch her a glass of wine and a steak, but it takes me fifty minutes to find them. When I return, she says she asked for oysters, which I take to mean sex. As we walk among the other kids, I keep my arm wrapped around her shoulders, and we talk tenderly. I sense she is trying to voice some regret about us.

"So, you're getting married?" I ask. Before she can answer, I add, "I'm going to be a writer."

In an instant, it dawns on us that Sally is fated to die, and there's nothing to be said or done.

I return to the hotel for a cleansing shower, moving from nozzle to nozzle in the communal space, colder to warmer to hotter. In a locker room I meet Steve, who had surrendered his driver's seat to John. Together we strain to puzzle out the Sally riddle. I'm on the verge of saying, I know what it is—it's our guilt!, when Steve says it first.

We move to a hotel room full of the other kids. John, the driver, is sitting alone, crying inconsolably. I take his hand and say, "We'll talk." Jane is by my side, sympathetic. Just as I'm feeling I need to protect John from exposure to too much intensity, a hotel official intervenes and intones, "This is a matter for the FBI."

"No," I quickly respond. "We know exactly what it is."

The dream reminds me of the day I wandered downtown into Toronto's Occupy Movement, encamped young protesters confronting the One Per Centers. Among the forest of signs, one arrested my attention: "You know exactly why we are here."

———

In May 2015, the Toronto Odysseyites assembled at the Jolly Miller for a mini-reunion. Steve had taken it upon himself to call a rogue meeting, and this time I was happy to let someone else drive the bus.

Over dinner, Steve in particular was bursting with spontaneous wit, and the laughter cascaded as in the old days, bringing our band of eight—Steve, Dave, Stu, Jane, Marywinn, Robin and Sean and me—close to tears. I passed on the news that George and I had donated $500 to Branksome Hall to install a donor/memorial brick with Sally's name together with those of other alumnae, living and dead, on a curving path outside the new, multi-million-dollar Athletic and Wellness Centre. (Though my inner curmudgeon bristled that Sally was reduced to just another brick in the road.)

The mood shifted when Steve began to recount his memories of the day of the accident, surrendering the driver's seat to John, and being the first to arrive at Sally's side after she fell out the door. I was struck that it was the first time, as a group, we had spoken of what happened that day.

Before we left, Marywinn roused Nan in B.C. on FaceTime, opening up the east-west circuitry. On the subway home, I accompanied Robin, George's cousin, and we fell into an intense conversation. She related a story I'd never heard: that when Bernie broke the news of Sally's death to her in the Paris hotel, she burst into a hysterical scream. Bernie had responded, "Now, now, Sally wouldn't want that."

The next day, I received an email from Robin. When she'd arrived at work that morning, the phone rang. Picking up the receiver, she heard the voice of a woman with a West Indian accent ask, "Is Sally there?"

It was a wrong number—or maybe the right one. Damn clever, these spooks.

I called George to relate the latest happenings. In turn, he revealed a recent dream in which he and Sally were simply talking in a relaxed, easy fashion, as was their way, except now both were in late middle age; within days, George was turning sixty-eight and Sally sixty-five. He awoke with the realization that he'd been perpetually competing with Dr. Wodehouse.

"I never felt so audacious in my life as when I was nineteen and courting Sally," he recalled. "I had no idea where the energy came from, but I kept standing my ground. Wresting Sally away from her father, I was not crushed but tolerated. Then it all evaporated."

Days later, I was contacted by Ross, who had been unable to attend the mini-reunion at the Jolly Miller. His recently deceased father had owned the travel business that organized the Odyssey itineraries, and while dipping into his father's files, Ross had found a legal document marked "Wodehouse." Emailing me a copy, I discovered that in 1968, Sally's father filed a lawsuit against Bernie and the Odyssey, but the case petered out in 1970. The file contained details of the accident, including the name of the Mercedes driver, Willem Huygh, and the West German village, Bengel.

On Google Earth, I typed in Bengel, and like a bird in a dream I swooped back to the German highway, enjoying my defiance of my mother's lingering, taunting phrase: "Some things you will never know." Contemplating the arc of my life, I connected all the events I was never supposed to know or see or feel or remember, talk or write about, witnessed and unwitnessed experiences I must dam, disown, dissociate or deny: my three-year-old brother preyed upon in the third-floor bedroom of the Balmoral house; my grandfather murdering himself in his bed at Toronto General Hospital; my father injecting his arm with a lethal dose of morphine in my brother's third-floor bedroom on Dunvegan Road; the multi-generational predations of all-boys private schools; Sally lying dying on a German highway.

In my sessions with Eva, the dreams and epiphanies proliferated apace. In the summer of 2014, she had been displaced from her office to make way for condos; she was now working out of a three-storey building at Yonge and Roxborough on the edge of Rosedale. Arriving for my first session, I realized that she had set up shop a two-minute stroll from Sally's home on Chestnut Park Road.

Three days after Ross emailed the legal file, I was walking up Yonge Street en route to a session with Eva, keen to decompress a new, hot dream. When I reached the front door, I glimpsed the blur of a red-headed man jogging past: it was, of all people, Ross. As we talked about the Sally file, I withheld my amazement, beyond surprised by the latest coincidence. Aren't we supposed to meet only once every ten years? If it were all a dream, how would I interpret it?

Again, related events seem to cluster in threes, like the throwing of the three coins of the I Ching. A few weeks later, I realized I had failed to notice the obvious: Eva's three-storey office building contained a rectangular open courtyard rimmed by balconies—my archetypal pendulum dream of my mother and the "courting yard" made manifest, echoing the courtyard living room of Sally's De Grassi cottage and the courtyard of death in the three-storey Paris hotel.

Then I heard the cool tones of my skeptical inner scientist. Surely my collection of coincidences could be reduced to a severe case of apophenia—the human tendency to find meaningful patterns in meaningless noise. I stood accused: Random. Anecdotal. Unscientific. Magical thinking.

Guilty, as charged. With an explanation.

TWENTY-EIGHT

"My Baby Wrote Me a Letter"

Dear Sally,

I feel I owe you a letter. I know, even you might say I'm a delusional necromancer to believe I can communicate with the dead. But even if you are not there, not listening, I'm prepared, or unprepared, to take the risk. I feel like a ghost writer who doesn't know what the hell he's saying, but must keep talking, no matter what, not only to reconnect with the live wire of a single, spirited, once-loved girl, but to the entire spirit of an age not entirely annihilated. What were we all falling for if not each other's potential?

It must strike you as strange, if you are still capable of being struck, that with the passing of your unlived life I felt compelled to flush George, your lover and my rival, into the open. You must be wondering, if you're still free to wonder, why it is not George, but James, the monkey in the middle, who is writing you now; let's face it, in the end, you chose him over me, if I may assume conscious choice was involved. With your loss, he bore a cross heavier than mine, but who would have blamed me if I left him to die at the crossroad of 1968? Were we not implicitly taught that our happiness depends on ignoring the suffering of others?

Stranger still that I am writing a letter in the digital Facebook world you never lived to see; long gone is the stamped, handwritten envelope borne through the slit of the brass letterbox, cradled in the palm, tingling with the thrill of the slow opening. How many times that summer did we dance to "The Letter"? How many times did the pair of us babble tableside in sweaty nightclubs, week after inseparable week, always you the first to slam down your drink, butt your smoke, push back your chair, always you the first to wing us across the floor, banging into bodies, pulling me out of myself? "Lonely days are gone, I'm a goin' home."

Was it the curl of your smile, the curve of your hip, the turn of your head? How you swung your body as you danced? Or simply the way you wailed the lyrics? Any which way, I let you convince me it was *our* song, *our* lonely days, *our* home, and that you were singing to me, and only me, not an invisible deity named George, whose bearded face I chose not to see embedded in the gathering clouds. You made everything not only work but work like a dream. You made me feel like a potentate at the banquet; I did not know or care if you were merely sweeping crumbs from the tablecloth, and maybe you didn't either. If you were playing me false, I was playing along and falling for you. When I look back now, why didn't I burn us down with tenderness that night in Florence? Why did I settle for my diary and the consolation of the scribbled word?

One of your lingering attractions is that you are forever fused with the best of the sixties, your fall out the door taking your flaws with you. That random cluster of bus-riding teenagers is nothing now but the stuff of fiction, and maybe in the end I prefer us that way. Maybe I am a romantic after all, pushing my hyper-ironic, hard-headed, left-brain, rational maleness into a corner for a spell, surrendering to the belief, the wish, the hope, the faith that you are not mummified in your nineteenth year but still listening, every so often delivering, if not a letter, then a sly gesture, a sign.

For if we care to notice, you *have* been putting out all these years, haven't you? We have, in fact, gone all the way. Maybe, all this time, you have been evolving down the road alongside the rest of us; maybe, wherever you are, you understand infinitely more than we do.

Back in 2010, as George handed me your last love letter, composed hours before your freak fall, I must confess I experienced something more than the frisson of the voyeur. You'd been gone for decades, but as I read the words I was not meant to see, I felt as if a rusty three-sided fence had been re-electrified, as if he was giving you back to me. I wondered if that qualified as a good idea. That's me—the radical doubter, but open to suggestion.

When George forwarded me the rest of your letters, the fact that I fail to exist in any of them was not lost on me. But my total absence revealed a close presence, and an ocean away George knew it in his bones. On the trip, you were cruel in your kindness; why hide me if I did not matter? Did you choose to be with me every night for six weeks because I was safe? Or did I choose you because you safely belonged to George?

But, dear Sally, we three blind mice *did* sense the truth: there *was* danger in the air.

Once there was a time when George and I, invisible to each other, wished each other dead. Yet it was you who died. Maybe that's the essence of the uncanny: we knew the ending, from the beginning, without knowing we knew it.

But what if you had believed George's premonition and stayed home? What if you had not been murdered by a Greek myth? Would you have lived your life any less mythically, not dying for art? Did your disappearance send me down a chute marked storyteller-by-proxy? Or was I doomed from the start?

For years, Sally, I thought you were my first love, my first sudden death. But I was wrong, you were my second, and it is you who made me see and feel it. I did not know it back then, but I was magnetized by you on the Odyssey in 1968 precisely because you were so *heim-lich*, so familiar, the grounded, witty girl I knew six years earlier at De Grassi, a vitalizing antidote to the Balmoral crypt in which I grew up. The Greek root of "catastrophe" is "overturn," and with your death, barely out of my sight, you joined the *unheimlich*—the unhoused generations of familial ghosts haunting my disowned body.

Your sporadic yet insistent cameo appearances in my dreams compelled me to look back and pick up the reverberations of some-thing older, something younger, something buried and forgotten. Dream by dream, I made my groping way down spiral stone steps into the blackness, drilling down into the Pompeii of the fragmented mother. Decades in the making, piece by piece my discoveries have yielded cold comfort, but comfort all the same, as I slowly perceived the cracked mirror of my mother's face.

It was no small victory, decades on, to spear an elusive truth: for most of my life, I was made to believe my feelings packed the power to destroy the ones I desired. I loved you enough, Sally, to hate you. I now understand how I unconsciously short-circuited my mourning of the loss of you, and the ones before and after you, lest I drown in the original psychic tsunami of my earliest abandonment. Slowly allowing myself to love and be loved by Katy, and others, has stemmed the tide. In releasing a ripple of compassion for my own mother, I knew that in her long life she never found a channel out of the tomb of her own flesh, right up to the winter day when her ashes were low-ered under the one made of stone.

As for George's premonitory dream, I am guessing it was something more than a lucky, or unlucky, guess.

In my years of digesting literature on the uncanny, the Dead Mother Complex, telepathy, synchronicity and quantum physics, I have swung on a pendulum between pie-in-the-sky Jung and meat-and-potatoes Freud and everything in between. Are trauma and repression the parents of the paranormal? Are all deaths death wishes? I tend to align myself with those who believe the seemingly magical synchronicity is best approached as a waking dream inviting interpretation, its mirror-like correspondences between our inner and outer worlds reflecting the creative, compensatory purposes of Mother Nature.

In his inspired essay, "Why Did Orpheus Look Back?," psychoanalyst Michael Parsons imagines Orpheus entering therapy as his client. True aliveness demands the capacity to dream one's own death, he proposes, and if I may continue to conflate ancient Orpheus with post-modern Orr, George's fateful dream might be read, via Parsons, as paradoxically "a dream about the failure of dreaming."

On Christmas night 1967, protecting himself against the unbearable prospect of losing you, Sally, to someone like me, George kills you off in his dream. His mother had given birth to him while in a state of mourning for the recent loss of her father, also named George; twenty years later, the dream of her Sally-smitten son might be seen as a deep memory, a pre-emptive strike against re-experiencing the original maternal disconnection—the loss of his first love, the sudden psychic death, that had already happened. His "dream that came true" did not predict the future but the past.

Over your two years with George, you had enlivened him, and after you sailed for Europe, he felt he was dying without you: "I'm never going to see you again." None of this made him "crazy," only all too human.

He experienced your trip to the Old World as a death and a descent into the underworld. To protect himself against such *unheimlich* dread, he insisted on a total separation between the upper and lower worlds of life and death, Toronto and Europe. Charming his way into the underworld, George, the letter writer, was allowed to have you back, like Orpheus, but on one key condition dictated by the god of the underworld: never deny the existence of the inescapably dark place that comes to us all. In the anxious dispatching of the proposal by telegram, he meant to rescue you, and himself, pulling you up from the dark dream of the underworld into the turbulent, synchro-charged crossroad of August 1968 and beyond.

His fatal look back, via the telegram, condemned him to watch you vanish forever. Instead of bearing the two-month wait until you returned home on August 30, instead of carrying you inside himself while he looked ahead to your future lives together, he could not stop anxiously looking over his shoulder to confirm that you were still alive.

Then the hinge of the bus door pops, and you die for real, and forever.

When he revealed his *unheimlich* dream of your death to me and others, George was once more reaching out for life. In leaving his birthplace and moving to the West Coast, in the slow acceptance of your death he earned a chance to dream his own death in a way that allowed him to be more imaginatively alive. As with George, so with James: on our prolonged journeys to becoming our own men, at last we were able to let in strong, loyal, generous, warm-blooded women, worlds removed from our Upper Canadian iceboxes, and find fresh meanings in our lives.

But still, why, finally, Sally, did you die as you did? Were you sacrificed for a larger good? Did George's path of self-realization—and even my own—hinge on your death? Caught between two Georges, a guard-dog father and a possessive lover, you ran into a third force, the familiar figure from De Grassi Point, like you the child of a doctor, a charged electron orbiting you in tentative circles. Or was the timing of your death, plain and simple, nothing but a coincidence?

My mother was right: there are some things I will never know. But allow me to suggest that the universe is influenced, if not ruled, by the unruly forces of human desire. The lingering, fifty-year-old guilt of those of us who loved you, Sally—the notion that somehow we each and all contributed to your death—may stem from the hidden and mistaken belief that we can control events to prevent calamity. But the calamity had already happened. If there's a secret, maybe it's learning to accept, if not enjoy, that nothing turns out as expected. As Picasso put it, "Only the unexpected sally makes you laugh."

TWENTY-NINE

Talk to Me

Just a few more stories, Sally, and then I'll let you go.

It was the autumn of 1962, mere weeks after I was entranced by the sight of you sunbathing on the De Grassi dock. Newly turned twelve, I was straining under the yoke of Tony Hearn, our Grade 8 master. With his glinting spectacles and black toothbrush moustache, he was a caricature of repression, an alcoholic middle-aged British bachelor partial to beating boys in the boarding house. Weekly he drilled us relentlessly in a spelling competition, dividing the room into two teams, the Morons and the Illiterates, and posting our mistakes. Frantically memorizing words out of fear of failure and humiliation, I stood first in the class, my perfect record not quelling but stoking my panic.

One day, sitting beside a boarder I will call Brian, I was puzzled by the sight of his hand thrust into the pocket of his grey flannel trousers; why were his stretched-out legs gently vibrating under his hinge-topped desk? In the precise moment when I realized what he was doing, a purple-faced Hearn vaulted out of his chair. Charging down the rows of desks, he raised his palm and slammed the boy across the head with such force that he crashed to the hardwood floor at my feet.

"I will not tolerate this behaviour in my class!" Hearn bellowed. In my splintering state of dissociation, I made a mental note to look up the word "tolerate," and, oh yes, to never touch myself *down there*.

Under Hearn's watch as head of the boarding house, the sexual predation of dozens of boys by resident master Doug Brown would be covered up, only coming to light decades later. Brown was eventually convicted and jailed. I like to think Hearn was not entirely lacking conscience: having quit drinking some years earlier, the childless old man donated his entire estate to the school and retired to the womb of Florida, where he killed himself.

Three hours after writing the passage above, I received out of the blue an email from Peter Page, a UCC old boy two years behind me. Over twenty years earlier, I had randomly picked his name from a leaving-class list as an interview subject for my oral history of the school. We talked for a few hours, then never communicated again. He did not bother to reintroduce himself after all this time; the first sentence of his perfectly crafted one-page message simply stated, "I have been haunted by Tony Hearn for over fifty years."

Smacked by the exquisite coincidence, I invited Peter to call me. Out came the wrenching story of the vulnerable ten-year-old Jewish boy abandoned to a WASP boarding school by his Holocaust survivor parents. Hearn beat Peter regularly, black and blue, on the flimsiest of pretexts or none at all, and when Peter complained to his parents, who bore scars of their own, they failed to intervene.

I related my 1962 memory of Hearn's mad attack on Brian the boarder. Peter revealed that he had lived with Brian in the same dorm—the same one my father occupied in the 1920s—under the tyrannical Hearn.

Mere minutes after hanging up, I heard a fresh ping in my inbox. This time the message was from Brian, of all people, last seen in the sixties. Now living in San Francisco, he was, incredibly, inviting me to join LinkedIn. I thought, *Why bother? We have all been linked in for a long time.*

At first I was enthusiastic about capturing your story, Sally, but something shifted as I dug deeper. I began experiencing the act of writing as increasingly onerous. Even when I knew that my earlier books had in fact been generously heard and appreciated, I could not shake off an ancient feeling of always falling short. At last the thought hit me like a slap upside my head: at root, I had always been writing to reach my implacable mother. As a child, I rarely spoke, for why speak if no one is listening?

As I think of the story I wrote for my mother as a silent six-year-old—about the boy starving for food and air on the surface of the moon—I now see more clearly than ever its psychological genesis. As a baby, I went straight to work on her, trying to get her to play. But it didn't work. Experiencing no nursing, no back-and-forth smiling and babbling, no kissing or humming or singing or caressing, I lacked a mother tongue. To reach my marble-cold mother, I dutifully did my homework, silently making my mark on scraps of paper as if to illuminate the vellum of her skin. Orpheus moved the very rocks to weep, but the rock of my mother would not be moved, and I missed an entire developmental stage. My spine bent over a keyboard, pegging into my diary the minutiae of my daily movements like a crib-bound game of cribbage, I sentenced myself to an obsessive and unnatural task. If no one would remember me, I must remember myself.

You of all people, Sally, you the happy yakker—I didn't have to spell it out for you, did I? You have survived as the vehicle that drove George and me down into deeper places inside ourselves. Even in death, you challenged us to evolve into better men, moving forward yet looking back, compelled by a will to understand, even as we understand we never will.

Still, year by year, George and I passed hours on the telephone, talking up a storm. Our conversations drove a book of atonement with your name and body adorning the cover. Of all that you have left us, I have grown to appreciate what you never got: the meaningfulness of a longer life and a slower death.

One night, I found myself circling a question I was loath to ask George, knowing the answer in advance. At last, out it came: "How bad did it get? Was your life ever at risk?" And George answered. Seconds after hanging up the phone, I felt guilty for pushing him to open up to such pain. But then back flowed the elusive obvious: George was not my father, locked in his box of pain, but a man of his word: *I will try to be an open book.*

As never before, I realized that exclusive devotion to the written word was a poor cousin to simply living in the sensuous world of the spoken and unspoken present. *Talk to me.* I'm breaking the spell cast on the isolated boy, sentenced to life to the crafting of perfectly straight British lines, a slave to the letter of the law and the law of the letter.

Two years after your death, Sally, my mother gave me a Super 8 camera. She did some things right; motherhood will forever remain the toughest job in the world. At the time, neither of us realized she was setting me free: the camera made me feel like Superman. Then I traded image making for wordsmithing. But it's not too late to turn back to the bliss I failed to follow; in the beginning was the image, and I now picture myself making them again.

Sadly, George was denied the late-in-life fulfillment of a dormant ambition. In 2016, when he offered himself as the B.C. Green Party candidate for North Vancouver in the upcoming provincial election, he hoped for the capping of a career in public service as a silver-haired, sixty-nine-year-old ecoconscious Canadian incarnation of

Bernie Sanders. The party led George to believe he was their man, and he launched a well-crafted save-the-planet campaign. When, months later, officials got around to formally vetting his candidacy, George declared himself an open book, as he had done with me. But when he revealed the extent of his immersion in the counterculture as a young man, along with his experimentation with psychedelics in the wake of the sudden death of his first love, he was suddenly dropped. The brazen hypocrisy of an ostensibly progressive political movement lent a cruel twist to the sixties mantra "the personal is the political."

Thanks for listening, Sally. I hope I have not, as we used to say, laid too heavy a trip on you. You were the first to bring out my best self, and I'm thankful you were not the last.

The publication of *Dreaming Sally* has been synchronized to happen in August 2018, a full half century since we all converged at the crossroad of 1968, the year of your graduation, the year of your betrothal, the year of your death. We will both turn sixty-eight, a fitting realignment with the *annus mirabilis*. What are dates, rituals and reunions if not tattoos, buffers against time and loss, an illusion of certainty and control? Or are they an impediment to the blessed self-forgetting we knew as children, barefoot on the grassy edges of the August dusk? Impossible, of course, to plan a surprise, but the conditions seem propitious: will our fiftieth reunion serve as a launch pad for a gush of coming-of-old-age stories? What will spark when all of our minds and bodies come together in the same space and time? Something big, something small? Something over-the-moon? Something unwritable?

I once thought, Sally, that composing a book would finish you off; I have merely finished myself off as a book writer. An isolated childhood predisposed me to a craving for meaning that would lead

DREAMING SALLY

me out of a dead-end street. Decades on, I release myself from the impossibility of finding the meaning of life in the landing of a mortal blow, by chance or design, on the back of a girl's head. I am a human, simply being, part of a privileged yet still-juvenile species, a Grand Tourist savouring his detour and his return. You are guiding me back to the roots I never knew, back to the sandy beach, and a chance at peace. I hereby tender my resignation and resign myself to tenderness.

The long, strange trip continues with and without you. We are all accidents meant to happen; joy and woe, gratitude and disappointment, guilt and redemption woven silken fine. Oh, what a time we had, are having and will have. Here you were, are and will be, a part of us all: a summer wind caressing the lip of the volcano, a sip of iced vermouth, a dictated letter, snooker-ball pebbles clacking on the Mediterranean shore, sky of crystalline blue blanketing a Swiss pasture, bird swooping through open window, Tuesday tears of afternoon rain, out-of-sync gas and clutch, pendular swish of windshield wipers, unhinging of door, falling of body, a haunted Parisian courtyard, a primal wailing in the Canadian wild, a healing chairlift over the Rhine Valley, the new tellings of old stories. Mothers, talk to the souls growing in your wombs. They hear your silence, they hear your voice. Stay in touch. *Mysterium tremendum et fascinans.*

I am now typing out the last words you wrote to George (the last words I will write in the form of a book), the letter he received just before August 18, 1968, the second anniversary of your blind date and the day before your funeral; the letter he gave me in 2010; the letter he could not bear to read, for on the back of the envelope, you wrote, "Don't forget August 18!"

Munich, West Germany
August 9, 1968

Dear George,

Boy, are you going to be surprised when you get this
letter and the strike isn't even over. Marywinn's parents
have a friend who is a pilot for Air Canada and if we send
our letters to Frankfurt, he will fly them home to Toronto.
I'm afraid this is going to be short cuz we're putting all our
letters in one big envelope and we want to get it off as
quickly as possible.

Our hotel is fantastic, really modern, nice big rooms,
each with a bathroom. Today we went to the concentration
camp, really morbid, but very interesting to see after seeing
movies about it.

So far I've bought seven pairs of bikini pants and one
with a matching bra. Got the bra in Vienna and found the
pants here in Munich. Was going to get a slip but they
didn't have any my size. I think you'll approve. They're
all kind of sharp.

My money is rapidly disappearing but I'm having the
time of my life spending it. You'll see what I mean when
I get home three weeks today, thank God.

Really want to write more but I'd rather write less
knowing that you'll get this. So this is the end of my
letter.

My love to everybody but mostly for you. Be good.
I am. Sending telegram Aug. 18. Miss you.

Love always, Sal XXOO

PPS. Just read the newspaper if strike is over so no telegrams 'cept our anniversary Aug. 18.

P.S. You can't reach me between August 16–20 cuz I'll be in Holland somewhere and I'm not sure where or when. So Paris till 3 o'clock Aug. 16 or London from 3 o'clock Aug. 20. Then T.O. 4 o'clock Aug. 30. Can't wait. I love you. Don't forget.

SALLY
          LOVES
                    GEORGE.

My money is rapidly disappearing
but I'm having the time of my life
spending it. You'll see what I mean
when I get home 3 wks today
thank god.

Really want to write more but
I'd rather write less knowing that
you'll get this. So this is the end of
my letter.

My love to everybody but mostly
for you. Be good. I am. Sending
telegram Aug. 18.

Miss you.

Love always

Sal
xoo

PPs. Just read newspaper & strike
is over so no telegrams 'cept Aug 11.
By for now Cordial

Miss Sally Woodhouse
c/o Miss Lu

P.S. You can't reach me between Aug 16 30
cuz I'll be in Holland somewhere and
I'm not sure where & when. So Paris
till 3 o'clock Aug. 16 or London from
3 o'clock Aug 20. Then TO. 40 o'clock
Aug. 30. Can't wait.

I love you. Don't forget.

SALLY

LOVES

GEORGE

Ending of Sally's last letter to George, August 9, 1968

ACKNOWLEDGEMENTS

I am grateful to the many people who served as sources of support and inspiration during the creative evolution of this book, but I will name only a few.

Borne along by her inexhaustible spirit of challenge and caring, I remain in awe of my editor, Anne Collins at Random House Canada. Over the making of our two books together, I came to see myself as a somewhat over-vigilant male of the species who, better late than never, learned to absorb the riches that women have to teach us. I'm also very grateful for Sarah Jackson's close reading and her work with me on the photo sections.

I never cease feeling buoyed by the dedication and enthusiasm of my agent, Hilary McMahon. The gifted poet, Nick Power, responded generously to my first working draft, while Katy Petre, Teressa Gold, Naya Kee, Steven Carter, David Kingsmill and my siblings, Shelagh and Michael FitzGerald, each added their own thoughtful perspectives to subsequent drafts. Throughout the process, Eva-Marie Stern has served as an indispensable emotional midwife, tending to my inner pendulum swings with the sensitivity of a born artist.

I also appreciated my fertile stints in the artists' community of Artscape Gibraltar Point on the Toronto Islands and the Pierre Berton House in Dawson City, Yukon.

Without my miraculously loyal, honest, patient and understanding partner, Katy Petre, I would not be the person, and writer, I have become.

As for my friend George Orr, there would be no book without his brave commitment. I consider him a co-author, and I know that at some indelible point on our converged paths, our shared love of words moved subtly yet permanently into a world of love, the place where the story never ends.

SELECTED BIBLIOGRAPHY

Philip Bromberg, *The Shadow of the Tsunami and the Growth of the Relational Mind*, 2011

Doris Brothers, *Toward a Psychology of Uncertainty: Trauma-Centered Psychoanalysis*, 2007

George Devereux, ed., *Psychoanalysis and the Occult*, 1953

Nick Duffell, *The Making of Them: The British Attitude to Children and the Boarding School System*, 1994

James Elkins, *The Object Stares Back: On the Nature of Seeing*, 1996

M.D. Faber, *Synchronicity: C.G. Jung, Psychoanalysis and Religion*, 1998

Sigmund Freud, *The Uncanny*, 1919

James Grotstein, *Who Is the Dreamer Who Dreams the Dream?: A Study of Psychic Presences*, 2000

Carl Jung, *Synchronicity*, 1960

Gregorio Kohon, ed., *The Dead Mother: The Work of Andre Green*, 1999

Roderick Main, *The Rupture of Time: Synchronicity and Jung's Critique of Modern Western Culture*, 2004

Victor Mansfield, *Synchronicity, Science and Soulmaking: Understanding Jungian Synchronicity Through Physics, Buddhism and Philosophy*, 1995

Iain McGilchrist, *The Master and His Emissary: The Divided Brain and the Making of the Western World*, 2009

Thomas Ogden, *The Primitive Edge of Experience*, 1989

Thomas Ogden, "Reading Winnicott," in *The Psychoanalytic Quarterly*, 2001

Thomas Ogden, "Fear of Breakdown and the Unlived Life," in *International Journal of Psychoanalysis*, 2014

Michael Parsons, "Why Did Orpheus Look Back?" in *Living Psychoanalysis: From Theory to Experience*, 2014

Leonard Shlain, *The Alphabet vs. the Goddess: The Conflict of Word and Image*, 1998

Gibbs A. Williams, *Demystifying Meaningful Coincidences (Synchronicities): The Evolving Self, the Personal Unconscious, and the Creative Process*, 2010

———

A more extensive bibliography is listed on the author's website: jamesfitzgerald.ca

European Odyssey 1968 video is accessible on YouTube.

PERMISSIONS

Educated at Upper Canada College and Queen's University, **James FitzGerald** spent over forty years in the fields of journalism and book publishing. His first book, *Old Boys: The Powerful Legacy of Upper Canada College*, was a controversial inside look at the attitudes and values of English Canada's ruling class families rendered in an oral history format. Revelations of the sexual abuse of boys at the school, first published in his book in 1994, sparked the criminal conviction of three former teachers and a successful multi-million dollar class action suit against UCC. His second book, *What Disturbs Our Blood: A Son's Quest to Redeem the Past*, was a multi-layered exploration of madness and high achievement within his prominent Toronto medical family. In 2010, the book won the Writers' Trust Non-Fiction Prize and was shortlisted for three other major literary awards. The last in a thematic trilogy of creative non-fiction, *Dreaming Sally* is a true story of first love, sudden death and synchronicity set in the summer of 1968.

A NOTE ABOUT THE TYPE

Designed in 1792 by Englishman William Martin, the Bulmer font family is not named for the designer (as was the practice of the time) but rather for the printer who first used the fonts in his Shakspeare [sic] Press editions. Based on the sharp letterforms of the Italian Bodoni and the French Didot (both of which were virtually illegible when used in smaller settings) Bulmer features a more condensed letterform, higher contrasts in the strokes, and a subtle bracketing of the serifs, thereby increasing the legibility at virtually any point size. Bulmer was revived and modernized by American Type Founders in 1928.